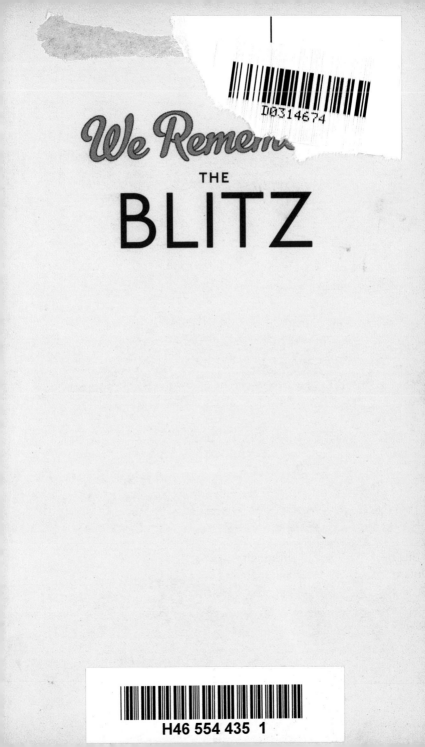

We Reme~~

THE

BLITZ

THE
BLITZ

FRANK & JOAN SHAW

EBURY
PRESS

1 3 5 7 9 10 8 6 4 2

Published in 2012 by Ebury Press, an imprint of Ebury Publishing
A Random House Group company
First published by Frank and Joan Shaw in 1990

The Random House Group Limited Reg. No. 954009

Addresses for companies within the Random House Group can
be found at www.randomhouse.co.uk

A CIP catalogue record for this book is available from
the British Library

The Random House Group Limited supports The Forest
Stewardship Council (FSC®), the leading international forest
certification organisation. Our books carrying the FSC label are
printed on FSC® certified paper. FSC is the only forest certification
scheme endorsed by the leading environmental organisations,
including Greenpeace. Our paper procurement policy can be found
at www.randomhouse.co.uk/environment

Printed and bound by CPI Group (UK) Ltd, Croydon, CR0 4YY

ISBN 9780091941567

To buy books by your favourite authors and register for offers visit
www.randomhouse.co.uk

Contents

Introduction

After the Royal Air Force broke the morale of the Luftwaffe and its command in the Battle of Britain in August and September 1940, the Luftwaffe's next tactic was to switch to 'terror bombing'. London became the first city to suffer these new attacks.

The first night raid on London followed the daylight bombing of the London Docks on 7 September 1940. For nine hours bombs rained down on a defenceless and unprepared civilian population. In that one night alone 1,800 people were killed and seriously injured. Every night that followed the bombers came over again with almost monotonous regularity and the loss of life and damage to property became horrendous. Without respite the raids continued throughout the remainder of September and then the whole of October. The onslaught was relentless and seemingly never-ending.

London was bombed that September by an average of 200 planes each night. In that period 5,730 people were killed and nearly 10,000 badly injured. Railways and railway stations were damaged, telephone exchanges put out of action, roads blocked, buildings destroyed, gas, water and electricity mains fractured and the whole city placed in what had become almost a state of siege. To add to the death and destruction, thousands upon thousands of homes were destroyed and damaged. It was the record period of the blitz-krieg – the knockout blow to be achieved by the destruction of civilian morale and the will to continue.

The attacks continued nightly throughout October with

the largest raid on the 15th, a night of full moon. On that night 400 bombers criss-crossed London and 430 people died with 900 seriously injured.

If you didn't go to work on the 16th everyone would have understood why. But go to work they somehow did. The trains ran; the newspapers were printed; the morning milk was still delivered. Life went on – that was the only effective and defiant answer that the civilians could give, and they gave it with a grim determination.

November nights at first told the same tale of destruction, but then the character of the raids suddenly changed. The provincial cities, which till then had suffered only marginal attacks compared to London, suddenly became the centre of attention. The new policy was inaugurated by the massive raid on Coventry on 14 November. Over 400 bombers were involved and more bombs were dropped than any part of London had endured in a single night. More heavy raids followed that month; two on Birmingham, one on Bristol, one on Liverpool and one on Southampton. While none compared in relative weight with the Coventry attack, each was a grievous blow to the city concerned. In the two Birmingham raids alone over 1,000 people died.

December saw a continuation of the same pattern. Southampton, Liverpool, Bristol and Birmingham suffered renewed raids. To the toll of misery and suffering were added the cities of Sheffield and Manchester. Over 600 people died in just two nights of the Sheffield bombing, and over 1,000 in the two-night bombing of Manchester, just two days before Christmas.

Throughout this period London was still being repeatedly bombed so that the strategy became obvious: to cripple the ports, destroy the industrial centres, and paralyse the will to continue. Because of weather conditions there was a comparative lull in the raids in January and February 1941, but still the cities of Swansea, Cardiff, Portsmouth and Bristol suffered enormously. Nearly 300 people died in Cardiff just one day into the New Year. In three nights of continuous bombing in February over 350 people died in Swansea. But it was already becoming clear that the blitzkreig was a failure. When flying weather improved in March the number of attacking planes went up to more than 350 in one last desperate gamble, but it was the last phase of the Blitz. Coventry had two more big raids and Birmingham one. In the months of March and April Merseyside suffered nine nights of bombing, Plymouth seven, Clydeside four and Belfast three.

In its final onslaught in May the Luftwaffe put up its greatest effort. Merseyside was bombed every night for the first week. Tyneside, Belfast, Clydeside and Hull all felt the thud of bombs, saw the leaping flames and knew the despair of death and homelessness. For Hull, until then spared the onslaught, March and May saw over 1,000 deaths. Then on 10 May came the Luftwaffe's final great attack.

Over 300 bombers droned over London as if in a personal act of hatred, revenge and retribution at being thwarted for over eight months. For over five hours the bombs rained down and over 1,400 people died with nearly 2,000 seriously injured. But fortunately this was effectively the end. Certainly the Luftwaffe left the people of Britain something to remember it by! Thousands upon thousands of buildings and homes destroyed. Thousands upon thousands of people killed, injured, maimed and wounded. Life disrupted. Strain, anxiety and discomfort. Fear, hardship and peril. This was the everyday lot of the ordinary people in all parts of Britain from autumn 1940 to the summer of 1941.

But they survived. They came through the ordeal. They endured it with both a stoicism and humour that no one could ever have expected. What individual private terrors were suffered as the bombs whistled down and the houses crashed? How were quivering nerves controlled and blind panic hidden? It is hard for anyone who did not actually experience the Blitz to ever comprehend the stark realities of intense fear, heartache, straining nerves and exhaustion that were constant companions every night.

In *We Remember the Blitz*, where over 150 people have written down for posterity their memories of this terrible time, we are in some way enlightened. Remarkably, we also see that out of this came positives. There is a determination to make no needless demand on your neighbours or fellow workers. Not to make a fuss. To carry on with your ordinary work despite fear, loss of sleep, falling bombs and debris, and the heartache of the loss of home and family. To help whenever help was needed.

In the period of the Blitz over 43,000 civilians were killed, including nearly 5,500 children. Over 50,000 people were seriously injured including over 4,000 children. Try to imagine that today – these figures for such a short period of time are horrendous and scarcely conceivable. But production continued, and even increased, and morale was, if anything, higher at the end than it was at the start.

The great German air offensive against the British civilian population finally ended in total defeat for the Luftwaffe. If the Battle of Britain was won by 'The Few', as surely it was, then the Battle for Britain was equally won by 'The Many'. Ordinary men, women and children going about their ordinary lives defeated, simply by their spirit and faith in the good things of life, a powerful enemy and a creed that believed that 'Might is Right', which had defeated and destroyed the other nations of Europe, and offered nothing but organised slavery.

Perhaps that spirit is best typified by the story of one raid when a milkman on his early morning round ignored the warnings and was told by the warden repeatedly to take cover. Finally he snapped, 'Take cover? Take cover? An' wot am I supposed to do wiv me 'orse?' And he continued his round.

We Remember the Blitz allows us ordinary people of Britain to remember again all that happened and in particular take note of what can be achieved when the determination is there. The entries were collected over 20 years ago, and it is a tribute to the writers that their memories speak to us still so vividly today.

Frank and Joan Shaw

Some Statistics

During the Blitz in 1940/1941 some 190,000 bombs were dropped; 43,667 civilians were killed; 50,387 were seriously injured. But all the figures given show only a small part of the full story. For example: by the end of April 1941, 70,000 houses in Coventry had been damaged. Before its first big attack on 28 November 1940, Liverpool had already been attacked 57 times and 520 people killed. In the London Region nearly 1.25 million houses were damaged in the nine months of the Blitz.

THE LONDON BLITZ IN 1940

	Civilians killed	Seriously injured
September	5,730	10,000
October	3,600	6,100
November	3,396	3,900
December	4,300	8,000

THE MAIN RAIDS ON THE PORTS

	Dates	Bombers	Civilians killed 1940/41
BELFAST	15 April 1941 4 and 5 May 1941 – 2 nights	100 110	946
CARDIFF	2 January 1941	125	299
CLYDESIDE	13 and 14 March 1941 – 2 nights 5 and 6 May 1941 – 2 nights	460 350	1,828
HULL	18 March 1941 7 and 8 May 1941 – 2 nights 17 July 1941	75 100 75	1,055
LIVERPOOL AND MERSEYSIDE	28 November 1940 20, 21 and 22 December 1940 – 3 nights 13 and 21 March 1941 1 May to 7 May 1941 – 7 nights	150 500 250 800	4,100
PLYMOUTH	20 and 21 March 1941 – 2 nights 21, 22, 23, 27, 28 and 29 April 1941 – 7 nights	250 750	1,073
PORTSMOUTH	10 January 1941 10 March 1941 27 April 1941	110 120 50	756
SOUTHAMPTON	23 November 1940 30 November and 1 December 1940 – 2 nights	60 200	558
SWANSEA	19, 20 and 21 February 1941 – 3 nights	250	352

THE MAIN RAIDS ON THE INDUSTRIAL AREAS

	Dates	Bombers	Civilians killed 1940/41
BIRMINGHAM	1 November 1940	N/K	
	19 November 1940	350	
	22 November 1940	200	
	3 December 1940	50	
	11 December 1940	200	
	9 and 10 April 1941 – 2 nights	250	2,162
BRISTOL	24 November 1940	50	
	2 December 1940	100	
	6 December 1940	50	
	3 and 4 January 1941 – 2 nights	150	
	16 March 1941	150	
	11 April 1941	150	1,159
COVENTRY	14 November 1940	400	
	8 April 1941	300	
	10 April 1941	200	1,236
MANCHESTER	22 and 25 December 1940 – 2 nights	150	1,005
SHEFFIELD	12 December 1940	300	
	15 December 1940	300	624

THE RAIDS ON OTHER TOWNS

	No. of Raids	Civilians Killed	Houses Damaged
ABERDEEN	24	68	2,000
BEXHILL	37	74	2,600
BOURNEMOUTH	33	77	4,000
BRIDLINGTON	30	24	3,000
BRIGHTON	25	127	4,500
CLACTON	31	10	4,400
DEAL	17*	12	2,000
DOVER	53*	92	9,000
EASTBOURNE	49	36	3,700
FALMOUTH	33	31	1,100
FOLKESTONE	42*	52	7,000
FRASERBURGH	18	40	700
GREAT YARMOUTH	72	110	11,500
GRIMSBY	22	18	1,700
HASTINGS	40	46	6,250
LOWESTOFT	54	94	9,000
MARGATE	47*	19	8,000
PETERHEAD	16	36	700
RAMSGATE	41*	71	8,500
SCARBOROUGH	17	30	2,250
WEYMOUTH	42	48	3,600
WORTHING	29	20	3,000

* In each case these towns suffered four years almost daily cross-Channel shelling so that the area became known as 'Hellfire Corner'.

We Remember the Blitz

I was 18 years old at the time of the Blitz, and a Volunteer Fireman. Consequently I had to be on duty during the raids, and I remember that one night I was standing in the middle of the road talking to two lads, one of whom was just 21 and married to a 20-year-old girl and they were expecting their first baby. Suddenly a bombing raid started, and almost immediately it seemed that we heard this bomb coming right at us and the lad that was married and lived just across the road shouted, 'My God that's coming close,' and he ran into his house to his wife. I and the other lad dropped to the floor, which is what we had been told to do because the blast would then go over you. It did, but when we got up the house that the other chap had run to wasn't there any more.

We both ran to the house amidst all the smoke and flames, and there we dug with our bare hands until help arrived, but when they were found they were both dead. We put a sack over their heads and tied it at the waist, and left both bodies on the footpath at the front of where the house had been until a lorry could get through to collect the bodies. They were there for about eight hours that night, and there were many killed.

Another time I remember that someone shouted that an air-raid shelter had been hit and was burning, and when they told me where it was I knew that my mother and sister were inside. I ran as fast as I could to save them, and in fact I managed to get them out, but I also went to six other fires that night helping to put them out.

There was a factory near to us, a three-storey place with a reinforced basement. One night during a raid everyone who worked at the factory went into the basement but the factory was hit and collapsed on top of the basement area. When we arrived we could hear everyone shouting because they were still alive, but the factory

building was down on top of them and then I remember hearing their shouting turn to screams as a water pipe had been hit and it flooded the basement area and everyone in there was drowned as we could not get in to rescue them. The war films you see are true to life because I can remember nothing but flames and buildings being demolished and fire-water pumps all over the road, and remember that after all that next day we still had to go to work.

We used to go over the road to have a bath because nobody had baths in that area in those days and we used to pay sixpence for a hot bath, towel and soap. One day I went to the bath and after I had undressed I could hear someone whistling. I looked round to see if I could see anybody about, but I couldn't and so I got into the bath and lay back to relax. However, as soon as I did I looked up and I saw a man putting in the glass windows that had been blown out the night before. I jumped out of the bath, put my coat on and my clothes under my arm and ran home down the street. My sister's boyfriend opened the door and couldn't stop laughing as I stood there dripping wet on the step.

There is another thing I remember. My sister and I went to town and as we passed the Odeon picture house a man came to us and asked us if we would like to kiss Clark Gable for £5! We looked to where he pointed and there nearby was Clark Gable in his army uniform with that same cheeky smile that you see on the films. But we couldn't afford £5 as we only got £2.50 a week at work, and in those days it was a lot of money. Apparently Clark Gable was raising money for the war effort, and as I look back over the years I often wish that I had had that money!

I got married on 7 June 1941. That was one day when the Germans were good to us, because that's about the only night that we didn't have any bombing! It may have all been a long time ago but we shouldn't forget it. I often think of the people I knew then. Billy who was aged 18 and in the Royal Navy. The young man who was killed running to try to help his wife and the baby that they were expecting. A young man who had both arms and legs blown off, and a gang of six boys I knew during the war and only two survived it to 1945. A little girl of four I remember with one arm blown off by a bomb. A mother and three children killed in an air-raid shelter. The faces of all those people particularly the young people will never leave me and the screams and cries for help of people who we were trying to save are always with me as well.

There were also however the good times. There was the kindness and help of people you didn't even know. Help and assistance given whenever you needed it without any thought for reward. One thing I remember about the war is how close people were.

Joan Adams

At the time of the Blitz I was nearly 16 and working as an errand boy for Wilson & Company in Brentwood. As the night bombing got worse fire-watching patrols had to be arranged in the streets where you lived. It was then decided that the older men who were doing skilled war work should get as much sleep and rest as possible and so my cousin and I, being 15 and 16 years old respectively,

Mr Ashman on left with his cousin.

were given the job of relieving the older men every night at midnight until the 'all clear' went.

One night I remember it had been quite a heavy raid on London and when we took over at midnight there were bombs falling all round us. So we spent most of our time in the shelter just popping our heads up occasionally every few minutes to make sure that the road was okay! At about 3.30 the same morning things quietened down but there was still gunfire coming from the London area.

My cousin said to me, 'Let's walk up the road and show them the fire-watchers are still about!' Looking back God knows who the hell was going to see us! We had walked about 50 yards when all of a sudden there was a loud whizzing noise through the air just as if something was coming straight for us. Of course we both dived over the hedge of the nearest front garden, which happened to be a holly hedge, and I can tell you it hurt! To make matters worse my cousin landed in a place where either a dog or a cat had been recently and did he smell! As it turned out the whizzing noise happened to be an anti-aircraft shell which had failed on its way up and had travelled back down to earth! This shell was not destroyed for a number of years after the war. It had gone straight through the stone step of a nearby front door and one day a hole appeared and there it was. The Army Bomb Disposal Team removed it. Going back to our patrol we did laugh afterwards but not at the time.

Another thing I remember is a landmine being dropped by a German aeroplane that was flying too low. The landmine exploded into the ground because the parachute had not opened properly and it caused a crater 500 feet across. My friend John and I were the first on the scene as it was only 400 yards away. We were lucky as the earth took most of the force and at the time it was the largest hole in Essex. When you look back and think of all the sleep you missed in those days and sometimes minutes seemed like hours and you had the feeling that you were the only person around and everything was coming your way!

George Ashman

Liverpool, as probably at that time our number one port, came in for prolonged 'pastings' of a night's duration and of days' and sometimes weeks' duration. Then there would be peace for a while before a series of raids would start again. Yet the people of Liverpool's sense of humour and spirit prevailed. My mother even cooked meat on an upturned iron when the gas mains were ruptured and bombs made craters in the roads. People did not whine. They got on with life!

I remember one night the raid had been both prolonged and frightening. The ack-ack guns near our house were adding to the noise. We like most people around us had *not* dug out our garden to install an Anderson shelter. There was no compulsion about shelters.

Anyway this particular night my mother lay tense in bed beside Dad, he being asleep and having his deaf ear uppermost. Deaf ears definitely have their uses! An ammunition ship in the docks had received a direct hit from the German bombers. The noise was unbelievable as was the damage. Rows of dockside houses and warehouses were obliterated. The sky was brighter than day on this dark and terrible night with burning buildings adding to the roar from the ammunition explosions.

My mother could stand it no longer. She woke my father asking, 'Andrew, can you please carry the bed downstairs?'

Of course he complied. My mother was always his 'bonnie wee lassie'! Fear lent my mother strength. Over the bannister went the mattress, and down the stairs they struggled with the base, the type that was

hinged in two. The base, jack-knifed against the living room wall, made a square tunnel! The mattress was inserted and in they crawled. The Airedale dog, a large neurotic creature, crawled in as well! The cacophony continued outside, but my mother felt much safer.

Then Dad sat up, knocking his head and grumbling away to himself, twisting this way and that. Mother put up with it for a while and then spoke. 'Andrew, what's the matter?'

He was one of the bravest and most rational of men, but there was one small creature he could not stand.

'Annie, I've got a flea!' said Dad.

Well, it broke Mother's tension. She started to laugh. 'Oh Andrew, the heavens are falling about our ears and you're worried about a flea!'

The Airedale, who was the prime suspect of being the original host of the flea, was pushed out rapidly and back upstairs went the bed! It was never brought down again!

On the long cold winter nights the men not directly involved with the war were called upon to do warden duties in their streets by rota system. Mother always had the wardens in for coffee and sandwiches and a quick warm halfway through the night. It was hard on the men if it had been a bad night of air raids, because they still had to go off

I was 14 when the war started and we lived in South-East London.

As raids usually started early in the evening, we had to set off immediately after the evening meal to get a decent place in the shelter. So we set off every evening, looking like tramps laden with our sleeping blankets and all sorts of other items.

Sometimes when a string of bombs were dropped, we could hear the echoes through the tunnels and as they got nearer you waited for one to hit some building above the tunnel. In fact, one did while we were down there. It hit a men's lodging house called Rowton House, which was built above our platform. The masonry and tiles and everything fell down on the sheltering population and one man was killed and several injured.

Needless to say, all the lights went out and we were petrified. My father drove for the Royal Mail, and so had to be at work by six each morning and so we usually came up and out into the open by 5 a.m., when the raid, if it wasn't over, was at least coming to an end.

That particular morning we were greeted by rows of dead bodies in sacks that had been dug out of the bombed buildings. From then on that particular shelter was closed for repairs and so each evening we had to leave even earlier in the day to get to Waterloo Station which was the next station on.

Sometimes we slept there and sometimes at other stations. Wherever we could get in for the night. We were actually down Trafalgar Square Station one night when a bomb fell and demolished the top of an escalator. We then went to Piccadilly and even as far as Regent's Park. When we were at Trafalgar Square or Waterloo, we used to walk home in the mornings. I remember coming out of Trafalgar Square one morning and seeing a landmine caught high in one of the buildings in Northumberland Avenue. On another occasion both sides of Westminster Bridge Road, including St

Thomas' Hospital, had been bombed and set on fire and to get home we had to walk amid fire engines and hoses everywhere all across the road. During a lull in the Blitz I attended a makeshift school at Morley College, which catered for children like myself who had not been evacuated. However, after only a few weeks, the college too was hit by a bomb and several sheltering in the basement died. So I decided to get my first job in an office just up the road from the college.

It was in an engineers' merchants. Around about this time we were getting raids during the day as well but not heavy ones. We were all issued with tin hats and gas masks (which you could scarcely breathe through) and had to take our turn in pairs up on the roof to watch out for incendiary bombs while everyone else was in the basement. It was scary seeing the bombers overhead and knowing that they hadn't come with any peaceful intent!

My best friend, whom I had known since we were four years old, was evacuated with the rest of the school to Devon but she returned during the Blitz because the family she was billeted with had an older son who was showing an unhealthy interest in her, and so her parents brought her away! She lived down a side street from Morley College and she too had a bomb fall on her house, but luckily the family were in the Anderson shelter in their garden at the time. They then moved to a house at Ealing and from then on we spent alternate weekends with her parents and mine.

Life then wasn't the same as it is now. My particular memory of those days is that you didn't know how long you were going to be around and so you enjoyed every minute of your life while you still had it. Everyone was everybody else's friend.

Of course we had a permanent blackout at night with wardens on patrol to make sure that no lights were showing. Those were also the days of 'pea soup fogs', as they were called in London. A yellow fog used to come down and it literally surrounded everything and this, combined with the

My memories of the Blitz are when Sheffield was bombed. I was about 18 years old at the time and worked at Arthur Davy's, a bakery in Castle Street, Sheffield.

It was on a Thursday night when the first bombing came and at that time I lived in Tinsley. I don't know the exact time it started, but at Brinsworth we could hear the ack-ack guns being fired as the planes came over. The funny thing is that I wasn't frightened. In fact I went to bed thinking somehow that it wasn't our city being bombed!

Well, the next morning I got up for work about six o'clock and walked down for my tram to Sheffield, but none came. Then I was told about the bombing in the city and how all the trams had stopped running. So I started to walk going to Attercliffe. There was myself and many others walking, but we all kept diving nervously into doorways as mains exploded and buildings kept collapsing all around.

Going along Effingham Road you had to pass two gas cylinders. Both were on fire and it was really hot as we passed by. When I reached work the buildings all around were on fire and any that had not been demolished were badly damaged. Amazingly, my own place of work didn't seem too bad. By then a few of the staff had arrived but we couldn't get in because our boss wasn't there. My friend and I thought we would go to have a walk round the block, but when we did I shall never forget the sights that we saw. I thought that they were logs of charred trunks, but they were human bodies. We were told a lot were drivers and conductresses from the trams that had got caught in the bombing.

There was a hotel called Marples in Fitzalan Square. It got a direct hit and the people who had gone into the cellars all lost their lives.

I went back into work when the boss arrived, but I was totally shattered by what I had seen. The most damage we had was from the hosepipes and we cleaned a lot up but then we were told we just as well make our way home and so this time I got a lift on a lorry.

On the Sunday night around six o'clock the sirens went again, but now I knew what could happen and so I went into the shelter in the garden. The bombers came over and it was as if they were starting where they had left off on the Thursday. They were dropping fire-bombs and one went on to the church roof and another on a haystack near to us. I remember a number of them falling in our garden, and my dad throwing soil on them to put them out.

Mrs Billington on the right, with her friend from work.

Suddenly almost as quickly as it had started it was all over but I will never forget that inferno, and the sight of all those bodies lying in the centre of Sheffield and what war had done to ordinary lads and lasses from our lovely city.

Doris Billington

I saw that you were writing a book about the Blitz and I am wondering whether the enclosed letter, which my husband sent to a friend of his living in India, would be of use to you. His friend never received the letter and it was returned to us many months later, having been to a number of places en route. Unfortunately we were never able to trace our friend in spite of many enquiries.

My husband died in 1985 and going through his papers I came across this letter and on rereading it I feel that it is a wonderful example of the stoicism of the British people during the ghastly period.

132 Brockenhust Avenue,
Worcester Park, Surrey

Wednesday, 9 October 1940

Dear Robert,

'Jerry' is cruising overhead in a lovely starlit sky, with a quarter moon half-cock in the south, and is being – for the moment – casually fired at by some of our smaller guns. We have many sorts of armament; at least that is what one gathers from the cacophonous emission each night. There is one some of us call the 'tea tray'. It seems as if an enormous tray has been dropped upon a concrete floor. We have too a 'Chicago piano' (why I can't tell) which is like a prolonged sharp-toned rattling bark. Then, of course, harking back to 'good' old days, we have a 'long Tom' and 'pom-poms' and I know that Nazi airmen are well aware of their effect.

For the moment (8 p.m.) after 30 minutes of the night raid, all is quiet. It's amazing, Bob, how used we have become to this raiding. We hear much of 'military objectives' but since we are all front-liners, I am afraid there are no specified non-military locations or folk. I have seen many ruined spots and am afraid that we civilians are carrying the baby. Personally, up to the moment of writing (because Jerry is back again), no ill fortune has come upon me and the disturbance of life is negligible. I can carry on like this from now till doomsday. There are a number who have lost everything and by jingo I take my hat off to the great spirit amongst them. Somehow some new basis is found quickly and although sorrowed, the folk go on living in an uncanny way, which makes me think that we are generally inclined to fix false values on life. You have read no doubt of 'Thumbs Up' and such headline stuff but I can assure you that though we have 'Dismal Jimmies', regular defeatists, we have more hearts, men and women with guts, which makes me intensely proud of my heritage.

I thank whatever powers there be for the advent of Churchill. It is a new Churchill free from political sniping and devoted to the waging of a great crusade – and, Robert, you must accept my unbiased word that aristocrat and labourer have joined well in this fight. I am confident of our success, 'ultimate' is wrong; in the New Year I hope to be released for service. My objective is Observer RAF but, as I have recently remarked to someone else, I suppose it will be Rifleman, Royal Ulster Rifles.

Jerry is over again and using one of his new two-engined planes – the B*** has just dropped a visiting card – it made us jump a little. This bombing business should be good fun if limited to a fight between AA and planes but is damnably disconcerting if one wants to carry on a correspondence. I tried, between raids in the evening, to swot trig. But although much interested, found it difficult to concentrate.

Where can all this lead? Wrapped up in all this war spirit, we are inclined to forget what we are aiming at. I think that generally it is as well because the prospect is fairly dark and unpleasant. There is to me a bright light which is an enlightened world and a rationalising of thought. There must and will come a vast overhaul of Britain and the world, which means an approach to socialism. No, not red-headed uncontrolled dictatorship of communists. An assumption by the State of its responsibilities to each of its members, whereby a decent standard of life is assured to everyone, and there shall be a little less *privilege through possession of capital. This also envisages the same cooperation of labour and above all the removal of distrust through a radicalised educational system. And Robert smiles sardonically and murmurs 'Blurb!'*

I am grieved, Robert. For two years now I have been a fireman – up to date I have not fought a fire. The nights I go on duty, Jerry gets funky and leaves my part of the world alone; at least so it seems. I do hope that when my time comes my game will not be at the expense of some poor blighter. The government, by the way, is about to introduce a comprehensive insurance scheme. It's tardy but most sensible.

You have not, I presume, seen an aerial 'dogfight'. Bob, it's great fun. The last I saw was a mass of German bombers pondering through the blue evening sky and suddenly set upon by a number of RAF fighters which, naturally smaller, sailed into their midst and then performed amazing antics in and around the bombers. I saw five planes descending. Four of which I know were Nazis and one of which came down about a quarter of a mile away. My brother, Alan, in the RA, has recently suffered injury too through a playful gun trail and has been laid low with a fractured tibia. At the moment I am slightly worried over him because he has been detailed in hospital for observation – I hear at a distance that 'heart' trouble is suspected but am incredulous. My family is well. All round your and my old home, a fair amount of damage has been done – that makes me so angry, the homes of poor folk who are hard put in peacetime let alone war.

Dorrie is great these days. Her spirit and sangfroid is a tonic and nothing I say can amply pay tribute to her.

I have just halted to hear the news, which is not extraordinary – at least four planes down today, an exposure of German news falsehood, news from Turkey, Romania, USA – also commonplace nowadays but only revolutions and victories of great magnitude will hold our attention. It has also come to my mind that I have not commented upon many of the great events, Norway, Dunkirk, Dakar. You have read as well as I, and can judge as well of their importance. I have endeavoured to give you a close-up of my little world. In these days of great propaganda one does at times query the veracity of true statements *but I want you to be assured that what I have written you is true.*

I must cut in here again and speak of beautiful London. By reason of damaged railway lines I had to travel otherwise on one or two days and chanced to go over Lambeth Bridge on the top deck of a 46 bus. The morning was a bright fresh one, blue sky and small clouds flecked here and there, and London rising away from the riverbank, with a vision of splendour and greatness. Oh Bob, I wish I had the eloquence of Wordsworth, for I would outshine even the brilliance of his sonnet 'On Westminster Bridge'.

I, and I should stress we, do hope that life has treated you fairly. Our interest is in your movement and action. Whether you have made yet another 15 applications for an army job, if successful, how and censor permitting, where? There is not room for expansion in this theme rationally. We do, most

*sincerely, long to hear of your well-being and that is
the pith of our enquiry. Give us a note sometimes and
if you come home we can assure you of a welcome.
We wish you good luck and safe wandering.*

*Thus, sir, as Englishwoman and -man, to
Englishman, we salute you and say long live freedom
and peace and honour.*

Sincerely,
Dorrie and Bill

Dorrie Bolding

We lived on The Green at Kew and I was 19 at the time of the Blitz. The Green had been dug up the year before and air-raid shelters put underground there. I was a shorthand typist in a factory on the Great West Road, Brentford, which was across the river from Kew, and I still lived at home with my parents and my sister, Audrey who was two years younger than me.

During the Blitz, when the raids were at their height, it seemed the whole population of Kew would trek to the shelters each evening, loaded with hot water bottles, flasks of tea, blankets and knitting. It meant I would be able to sleep with my boyfriend Don – very daring! Fully clothed and in full company of family and friends but under the same blanket just the same!

He worked at an office in Richmond and joined the ARP (air-raid precaution) so he was sometimes on fire-watch duties at night. But then I would go into Richmond and visit him!

My sister recalled that her boyfriend, Eric, also on fire-watch duty, offered to take her to see the street's fire engine. Greatly intrigued, she was disappointed to find it was only a window-cleaner's barrow, equipped with ladders and hung about with buckets of sand, which would be used to throw over an incendiary bomb careless enough to drop within reach!

Jean Bolton (centre front holding baby Christopher) at the V.E. Day Party, Bushwood Road, Kew, 1945.

Sometimes we would visit a cinema in Richmond, walking home along the Kew Road with fish and chips in newspapers, eating as we went, and laying odds on how far we would get before the sirens sounded. Our parents must have been worried stiff, but somehow danger didn't figure in our lives then. I remember walking back to the office one lunchtime when sirens sounded and a plane droned overhead. We had been told to lie flat in the road on such occasions to escape the blast of any bombs that didn't actually fall on us. But all I remember thinking was how silly I'd feel actually lying there all alone on such a beautiful sunny day and so I walked on! I can clearly remember thinking also, how could anything happen to *me*?

I remember particularly 7 September 1940, which was my birthday. As a birthday treat my boyfriend Don and I went to the West End to see *Cottage to Let*. The play was performed by the now late lamented Leslie Banks, Alistair Sim and a very youthful George Cole! The programme I remember said 'Don't be alarmed by bangs and sirens during the play – it is part of the plot'. Actually, that was the night that hundreds of tons of bombs fell on the London Docks, so bangs were going on both inside and out of the theatre! When we came out we found that all Underground stations had been closed and so those of us who couldn't get home were invited to spend the night in the theatre's basement bar. Of course, we did this, and we were very thrilled to be so close to the stars of the show. When we arrived home next morning at dawn we were greeted by frantic parents who had witnessed the blazing skies from Kew Bridge and knew we were in the midst of it all.

'Why all the fuss?' we wanted to know.

Of course we were *all right*. The young don't change do they?!

As a shorthand typist I remember I had to spend a lot of time copying out all the documents in the business. These then had to be stored in a safe place in case our building was blown up! What a job – no photocopying in those days! But eventually they were all done and we were then informed that a new factory had been built for us in the wilds of Gloucestershire and we were all going to move down there for the duration.

Friends and relations willingly gave up their precious clothing coupons so that we could evacuate with as many respectable items of clothing as possible, but what I particularly remember is joyfully buying pink bedroom slippers and somehow or other I got hold of some silky material to make some glamorous undies! However, when all was ready and farewell parties over, would you believe it a bomb dropped on the new factory and so we all went back to square one! But I do remember that we kept all our new clothes! My boyfriend joined the Royal Air Force but as our factory was on war work, I was in a 'reserved occupation', even though I was only a typist!

In 1942 Don and I were married – 'It will never last – you are too young' etc etc. A year later our first baby – Christopher – arrived and we lived in two rooms in my mother-in-law's house, and during air raids slept under the Morrison shelter in her dining room.

Mother-in-law took her Post Office savings book each night and put it under her pillow! That was when the war really began to get to us – having the baby made me realise how dangerous it all was and all you could do was pray that you wouldn't be hit. It all became beyond a joke, as my granny said!

Till then, as a young girl, I quite enjoyed the war. Little did we realise what it was all about. I don't remember seeing any of the films which have been shown lately of the horrors of the first war and certainly we knew nothing of the ghastly goings-on in the concentration camps either. I suppose it was important to keep up morale but I often think a greater sense of urgency would have been engendered and we would have put more effort into our work if we had known more.

Jean Bolton

In 1940 my family faced the Blitz. There was Dad, who was a steel mill worker and a volunteer fireman; Mam, with five children – myself and four others – and pregnant with another one; Dad's father (who was in dementia) and Gran, who was aged 73 and had only one leg. I was 12 at the time and Mam certainly had her hands full! Teesside was not Coventry or London but it was a very important industrial target and well defended with anti-aircraft guns, barrage balloons and smoke screen devices.

I was nearly 13 when the Blitz really got under way. Just the right age for adventure! I can't remember myself and my younger brother, Peter, feeling afraid of the Blitz. Excited, yes, but not afraid.

One of the most vivid Blitz memories for me was of coming out of the cinema after seeing *Mutiny on the Bounty* with Clark Gable and Charles Laughton. We lived maybe a mile and a half  from the Hippodrome, normally 20 minutes' walk away. That night action started early. 'The air-raid siren has sounded' sign had appeared at either side of the cinema stage at about 9.15 p.m. Some patrons walked out but others stayed. Amongst them were Peter and me.

After about 15 minutes, as we watched Clark Gable lead the mutineers away from Tahiti and the vengeful Bligh, a burst of gunfire sounded. It was so loud that we could hear it even inside the cinema. We stayed until the end of the picture but then left to find our way home.

The gunfire was deafening. There was a mobile AA gun on Teesside and it was fired often from sites around Middlesbrough. As we ran from shop doorway to shop doorway, sometimes crawling on our hands and knees, we could hear the shrapnel falling like rain and hitting the rooftops all along Linthorpe Road, the main road of Middlesbrough.

We eventually arrived back home at the family brick street shelter to a worried mother and neighbours to whom we related the story of our hands and knees journey home!

When the 'all clear' sounded we immediately left the shelter to start collecting shrapnel for souvenirs. It was one of many exciting nights for me.

Another occasion was one night after the air-raid warning had sounded about half past 12, I think. Within minutes and before we had had the time to get out of the bedrooms and down to the shelter we heard the bombs coming down. I think there were five or six in the stick. They fell across the part of the town where we lived, starting about 200 yards from our home and ending on the other side of a public park. We heard them coming and we ducked I can assure you!

The worst night for me and one of many bad ones was the night our biggest co-op emporium, along with a paint shop and a filling station, and a block of shops opposite, were bombed and set on fire just at the bottom of our road. Dad had come home from the two to ten shift and had turned out to fight the fire. It was a very long bad night. When I saw him it was about 7.30 a.m. the next morning and he was wet, black and tired out and white-faced. I realised then that he would have to turn out for work in another six hours! I grew up a bit and started to get frightened at last. I could go on. There were other nights. Some worse. Some better.

Joe Bradley

War was exciting! Who amongst us youngsters could deny it? Air-raid sirens, gas masks, periods to be spent in school cellars, and Anderson shelters were all diversions welcome to the younger element. A raid after midnight meant no school until 10 a.m. the following morning and, while school shelters were being built, only half-day schooling was in vogue. Ignorance was bliss, and the knowledge of the true horrors of war had not yet reached us.

If the days were full, our nights were often disturbed by the regular air raids over nearby strategic targets. Sirens and the sound of falling bombs and the anti-aircraft fire became part of our normal lives. Soon these became commonplace and it was not unusual for us to fall asleep in our beds until woken in the Anderson shelter. For everyone it was the job of a father or older brother to expertly execute the transfer from one to the other of our places of repose.

One night was different, for the sounds of war were even closer, and none but the deepest of sleepers could have been insensitive to the earblasting cacophony of sound. Blast upon blast rent the air. The sky was lit by not-too-distant fires and a German plane now obviously off course was caught in the beams of searchlights overhead. It circled the village, no doubt attempting to avoid the heavy flak over its original target area, and seeking for an escape route back across the North Sea. It circled once more and then ditched its bomb load and headed east.

Every window rattled and some shattered as the sound of two massive explosions reverberated, it seemed for ever, to be followed by the drone of the lone aircraft and the crack-crack of anti-aircraft guns. We speculated as to direction and distance of the explosions as we stood outside the shelter.

Our curiosity had outweighed the fears of adult and child alike. All agreed that there had been some that were 'pretty close' but only morning would tell.

Morning was a Saturday and we were all up well before time to learn that the prime target had been an engineering works some four miles to the east. This had been damaged, as had the nearby goods station, but *our* bombs had fallen much closer. The Fells above the village had been the unwitting target, as we soon learned, and we hastened to the scene.

The two high-explosive bombs had fallen on and had felled a good portion of a plantation of conifers!

Wide spaces amongst untouched trees were littered with charred debris ranging in size from whole tree trunks shorn of their branches, to splinters of less than an inch. A souvenir much coveted and admired by the young boys who swarmed over the area was a piece of bark in which was embedded a jagged piece of shrapnel. The whole situation created a great deal of consternation to the handful of air-raid wardens and auxiliary firemen and a single policeman who were trying to control the situation!

A small farm near the plantation had escaped any damage, despite its close proximity to the explosions. However, it had been completely encircled by incendiary bombs! Their presence was marked by the rings of burnt areas of grass and gorse, some of which were still smouldering. I have to admit that I remember that the firemen and volunteers were hampered in their task of damping down the area by the ever-curious and excited boys continually on the lookout for souvenirs!

Consternation approaching panic was experienced by the local schoolmistress on the following Monday morning when one of her older pupils turned up with an unexploded incendiary. Apparently it was his relic of Friday night's raid! Gold-silver in colour and some 12 inches in length and three inches in diameter, it had been retrieved from a small crater that it had created amongst the gorse.

A hurried message to the local constabulary was followed by the sight of the bomb, nestling on a bucket of sand, in the furthest corner of the schoolyard. Guarding it were two timorous members of the staff, ably and proudly assisted by two of the 'big boys' with stirrup pump, water bucket, sand shovel and a piece of soaked sacking at the ready.

School was hurriedly dismissed for the day and the cheers which accompanied this announcement were concurrent with those for our intrepid souvenir hunter. The fate of that bomb was *never* determined!

Much later we learned that our neighbouring village was

visited by the same retreating bomber and had also received its quota of two high-explosive bombs! But its trees and gorse were real flesh and blood as the bombs fell on its local pub and houses.

Aidan Harrison

One morning two of my friends and I were cycling to work and as we were rounding the corner into Ilford Lane, where the factory was located, a postman said, 'Don't bother to go to work this morning, girls, your factory isn't there any more.'

Apparently the Germans had dropped a load of bombs on it during the night. The only thing left standing was two brick air-raid shelters!

However, our boss was not going to be beaten. He told us to give him a couple of weeks and he would set up some machines in the shelters. This he did and it was business as usual in no time. He started a night shift and we worked two weeks on days and two weeks on nights.

The worse part was cycling to work at night because the sirens always sounded before we had reached the factory gates but we used to just cycle on like bats out of hell, and we

Outside John Ismay & Sons, Eileen Morrison far right.

were always pleased to reach the warmth and safety of the shelter.

Towards the end of the Blitz, Mr Deshaw, our boss, announced one day that he was so pleased with the way that we had rallied round and hadn't missed a day's or night's work except for illness, that he was going to give us all a medal each!

He was true to his word. He had eight gold medals struck and the rest were silver, and as he considered that we had all been equally brave and conscientious, he drew our names out of a hat for the eight gold medals and to my delight I and my two cycling friends each received one. Each of the medals had the inscription 'For Courage and Devotion to Duty During Intense Aerial Warfare'.

The firm was John Ismay & Sons and we manufactured electric lightbulbs. I left the firm in 1942 to join the ATS, and was stationed in London just off the Tottenham Court Road. So far as I was concerned I was out of the frying pan into the fire!

Still we survived and it wasn't all bad.

Eileen Morrison

I was a schoolgirl in the Blitz and living in the city of Norwich in Norfolk with my older sister and my mum and dad. My two brothers were in the Forces.

Norwich had been bombed many times but the time I remember most was when the city was bombarded with incendiary bombs. The siren had gone – and the crash warning came almost at the same time – leaving us no time to vacate my parents' public house and retreat to our 'safe' shelter under the Roman Catholic church/cathedral into one of their vaults which had been turned into an air-raid shelter. With hindsight I shudder to think how we would all have been buried under tons of masonry had the church been hit. Fortunately, for us it never was!

Bombs were dropping all round our pub. There was a garage opposite to us and this was ablaze with enormous ferocity. All the windows in Dad's pub were blown out by explosives and we stood at the top of the cellar steps, huddled together and witnessing destruction and fire all around us. Our old dog, a Labrador called Niger, was actually crying! The noise was deafening. Bombs 'whistled' as they came down before their inevitable crash. The few guns we had around Norwich were doing their best, but we were all terribly frightened.

Suddenly my sister started to sing 'There'll always be an England' and I remember my mum and dad and myself joined with her, singing our heads off as if somehow we would be letting 'Jerry' know that he wouldn't beat us anyway!

As if by a miracle the raid stopped. Everything went quiet except the noise of the burning buildings and the firemen's voices and hoses of water trying to put out the fires of Norwich.

My father started pulling pints of beer and was handing these to the firemen through the window frames. The 'all clear' came and we were told we would have to evacuate from our home as there was a 500-pound unexploded bomb on the other side of the road! There was an army billet quite nearby and I don't remember how, but suddenly an army vehicle appeared and we were driven through the city to go to stay with my auntie who lived at the other end of Norwich at Thorpe. The ride in that army vehicle, although quite exciting for a 12-year-old, was like a ride into Hell. We went over firemen's hoses and the whole of the centre of Norwich seemed to be on fire. My favourite theatre – The Hippodrome – was a raging inferno. Chamberlains, which was a high-class store, stood like a gaunt shell with great flames shooting through the store and right up through the roof. Wherever we looked all we seemed to see was fire and chaos.

As we came to Prince of Wales Road it suddenly seemed as if Norwich was 'normal' again. The raid had not affected this part of Norwich at all. We arrived at my auntie's house.

Hazel Carey with her father in the Home Guard.

Her and my uncle also ran a pub called The Redan at Thorpe, and we had to knock to awaken them. They had slept right through the Blitz, and didn't even know there had been a raid! Would you believe it! The best part was that after our frightening ordeal I can remember my feeling of utter anger as my auntie fainted! She had been tucked up in bed and didn't know anything about the dreadful happenings going on, and yet had the nerve to faint at our unexpected arrival in the early hours!

The unexploded bomb was eventually defused and we were allowed to go back. I seem to remember it was after about three days. Everywhere and everything had changed. And the smell of burned buildings was everywhere. Our pub, the Tuns Inn at St Giles, managed to survive the war and being hit by any bombs and still stands as the second oldest pub in Norwich.

I grew up quickly during the war, and although I was extremely frightened lots of the time my strongest feeling is of a time when everyone was friendly and helpful towards their fellow man, and although we went short of many things, we never went without friends.

Hazel Carey

My story is of the Manchester Blitz although I was at the time in the Eston Fire Brigade. Eston is situated to the east of Middlesbrough. Manchester had already suffered badly from a raid on Sunday night of the 22 December 1940, and on Monday, 23 December a call was received at about half past three in the morning from our chief officer, Tommy Donaldson, to our section leader, Stan Haggath, ordering him and a crew of four men with a heavy trailer pump and towing vehicle to prepare to leave for Manchester. The remainder of the crew was made up of firemen, Dick Bean, Ken Brown, Jimmy Wilde and myself.

At about quarter past seven that evening, air-raid warnings were sounding all over the city, and officers in charge of units were told to report to the control officer in the dining hall. Our crew was detailed to reinforce Station 30 of the Central Division, with a Manchester fireman as our escort. By the time we arrived at Station 30 the Blitz was well under way, and flares illuminated the city. Bombs were dropping and the glow from incendiary fires lit up the sky. Patrol Officer Sturgess, who was the officer in charge of the station, informed us that we were the next turnout.

Fire call came. We were ordered to proceed to the Corporation Street district with again a Manchester fireman as pilot. We arrived at the scene of the fire where four- and five-storey buildings in the shopping centre were involved. Immediately we had difficulty in locating a hydrant because some crews were already in action using them. Eventually, however, we found a burst main and utilised the floodwater as though working from a dam.

High-explosive and incendiary bombs were falling around us and we had barely vacated one point between two burning buildings when a bomb fell within yards of the spot and the blast almost extinguished the blaze with which we were contending!

By the morning of 24 December we had the fire completely under control and made up our gear and realised that the initiative was on the officer in charge of units, because it was obvious that when one fire was extinguished the best course of action was to move on to the next nearest blaze and take action rather than return to the station for further orders. Almost every street in that area was strewn with used and abandoned hoses. In some cases they were still connected to standpipes with the branch pipe attached. We continued into action on a block of shops in an adjacent thoroughfare, and it was about 5 a.m. on the morning of 24 December that we finally got this blaze extinguished.

We were then directed by our Manchester pilot to Piccadilly. This was an extensive job involving six- and seven-storey buildings on which numerous pumps were in action, including appliances of the regular brigade. On this scene a crew of Auxiliary Fire Service men lost their lives as a result of high-explosive bombs, which also wrecked their trailer pump. Our own appliance was in danger of being buried by collapsing walls or by firing through heat radiation, and we were ordered by a Manchester section officer to abandon our pump but leave the controlled branches in position on the fire.

At first we obeyed the order and retired to safety, but within minutes we had our own rethink, and decided on trying to save the pump and acted accordingly, being successful in dragging the complete unit to safety without closing down our water delivery.

At 10 a.m. the same day we were replaced by another crew and returned to St Josephs for a meal and a rest. We had been continually fighting fires in three different areas of Manchester for 15 hours without a break. However, despite this when we returned to St Josephs we found that the catering arrangements were decidedly poor because we then had to queue for 35 minutes for a slice of bread and some unidentified meat roll and a mug of tea!

After four hours' rest we left for Piccadilly to find our pump unit still in action but beginning to become overheated

due to a stoppage in the cooling system. After repairs we were able to remove our pump from the fire ground and were ordered back again to Station 30. Most of the larger fires were now under control so we were able to standby at the Muster House. The next day of course was Wednesday, 25 December. On the previous night there had been no enemy action, and we began to believe that perhaps the spirit of Christmas had reached the Germans! We reported for duty at 8 a.m., but by midday we received our first call out to a clothing factory. I vaguely remember being lashed by ropes to a pillar above burning materials to prevent me falling while directing a jet of water into the fire. That fire was under control in about half an hour, and we then returned to Station 30.

Still on the same day, Christmas Day 1940, at about 6.20 in the evening we received a return call to Piccadilly to deal with fresh outbreaks of fire mainly caused by fractured gas mains. I believe that it was on this call that I first realised the dangers of firefighting, for not only had we to risk the danger of escaping gas, but also to be aware that large coping stones were dropping around us from the top of this seven-storey building. I should point out that our reason for extinguishing the gas flames was not only in the interests of public safety, but to prevent enemy bomber crews from seeing the flames from above. That night fortunately there was no further enemy action!

It was on Boxing Day 1940 that our section leader, Patrol Officer Stan Haggath, was able at last to get through to Eston by telephone and speak to Chief Officer Tommy

Donaldson. By that time of course the chief officer had been inundated with calls from our wives who had up to that time been unable to find out what was happening and if we were all right. Incidentally at this stage I ought to mention that Christmas had now passed, but that instead of turkey and all the trimmings for Christmas dinner we had gorged ourselves with a marvellous meal of Oxo and two cracker biscuits each!

At three o'clock on 26 December we were informed that a convoy was believed to be leaving from Manchester, and we rang Central Control for confirmation, but we were then informed that this was not the case although we would be released from our duties with the arrival of a relief crew from Oldham. The control officer asked about our condition and Stan Haggath said that two of his men were unfit due to fatigue and lack of food. The control officer apologised for the lack of food and said we were to be relieved from duty very soon. We would then be able to return home at our convenience.

At six o'clock that evening we left Station 30 for home after reporting out at the Auxiliary Fire Service Headquarters. Driving conditions were very poor owing to the heavy fog so we decided to find billets outside of Manchester rather than travel by night over the Pennines. We found a billet at about nine o'clock that night at Marsden, near Huddersfield, and we eventually arrived back home at Eston at one o'clock on 27 December 1940.

In 1940 Eston Fire Brigade consisted of just five 'regular' firemen and about 100 auxiliary firemen who manned the Central Fire Station and other satellite stations in the area. Eston had already experienced wartime bombing when the Blitz on the larger towns and cities in England began. I just thought you might like to know that this story shows that many small fire brigades like Eston's were ready to assist the much larger brigades when the need arose.

There were many horrific happenings during the war

period, but one of the pluses was the nationalisation of the small fire brigades, particularly in the standardisation of equipment. When we arrived at Manchester our standpipes did not fit their hydrants! This at least was sorted out when the fire brigades were nationalised.

George Clark

I have a little anecdote to tell you about my childhood in London during the war. My sister, Betty, and I were running home from school one day to have our midday dinner. We were running along the main road called Lewisham Way when we suddenly saw two planes flying very low. They were so low that we could even see the pilots' heads and a black cross on the body of the planes.

Then just as suddenly we realised they were German planes. A soldier who happened to be passing by suddenly pushed us both against the church wall of St John's Church, and covered us with his body. At that moment we heard a shrill whistling noise and then the crunch of a bomb exploding about a quarter of a mile away.

The soldier told us then to run on home to our mum, which we did. Then we had our dinner and though we were very frightened and still shook up, we decided to go back to school that afternoon. Weren't we good children!

I shall always remember as we ran up the steps to our school that the headmistress, Mrs Peake, was standing there and she opened her arms to us and said 'oh my brave British children'.

We discovered later that the bombs had crashed on to a street *right* next to our school and two sisters who had just gone home to dinner, like we had, were killed with their mother and younger brothers and sisters. One of the sisters was called Jean and was in my class and the other was called Audrey and was in my sister's class. Of the whole family, only their father and older brother escaped because they were both at work at the time. They were the Peckham family from

Oscar Street, Deptford. How very sad it all was.

Also that very day was the day that a school at Catford in South-East London was bombed at dinnertime and many children and some teachers were also killed.

Our school at Deptford, which was Lucas Vale School, was exactly the same type of building as Sandhurst Road School in Catford, which was bombed also. We often wonder if those pilots, one having just got the Catford School, were aiming at our school at Deptford, which would have been very near each other from the air.

Betty on the left with her mother and Helen.

I was 11 years old at the time and my sister was nearly 14. Strangely enough I happened recently to find some old school books. As I was glancing through a poetry book I noticed that I had put above each poem the name of a girl in my class.

There, very poignantly, so that it brought tears to my eyes, was Jean Peckham's name. God bless her and I hope she rests in peace.

Helen Clarke

My most poignant experience of the whole war, and one that haunts me still at times, took place at the dawn of a perfect June morning, with the sun just starting to blaze down on us.

It is indeed remarkable how the Good Lord gives us the best weather in times of crisis, such as the Retreat to Dunkirk and the Battle of Britain.

In this case Colonel Robinson and I were just leaving the main ARP Centre in Southampton after a night's raid when one of the officials came up to the colonel and said, 'Sir, there has been an incident of a serious nature in a close on the outskirts of the town. Would you care to go and have a look at it?'

'Think you can find it, Collier?' said Colonel Robinson to me as I went back to my car and proceeded out of the town towards Reading and found it down a side turning off the main road. I was glad about that as I was already getting very tired after a full night's work.

The Close was a pleasant recently built estate with a high-class underground air-raid shelter which the families had clubbed together and built privately for themselves.

The Luftwaffe had come over and when the sirens went, the inhabitants of The Close had just trooped down to it almost automatically.

Jerry's tactics were always the same. They would come over the town, turn round and release their bombs as they swept out to sea. In this case, by a million to one chance, one of the bombs scored a direct hit on this underground shelter and killed every one of the occupants, about 20 of them.

The ARP were hauling out the mangled bodies as we arrived on the scene and the only survivor of the estate was an old man of about 70 who was standing on the pavement of his house with tears streaming down his face.

'I went through the whole of the 1914–18 War,' he said to me. 'And I was determined that no Bosch would get me out of bed so I stayed there and this had to happen.'

All the houses were absolutely intact with the exception of one slate dislodged off a roof. I had never been in an air-raid shelter during a raid, and I can tell you that this convinced me never to do so.

But we had our funny things as well. I was in the regional headquarters of the southern region in Reading. I well remember being taken to the great fire in Leatherhead when Jerry had dropped some bombs late at night on to what I think were some oil storage tanks, and it was indeed ablaze for very many hours.

We had most of the fire services from southern England there helping, and I had a well-earned cup of tea at about 4 a.m. with a leading fireman who I remember said genially, 'This was a nice little fire, but you should have seen the one at Liverpool recently. We kept that one alight for 14 days and nights!' Such was the cheerful bonhomie of those wartime days.

Michael Collier

During World War Two the great port of Liverpool was naturally high on the list of enemy targets and at one time the city suffered eight continuous nights of bombing. The Docks in the Mersey Estuary stretched from Liverpool right up to Bootle and at this time I was a young girl of 16, living at Balfour Road, Bootle, within half a mile of Gladstone Dock, the last one in a long line stretching from Liverpool.

One Saturday evening, in the middle of the eight-day Blitz, I was sitting in the lounge with my younger brother and my grandfather, when we heard the whistle of a descending bomb quite close at hand. My grandfather, with great presence of mind, pushed my brother and I quickly under the table and within seconds the large window frame crashed into the room right on to the sofa where my brother and I had been sitting. It fell with such force that the sofa was split in two and the whole room was littered with splintered glass. As I emerged from the table, I saw that the blast had caused five doors to implode into the room. It was a lucky escape.

Later that night, a huge timber store at the back of our house caught fire, and on the same evening, Bryant & May's match works went up in a terrific blaze. The timberyard fire caught a corner house in a cul-de-sac and a sudden change of wind caused the flames to spread quickly down three or four houses in a row, with a common roof, to our house at the end.

It quickly blazed furiously back and front. My father dashed up the street to try and rescue some horses which he believed were trapped in a stable and my mother and I went upstairs to see what we could salvage. She went into one bedroom and I went into the other. As we came out on the landing a flaming beam crashed down between us, just missing me but catching my mother's forehead slightly.

Next day she decided to go to hospital for treatment and her sister-in-law offered to accompany her. While the two women were away, their two young sons, both aged 11 years, went to investigate the damage of the previous night.

As young boys will do, they were tempted to stray on to an area of the estuary shore above Gladstone Dock, which was fenced off with barbed wire and which had 'Danger – Mines' notices displayed pro-minently. One of the boys slipped through the barbed wire easily but the other, my brother, caught his clothing on the barbs. While he was extricating himself, he still claims that he saw a bomb coming down, followed by a large explosion, but the coroner later said that he believed that what my brother

saw was the body of his cousin coming to earth after he had trodden on a mine. At any rate my cousin was killed. They later found his head and shoulders separated.

Later that morning my grandfather was on his way to church when he met an acquaintance and stopped to shake hands with her. While they were greeting each other, a delayed action bomb suddenly exploded. My grandfather's friend was killed instantly as she stood next to him, but he escaped with nothing more than a cut to the head where a brick caught him. Such are the tricks played by a blast from a bomb.

There is also a note from John Godwin, the husband of Elizabeth Godwin, which, while not a matter strictly of the Blitz, is nevertheless of interest. His record is as follows:

One day in 1944 while I was living in my parents' house in Hednesford, Staffordshire, we experienced a tremendous rattling of all of our windows and it was only later that the full details came out as to what had happened. In a little hamlet named Fauld, near Burton-on-Trent, an underground dump of Royal Air Force high-explosive bombs had been triggered off accidentally and the result was the biggest bang that England had ever experienced. In fact, it was the biggest man-made bang in the world apart from Atom Bombs.

In all, about 3,500 tons of high-explosive bombs went up. Farms were wiped out and about 70 people were killed. Had the store not been in the country, many more people would have been killed. Even today there is a huge crater about three-quarters of a mile long still visible and about 70 feet deep.

John and Elizabeth Godwin

As a private in the 7th Worcestershire Division I was stationed in Hull in Yorkshire when at that time the Blitz was in full swing with raids practically every night and also on many days as well. I met my wife while I was at Hull.

From the start of the Blitz until we got married my wife hadn't slept in a bed, but had spent every night in the shelter. One night we went to see a picture at the Mayfair Cinema and we always picked a

Mr Lench second from the left.

seat against a pillar in case of an air raid. There was one that night, and believe me the whole cinema shook, but I passed it off by saying that they were the big naval guns going off.

Anyway when we left it was like daylight in the street. Everything was bathed in moonlight. All of a sudden a plane came just clearing the rooftops and I can clearly remember machine gunning and that the bullets were rattling on the slates. We rushed to the nearest shelter and I pushed the wife down and as soon as the sound had died away we ran to the next shelter and so on until we got home.

I returned to my unit one night during an air raid and I can remember that the centre of Hull was in flames. Just as I came out of the station entrance a plane had been hit and was going down, and I actually saw the German pilot disappearing into the flames of Hammond Stores in his parachute.

That same night I saw the shape of a policeman on duty outside the Shellmex building. He was there one second, and the next he was gone. I remember that all they found of him was his helmet, about 500 yards away on Paragon Street.

The people of Hull were the bravest, good-natured people I have ever met and believe me until the end of the German Airforce I don't think they had many peaceful nights' sleep. But they were always up and ready for work the next day.

For the size of the city in those days they must have had the worst bombing of the war.

Edward Lench

I was nine years old at the time of the Blitz. Home was a terraced semi somewhere in Felixstowe. Coal fire, tin bath, scrubbed and hosed down once a week in front of the fire. Light was provided by a gas mantle.

Suitably attired in an old shirt of my father's, I can remember being marched upstairs, equipped with a candle to light my way to bed. My bedroom today would be called a fridge! The sheets on my bed were like sheets of ice. In winter, icicles formed inside the window frame.

By the end of the war we had moved house four times as a result of bombing and machine gunning. My uncle had been killed serving in the Royal Navy. His ship had struck a mine just outside Harwich Harbour. In fact, I believe two went off together. After all these years the explosion still rings in my ears. A second uncle had his legs shot from under him at Dunkirk.

I remember as a child being kitted out with a gas mask, and all sorts of information was broadcast on the radio. Everything was then repeated at school, followed by the appropriate drill: 'Don't pick anything up in the road.'

I was soon to learn the wisdom in that. One of my school chums, slightly older than me, had his hands blown off by what he thought was a pencil. As the war progressed we were moved from Felixstowe to Leicester, and then from Leicester to Ipswich, where it seemed that every day and every night we found out what saturation bombing was.

Ipswich was splattered. Bombers came over in waves like big clouds and very high. One evening it seemed the bombers outnumbered the stars. Bombs came down like confetti and searchlights and tracers criss-crossed the sky. 'Bread baskets' came sailing down. These were bomb-shaped containers designed to deliver large numbers of incendiary bombs all at once, opening up while on the way down. During time off from school we used to wander around the fields and streets looking for unexploded incendiaries. If we found any we found it quite easy to dismantle them by unscrewing the detonator and removing the spring and kicking them off with a long cane out of harm's way.

To us it was harmless fun, but looking back it was deadly dangerous! In addition to this little pleasure there were on the heath ack-ack batteries, close-range weapons such as Bofors, pom-poms, armed Bren gun carriers, all designed to deter low-flying aircraft attacking the factories and airfield.

My parents, being occupied on munitions work, had no control over us kids. We were left to fend for ourselves! I remember one day we were up on the heath with the soldiers, passing the ammunition to the gunners while they were gunning the enemy aircraft overhead. It got so intense one day that the soldiers ordered us to run home and shelter. We were accompanied by two more youngsters who were our school chums. They were deaf and couldn't speak so well. We charged down the road, arriving at my gate, but I saw that one of them had blood pouring down his legs. I was trying to tell him to keep running and get home to his mum but we had been gunned running down the road home. The bullets hadn't hit him, it was tarmac spitting up from the bullets that had actually punctured his legs.

That night my mother had attended a canteen dance at the factory with the elder sister of these same two boys. At 10 p.m the bombers arrived to give the factories and the nearby airfields a thrashing. My parents eventually arrived home with the boys' sister and I can remember just having a quick cup of tea and saying goodnight to her before being whisked to next door's shelter! This was a magnificent concrete dugout. The concrete must have been a foot thick and there were three tier bunks with all mod cons. It has got to still be there. No one could take it apart!

The bombing that night frightened me. I had been thrown out of my bunk by the explosions. It was horrendous and so intense and so loud that you couldn't distinguish between gunfire and bombs exploding. Then the 'all clear' sounded so Dad and I ventured into the road. There were incendiaries burning all over the place. It was absolutely deadly danger-ous and the odd straggling bomber was still just as likely to give you a farewell pasting, or leave some 'presents' for the kids to pick up.

The road was well lit and burning, so Dad and I went down the road to help with whatever we could. You could smell death. It had a certain smell about it. It got up your nose and in your mouth. There was a horrible 'cut-up' flesh smell. Indescribable, but anyone who has experienced this never forgets it.

My friends' house at the corner of Landseer Road and Nackton Road had vanished. I set to clawing at the debris on my hands and knees and looking to find my friends. A stock-inged foot protruded through the rubble. I pulled feverishly at it and the whole leg came out, with all the pieces and guts hanging by threads of torn flesh. That was all that was left of my mother's friend, the girl I had said goodnight to just a few hours earlier. After all these years I can still see in my mind's eye that leg as if it had happened yesterday. The whole Nunn family had been blown away and a lone soldier son came home to bury all his family.

Later my father and I set about digging our own air-raid shelter. We shared this with the old lady next door. We were reasonably safe and away from the town, and so I was allowed out at night with my mates, under strict orders to be in by 9 p.m.! 'If there is a raid get home fast.'

I saw bombs falling and often wondered which way I would run if one came my way!

One night I heard crying. A little girl was sitting on her front doorstep across the road, quite alone. I ran over to comfort her. Her mum and dad had slipped out down the pub for an hour and so I stayed with her holding her hand and waiting till they got home. I wasn't brave. I was just as frightened as she was. There was a raid on at the time, and I can remember the ground shaking as the bombs whistled down.

Towards the end of the war I had had enough. I used to go to bed and cry if my father came to me to get me up during the air raids. I know now that I must have been close to a breakdown. I can remember saying to him that if a bomb hits this house, I want to be in bed!

Just a few years ago I took my wife to the street where we lived. I stopped my car outside the house, just to be there again. Then amazingly I saw the same girl whose hand I had held! I called her using her Christian name, so as not to startle her because I was a stranger. I asked her if she remembered that it was me that used to hold her hand!

'Of course I do,' she replied, tears rolling down her cheeks. 'I never forgot you or that night.'

Sidney Davies

I was the manager of a bakery in South-East London in September 1940. Then came that great Saturday afternoon raid on London by the German bombers who had broken through our air defences. My wife and my two little boys and myself were in Lewisham shopping, and I remember we were in a large department store when the siren went. There was no panic. Everyone was advised to go to the basement area. This we did and there we listened to the explosions going on above until all at once there was a tremendous crash overhead and suddenly we found ourselves enveloped in dust and debris.

The store had suffered a direct hit but thanks to the management's advice in directing us all to the basement, no one was injured. Many suffered shock, as might be expected, but then eventually the 'all clear' went and we all came out into the bright sunlight.

What a mess. The whole street was a shambles. About half a mile up the main road leading to Deptford were the crashed remains of a German bomber. All the shop windows had been blown out and their goods were scattered far and wide. We had never seen anything like it.

Then the siren went again and we all made for the large public underground shelter. Here I stood next to an old lady who was sitting on a seat rocking to and fro. I asked her if she was all right and then amidst her tears she replied that she was all right, but she felt upset. Her only son had been killed 22 years before fighting in a war to end wars, and now she realised that it had all been in vain.

Then came the 'all clear' again and we made for home and when we reached the top of the hill below where we lived, we could see right across Docklands and the East End of London, and it was just one mass of flames as far as the eye could see. It was then that I decided it was time for my wife and children to leave London, so the next day I took them to Euston and put them on the train to my wife's sister at Wellingborough, who had been begging her to come for days. I remained in London to carry on with my job.

From that Saturday in late September 1940, right up until Christmas, we suffered air raids every night. We were unable to go to bed properly, we just used to crawl into an improvised shelter built out of stout timbers from bombed buildings and tried to get some rest. The government issued us with earplugs to deaden the sound of the guns and bombs. Our bakery was hit twice, but we never stopped baking for more than 12 hours at any time and this was only to carry out repairs to the machines and building. At this particular time 26 bakeries were completely destroyed in our area, and so it was vital that we continue in order to meet the needs of the people. Although we kept up production, we lost a number of our staff during this period who were either killed or injured.

I remember that on the night of 20 September, my staff were working but they were nervous because the warning siren could not be heard above the noise of the machinery. So I agreed to remain outside and call them if things got too threatening. There was a raid on, and I could hear the planes approaching and the crunch of bombs as they fell. When these sounds got too near for comfort I called the staff out, and we made for the shelter, but before we could reach it we heard the scream of a falling bomb.

So we all flattened ourselves on the ground. Seconds afterwards the earth seemed to lift up as the bomb hit the road in front of us and exploded. We were totally enveloped in dust and choking smoke but we had no casualties and we made it to the shelter just as a second bomb fell about 100 yards further on. The shelter was crowded with people and some women had fainted and there was a cry for water. I knew where water had been available in the bakery but whether it was still obtainable now was impossible to say. However, I borrowed one of the ARP warden's steel helmets, and in company with another warden we picked our way in the total darkness over the rubble and eventually found the tap. Fortunately the water supply had not been damaged and we were able to take sufficient water for everyone who needed it. After all this I remember one of the men started everyone singing and I can still hear those voices singing that very popular song of the time 'There'll Always Be An England'. Even a night like this could not destroy the people's spirit!

When daylight came we went out to view the damage. The roof of the bakery was gone. A large furniture depository at the rear was half gone, and all around houses and buildings were shattered. In the bakery at the time we had to vacate it, we had nearly 800 loaves in the ovens, and six bowls of dough made for the next batch. Each bowl contained six hundredweights of dough, almost two tons in all! This had risen and spilled over the side of the bowls and flowed all across the floor. This was the sight that met our eyes on our return. All the bread in the ovens was burnt black. It was a daunting sight, but every man just got his coat off and we all worked non-stop to get the place cleaned up and working again. Twelve hours later the council had covered the roof with tarpaulins, the oven builders had repaired the damage to the ovens, and the staff had cleaned up all the mess. The dough had been shovelled and deposited on a piece of waste ground between the bakery and the shattered depository!

At six o'clock that evening we started baking again and then, would you believe it, it started to rain! The tarpaulins on the roof sagged and filled with water and then the wind started getting under them and lifting them and down would come gallons of water all over us. The best part was that the dough on the waste ground started spreading and flowing in all directions! Yet, despite all this, the men carried on and I never heard a grumble from any of them. But the next morning we were all rewarded with a little comic relief. The owner of the depository arrived on his motorcycle and he came in rather too fast and ran smack into this sea of slimy dough. His feet were stuck in it, his motorcycle was stuck in it, and I can see him now trying to extricate himself from tons and acres of dough while everyone stood around helpless with laughter. I suppose it was not so funny really, and he was livid, but that was the fortunes of war!

There is also one sad and also very strange story that I must tell you that happened. After we were bombed out near my place of work in London I decided to move to the outskirts and travel to and fro by train from Old Coulsdon to

Lewisham. On this daily journey it happened that I became friendly with a fellow traveller and we became in fact close friends. He was an extremely nice fellow, but he was a Christadelphian and did not believe in war or killing and so when he was required to register for service he stated that he would only serve in the RAMC where he might be able to save life, but he would not fight. However, he was rejected on medical grounds so that that problem never arose.

However, one morning on the train he was verbally attacked for his beliefs. His reply was: 'I have a wife and a 12-year-old daughter, I have no wireless set, I do not read the newspapers, and I do not have an air-raid shelter. We take no precautions whatever except those required by law such as the blackout.'

They all labelled him as mad and said to him, 'If your wife and daughter get killed by a bomb you will wish you had provided some protection for them. Alternatively, if you get killed your wife and child will be left alone because you failed to protect yourself.'

He replied, 'I have sufficient faith to believe that I am right and I know that if we are to be destroyed we shall all go together.'

Some weeks later there was an air-raid warning and there was quite a lot of gunfire and I heard the distant explosion of a bomb. Then all went quiet and the 'all clear' sounded and I went home. The next morning my friend wasn't on the train and later that morning our foreman came into the office with a daily paper and said to me 'Is this your friend?' and handed me the paper pointing to the stop press news where it stated 'A lone raider dropped a bomb last night on the outskirts of London. Three people were killed, a Mr Harold Crosskey and his wife and daughter.'

I immediately phoned the man's brother and he confirmed that this was so. I have never understood how a man could have such a faith as he had nor have I ever been able to understand why such a strange thing should have happened.

This is perfectly true although it is almost unbelievable, and had I not known him or the circumstances I don't suppose I would have believed it for one moment.

Well, those are just a few memories of one who spent the whole of the war in the real war zone where we suffered great deprivations, worked long hours, and carried our life in our hands day and night with death and destruction all around us. But we never complained, we never went on strike, we played our part in feeding the public. We passed through periods of laughter and tears and we lost many dear work-mates, but when the war ended we of the civilian services who provided all these supplies were forgotten. We received no medals, no reward, no mention in despatches, but we had done our duty, and to me that was all that mattered.

Raymond Forcey

We lived in Plymouth at the time of the Blitz and my memories of it are both humorous and sad. I can remember my father being 'on guard' outside the Anderson air-raid shelter in our garden, with a colander on his head for protection! He did that because he didn't have a tin hat!

Also Father challenging an airman approaching in the middle of a heavy air raid at night, only to discover that it was our oldest brother home on unexpected leave!

My other teenage brother was in the air cadets and had been at a meeting one evening and was on his way home when he got caught in one of the air raids. The result was that he was asked to help the rescuers who needed someone slim to crawl through a small hole of a bombed house to see if there were any survivors. All he found inside were dead bodies. He could not talk about it when he got home and was gently bullied because he suddenly went so quiet, which was most unusual for him.

This same brother and I attended our middle brother's wedding in Bristol. He was in the navy and only had weekend

*The wedding at Bristol. Hetty and her brother Harold
next to last couple.*

leave. I was a bridesmaid. On our way home we could see a lot of damage in our avenue, only to find we had hardly any roof or windows left and a huge tarpaulin draped over the house. From then on we had to sleep in the Anderson shelter with candles in plant pots, and another inverted over the top for warmth.

Meanwhile Dad's works was bombed in the same raid and so he went on his way to St Albans to set up work and accommodation for the men. So when we arrived home from Bristol it was to find Mother clearing the debris!

Hetty Duncombe

I remember when the war started in September 1939 that I was 14 years old in January of that year, and had been working already for eight months. My younger brother Dennis was 13 years and still at school in Briton Road, Coventry. When the war started he was evacuated to Bishop's Itchington, with another boy. I think his first name was Billy. They stayed with a very kind couple, a Mr and Mrs Kendrick.

We were able to visit them once or twice, and it was lovely to get away into the countryside. The Kendricks had a poultry farm, and all the poultry ran free; hundreds it seemed to me! There were no battery hen houses in those days.

I remember catching a little wild rabbit which was hiding in the long grass at my feet. My young brother carried it into the village to show his friends, and then brought it back and let it free again. I remember Mr Kendrick saying, 'If you let him go at the spot where you found him, he is sure to find his way home.' I often think about that time, because Billy later went into the army and was killed in Belgium.

Then one Tuesday night in April 1941 our house was hit while we, Mum, Dad, my brother and myself, were inside. This was at Littlefields on Stoke Heath at Coventry. Luckily we were not badly hurt. However, I will never forget the awful darkness and the terrible noise! My father somehow managed to get us together and we clawed our way out through rubble and bricks. They had been blown down the stairs and across the hall, wedging the door open. We had been making tea for the firefighters and wardens, so luckily we left the door open.

We had to step over a man who was obviously dead. He lay across our gateway. I never did know who he was. We made our way to the shelters on the heath near the Barras House Hotel. It was very crowded in those damp shelters,

Nora on the left with Joyce next to her, Joan next to last on the right.

and some people had bandages on their heads already. We had very poor lighting, but we could still hear the whines and thuds of the bombs. I remember feeling 'closed in', and wishing I was outside again, and a feeling of being trapped. Then I began to feel angry that such things should happen, and I suddenly felt less afraid. After that awful night we realised we were among the lucky ones. We stayed with my aunt for a month and then we were rehoused in Barton's Meadow at Stoke Heath, very close to our previous home.

In spite of what I have written we young people had some very happy times then, like the concerts we used to get up in our dinner break at work. And there were some wonderful songs. One of our friends Alma Eaves had a wonderful voice, but I have lost touch with her long ago. However, I have never forgotten her and the dancing to Oscar Rabin's Band at Exmouth. I and my two friends Joan and Joyce who travelled down, crushed together on a luggage rack, in a train packed to bursting mostly with men and women in the Forces.

We had our bicycles in the guard's van and what a journey! But it was lovely and well worth it to be cycling around the Devon lanes almost free from traffic and certainly at that time free from bombs. Oh yes, there were some very good times!

I could go on and on, but I have probably written too much already. There are so many memories, most of them happy. Or was it because we were young? Perhaps it wasn't so nice for the elderly or the sick.

Nora George

I remember the Blitz very well. We are Leicester people born and bred. I was seven years old when war broke out and was not to meet my wife Dot for another ten years.

The first few days, or rather nights, my sister Mary and I had a mattress under the dining table. It wasn't much protection but it shielded us from flying glass should the French window break through blast. A further precaution was all

WE REMEMBER THE BLITZ

our windows were criss-crossed all over to prevent them shattering. We also had blackout curtains at all windows, which were made of black material. The table was used until the council provided everyone with gardens with an Anderson shelter. These were steel corrugated sheets overlapped and bolted together and set in a solid concrete box sunk below ground level. Reinforced brick and concrete shelters were erected in streets for folks without room for an Anderson shelter in their backyard.

Due to the brook at the bottom of our garden, our shelter occasionally flooded. When this happened we went to a neighbour's and shared Sam and Win Orridge's shelter, which was marvellous! It was carpeted, with good seating, and in fact just like home! Mary and I actually enjoyed the tummy-turning thrill when the warning siren wailed, warning us that German bombers were coming. So Mum, Dad, Mary and I rushed to the Orridges' shelter.

They had a big tea urn with hot, sweet tea. Bliss! We would sit at the open door. The men would stand outside having a smoke and we all watched the searchlights lighting up the sky and occasionally picking out the German planes upon which the ack-ack would open fire. If it was shot down there would be loud cheers all around!

Then the war really came to Leicester with the Blitz and it all ceased to be a game. I remember a shoe factory, Freeman, Hardy & Willis, caught fire at Humberstone Gate. The waves of German aircraft heading for Coventry to bomb munitions factories and other factories making army lorries, tanks and aeroplanes, mistook the FHW blaze for bomb damage and unleashed a deluge of bombs on Leicester. In fact, Leicester took a pounding for several days and quite a lot of damage was done and many people lost their lives.

I remember one evening after the warning siren had gone, we had gone down to the shelter and lay there in our bunks listening to the bombs whistling down. There were crumps and thuds and bangs as bombs landed, and hissing as incendiary bombs fell in the brook. One incident I well remember. Our house, 35 Broadway Road, was separated from Holmefield Avenue by a tennis court and the brook. The sirens had gone and apparently the occupants of a house in Holmefield Avenue had gone to their shelter. As a man returned to the house for a pair of socks, the house received a direct hit

and he was killed. About that time an English aeroplane crashed on a house in Dugdale Road.

I remember that Mary and I walked from Broadway Road to Medway Street School and observed the bomb damage. Highfields was particularly badly hit. The beautiful pavilion in Victoria Park was flattened and a lot of big houses belonging to Jewish clothiers and furriers and jewellers in Tichborne Street were hit and houses damaged in Mere Road, St Stephens Road, Saxby Street, Diseworth Street, Ashbourne Street and Percival Street and Parry Street. Spinney Hill Park had huge craters and the nearby Steeles & Busks factory was hit by a landmine, blowing windows out for some considerable distance around.

For all this devastation, the people of Leicester were great, much as they are still today! There was a wonderful atmosphere. We were all in the same boat. We respected and loved each other and observed the law and helped each other.

I think a lot of people actually loved the war because we were all *somebody*. It does seem a pity though that it takes a world war to bring out the best in people.

Brian Johnson

I was 22 when war was declared. I wasn't married but I was living at home with my mother and stepfather and half-sister, who is younger than I am. At first when the war started things were quiet, but then gradually the raids started so that several times in the night we would have to get up and make our way to the shelter at the bottom of the garden. That is until, in the end, we decided, like many other people, to sleep in the shelters. We made them as comfortable as possible and so we were able then to snatch a few hours' sleep when there wasn't any raid, which by now was becoming rather rare!

At work during the day the same thing was happening. Work was constantly being disrupted but, of course, that was the idea, to stop production. I worked for the Plessey company at Ilford, starting there just before the war and just before they switched to armaments. So with the armament production it was essential for work to carry on as long as possible. With these 'nuisance raids', as they were called, we were eventually told that we must carry on working for as long as possible but when real danger was imminent then the 'danger signal' would be given and we must get to the shelters quickly.

The first incident I recall was one night when a bomb dropped on two shops at the top of our road leaving, all of a sudden, just one large crater. The two shops, one a green-grocer's and the other a fish and chip, belonged to the same family. At the back of the shops was a stable with two horses in it and my stepfather and another man helped to get the horses out. Naturally the horses needed calming down but fortunately my stepfather and the other man were used to handling horses, so I suppose that helped a lot in getting them out.

The second incident happened early one Saturday evening. Suddenly the warning sounded, and almost immediately it seemed the German planes were overhead. I remember that the guns were firing and shrapnel was falling heavily, so we stayed in the house, hoping that there would be a lull in the firing and enough time for us to run from the house into the shelter. There never was any such lull. Bombs came whistling down and thudding into the ground, and each time we held our breath, waiting and wondering if the next one was going to land on us. When it didn't we silently thanked God that it had missed us but sympathising with the people around who had been killed or injured. Finally, early on the Sunday morning, which was 20 April and Hitler's birthday, it became very quiet and we thought soon the 'all clear' would sound and we would be able to go to bed.

My mother had asked for the time and I had just said, 'Twenty minutes to four,' when suddenly there was a dull thud, like an old enamel bowl with something in it being dumped on the ground. My mother said, 'I wonder what that was,' so I said, 'When it gets light I'll go and have a look.' Suddenly there was a loud bang and a flash, and it seemed as if everything was flying about us. Windows were blown in and ceilings came down, and one door hit me on the side of the head and another was blown across the room, hitting me on the back of the head and pinning me down, with dust filling my eyes and mouth.

I started to scream. I thought my mother had been killed and everything was in black darkness. I couldn't get up or see to get to her.

Suddenly I heard her say, 'Stop screaming.' Then I thought about my sister. She had gone in the other room to lie down on the settee. Suddenly she came out unhurt but, like the rest of us, shocked. My stepfather, who was also in the same room, managed to get over the rubble and round the furniture and lift the door off me. He had a cut on the side of his face and he was very lucky to have got off so lightly as he had been sitting by the windows that had been blown in.

Then my mother said that her head was bleeding badly. We managed to find our way out of the house and into the shelter but then we found we hadn't got a match to light the candle! I made my way back to the house to get the first aid box out of a cupboard where the door had been. Going back

to the shelter I tore off a large piece of cotton wool and laid it over my mother's head to soak up the blood. In the meantime my father had gone to find help and get some matches. He managed to get some but was told by a warden that if my mother could walk, we would have to take her down the road to the first aid centre, as there was no one available to come and see her. They were all out attending other people because, apparently, a high-explosive bomb had fallen in the next road killing and injuring dozens of people.

We got my mother to the first aid post but then she had to be taken to the town centre to an underground first aid post where doctors and nurses were in attendance. I remember that there were many many casualties there. Some of them were severely injured, some had terrible wounds and some were dead. My mother had a very bad gash on the top of her head and she had lost quite a lot of blood.

We lived next door to a junior school and there was a nine-foot brick wall between our house and the school playground. Two days after this explosion some men from the War Ministry came down and made an inspection of the cause of the explosion, and then told my mother that we were really lucky to be alive. The missile had been a landmine but the blast had gone the other way and demolished the little school. We thanked God it happened on a Sunday and not a Monday when there would have been hundreds of little children in the school.

When I went back to work after taking two days off to take my mother to hospital and clear up the mess, I just sat at my bench looking at my work. It sounds unbelievable, but I just couldn't remember what my job was! Actually, I was on some delicate work connected with the Spitfire. Eventually I was sent to the first aid. Even at that time my head was still spinning round and when I told the sister in the first aid post my story, she said it was all caused by shock. It was all a terrifying experience and after that, every time I even heard the air-raid siren warning, I was petrified.

Some time after that I was transferred from the main factory to a subway, which was being built as part of an underground railway. I think it must have been almost completed when the war started, so that the building of it was stopped and the government took it over. Plesseys transferred a lot of their machinery and workers down there and I was one of them. I had never worked on a capstan machine, but we were told that if we refused to go we would be sent up to the Midlands to work. I had no wish to go away from home so I went, but it was all rather depressing down there and very noisy, being in a tunnel. It was also damp and often we would see large rats running about. Every week the rat catcher would come round and put poison down in the vents in the floor where the rats came up but they still came back!

My third incident, and a very tragic one, happened when I was on my way home from work one night in the summer. I was alone as I had left all my workmates behind when I was transferred to 'the tunnel'. The warning sounded and I was about ten minutes' walk from home when that happened. That was also where the nearest shelter was so I started to hurry, hoping to get there before the German bombers came over and the gunfire started. I didn't make it. The bombs started coming down and I remember that a bus rounding a bend in the road had stopped and the passengers were crouched down. I was passing some shops with plate glass windows at the time and I certainly wasn't very happy about that! So I thought if I didn't want to chance getting my head blown off, I'd better crouch down like the people on the bus.

I covered my head with my hands as everyone had been instructed to do in these circumstances, when a bomb dropped just a couple of streets away, and suddenly I realised it would be near where my step-cousin and her family lived. After I got home I learned that my cousin's house had been hit and six people killed. That was her husband, three of her four children, and also her young niece and nephew who had previously been bombed out and were staying with her, along with their parents.

There was an awful lot of bombing going around all the time where I lived. But it was something we had to accept and we just got on with our life and our work, like many other people who lived in towns and cities and who were experiencing the same dreadful war and the same dreadful bombing.

Even to this day, when I wake up in the morning, I remember that dreadful time when that landmine fell and the whole world seemed to explode with it. Often I dream I am running for a shelter to get away from the bomb, and I pray that my children and grandchildren will never have to experience war. I have lived through two world wars and, apart from my own terrible experiences in the Second World War, I lost my father when I was just two months old in 1917.

Helen Hawkins

My memories of the Blitz are of the bombing of Clydebank in Scotland. It was a long time ago, but I remember it very well. At the time I was serving with a heavy artillery battery, stationed at Bearsden, which overlooks the Clyde Valley and Clydebank.

It was about nine o'clock at night with a clear night and a full moon. We got a 'stand to' just before the air-raid sirens sounded, so we were manning the guns and waiting as the bombers came in. As we stood there we noticed in the distance and over Glasgow, ack-ack fire in the sky as the guns followed the planes heading for Clydebank.

When the planes came within our range we opened fire and got off quite a few rounds at them. What we didn't know at the time though was that these planes were the Pathfinders. As they got over the town of Clydebank, they dropped flares, and then incendiaries which started many fires.

Then came the bombers, following them in wave after wave.

You could hear them droning on over the targets, releasing parachute mines and bombs. While that was happening we were firing like mad. At one time we were lit up by flames, and I remember that in the flames I could see a parachute mine floating down and it dropped in a nearby field and exploded.

It went on like this late on into the night. At one time I thought that my ears were bleeding with the gunfire! By now Clydebank was lit like an inferno and we realised that however much we fired at them we just couldn't stop them. The red glow in the sky told its own sad story.

The next night the bombers came back and it all started again. The people of Clydebank suffered so much in those two nights and still came out smiling, that I really wonder how they did it.

Joe Fairfield

When war was declared I found myself a 16-year-old messenger boy in the Auxiliary Fire Service, ready to take messages by cycle that under normal conditions would have been telephoned. It had been realised that the telephone system could well become inoperative in air raids, and our job was to replace that system.

It was a long hot summer in 1940, and boredom had set in and the term 'phoney war' was being used and then suddenly, almost 12 months to the day after the Declaration of War and late on a Saturday afternoon, the sirens sounded. Eyes were raised towards the blue skies to the south-east, and we could hardly believe our eyes. Distant specks in the sky slowly materialised into large formations of bombers leaving vapour trails in the clear sky. Around these formations fighter planes circled like angry hornets.

It seemed that almost immediately they were overhead and then we heard the scream of high-explosive bombs and plumes of black smoke billowed in the air as the bombs exploded with a thunderous crash. The streets rapidly emptied except for the Fire and Rescue vehicles answering their first real call, and putting all their months of training to the test.

Within a few hours roads were blocked by bomb craters and fallen buildings, and water mains were fractured and electricity cut off. The only water available to fight the huge fires that were raging was the surrounding river and docks. Lots of the smaller fires had joined together and stretched from one end of the Isle of Dogs, where I was, to the other. Bombs continued to fall throughout the night as incoming bombers used the huge fires on the ground as their target, unloading their cargo of death and thus adding to the carnage and destruction below.

Came the dawn and the whole area could be seen as a mass of smoking debris, and we realised that the war for us had really begun. What had been exercises had become a reality. The 'phoney war' was at an end and the battle for London had entered its first stage.

You must remember that whole families and children who had been officially evacuated at the outbreak of war had returned to their London homes when the threatened air raids had not materialised. The morning following that first big air raid on London's Dockland thousands of people packed a few essential belongings and joined the rush to get out before the bombers returned.

My mother had been given an address at Hitchin in Hertfordshire of a person who could offer her and my young brother and sister temporary accommodation. We walked from the Isle of Dogs to Aldgate, some four or five miles, picking our way through piles of debris along with hundreds of other people. Arriving at Aldgate we saw thousands of people standing around. There were no Tube trains running and it seemed that the escape route had been cut off. Being late afternoon by then some were looking anxiously at the sky and expecting the return of the German bombers at any moment. Nobody knew what to do to get away, and one could feel an air of panic beginning to set in. Nowhere to go and no means of getting there.

Suddenly in the midst of all the mayhem appeared a military brass band resplendent in their dress uniforms and somehow managing to march through the clogged debris-strewn streets. I can clearly remember that everybody suddenly stopped and clapped and cheered and the panic that had at one stage been starting to set in was instantly forgotten, and somehow fresh hope seemed to be offered. I don't know whose idea that band was, but it was certainly a masterstroke!

We decided to try Liverpool Street Station and while we were shuffling along Commercial Street a small lorry emerged from a side road and the driver called to me asking for directions to the A10 Cambridge Road. I asked him where he was going. Would you believe it he replied, 'Hitchin.'

'Will you take my mother and the two small children?' I asked.

'Jump on,' he said.

As I stood in the road waving them goodbye I found myself wondering if I would ever see them again. But most of all I remember marvelling at the stroke of luck that had provided transport to Hitchin out of the blue.

The next particular memory I have is the fire at Rum Quay. It started as just another air raid but as the night wore on the intensity of the raid increased. It seemed that bombs were falling without respite. Incendiary bombs, came down in clusters, hundreds of small fires started and these being unattended rapidly spread into large fires.

The whole of the Rum Quay in West India Docks was soon ablaze with one huge fire a quarter of a mile long and four storeys high. The area was full of stored rum and sugar, and blazing molten sugar mixed with the rum and ran along the gutters, filling the air with a sweet sickly stench. Fire pumps had been called into the area from as far afield as Potters Bar and Chelmsford some 30 miles away. They had been instructed to report to Millwall Fire Station where they were formed into small convoys and I on my motorcycle led them to the control point set up in West India Docks.

The officer in charge decided that travelling time could be saved by stopping the machines passing along West India Dock Road and directing them straight into the docks. He handed me his last flashlight and stationed me in the middle of the road where I proceeded to stop every fire appliance that approached and re-routed them directly to the docks. I remember I was stood opposite the well-known Charley Brown's public house from about eight o'clock that evening until five o'clock the following morning. A lone figure, 17 years old, feeling extremely frightened but nevertheless very important! A 17-year-old messenger boy giving instructions to fire crews on the most dangerous duties you could imagine.

Just after five o'clock I heard the bell of an approaching fire vehicle through the thick smoke haze. I waved my torch and found I had stopped a large black car with a silver bell on its side. Out of the car stepped two fire officers with gleaming silver epaulettes on both shoulders. One asked what I was doing and I dutifully repeated my instructions and directed him into the docks. I remember that he glared at me and shouted, 'I have a row of tea warehouses on fire at St Katharine Docks. All the appliances I have sent to this location have been redirected by you to the West India Docks. I have not had a single engine report since the first call and a whole tea warehouse complex is burnt to the ground – gutted, and it's your fault.'

I stood there, covered in black soot, a young lad who thought he had done a good night's work and wondering what now would happen to him! Of course, nothing did, but a few weeks later when it was officially announced that the tea ration was being cut, I remember that I did have a very strong guilty feeling!

I remember clearly the fire blitz on the city. Like the others it had started as yet another raid. The sirens had sounded just after sunset, the bombers had circled overhead in ones and twos, and a few high-explosive and a few incendiary bombs had fallen. It was just another nuisance type raid, we thought.

Then the pattern changed. The direction of the raid suddenly switched away from the East End of London to the City of London, just a few miles upriver. Wave after wave of bombers came over and dropped thousands of incendiary bombs on the City. There were some high explosives, but obviously the intention was to destroy the City by fire.

My job was to lead convoys of fire engines arriving from outlying districts into the city centre. Around midnight I found myself in Queen Victoria Street. Next to me were two very senior fire officers discussing the situation. One turned to the other and said, 'The situation has gone beyond being desperate. It's out of control.' I clearly remember the other replied, 'Yes, and there's nothing we can do.'

I sat there astride my motorcycle, surrounded by a sea of fire, and really believing and thinking that this was the end of London. Looking up I saw the dome of St Paul's silhouetted against a blood red sky. By a miracle it hadn't been touched. It stood out like a symbol of defiance, with the gold cross on the top of the dome reflecting the surrounding flames, and I can clearly remember looking at it and thinking that after all there would be something left.

The next air raid I particularly remember started as usual just as the light was fading. It seemed to consist of an endless stream of planes dropping a whole variety of bombs. High-explosive, incendiary, oil bombs, landmines, aerial torpedoes scattered over the area, starting innumerable fires over a large area stretching resources to the limit and beyond.

Although a despatch rider, such was the situation that I had been left with a trailer pump with one branch hose damping down what had been a large fire at a paper warehouse. Large rolls of paper stacked on top of each other from floor to ceiling. Every so often flames would bounce from the centre of one of the rolls, and I would turn on the hose until the flames subsided, by which time another roll would burst into flames and it seemed an endless task as the whole night passed away.

About 4 a.m. I was relieved and joined the rest of the watch around a canteen van that had just arrived. Being the youngster I was handed the first cup of tea by the lady serving when a shout went up: 'The Tooke's on fire.'

To a man the whole watch turned and ran off, leaving me standing with my cup of tea.

'What a brave conscientious bunch' said the tea lady, 'out all night, soaking wet and tired and yet as soon as the call comes they dash off.'

I hadn't the heart to spoil the illusion! You see The Tooke was our local and we would have nowhere to congregate for a pint and a sing-song around the piano on our quiet nights if it had burned down! I am happy to say that they managed to confine the fire to the roof space!

Stan Hook

At an early age I encouraged my daughter to write wee letters to members of the family serving in the Forces and I always read them before posting. I suppose I thought this letter would interest her father in Burma but held it back as it might worry him.

My daughter's letter has not been altered and, as you will see, I have left in the spelling mistakes – dreadful! Incidentally, her previous school was destroyed one night in a bombing raid. The letter reads as follows:

6 Faraday Avenue, Sidcup, Kent
9.3.45

Dear Thelma,

Thank you very much for your letter, I think it is very interesting.

I am writing this letter on Friday afternoon at 1.20. I am not going to school, I haven't a cold or cough or anything the matter.

Early yesterday a rocket fell near my school, I will tell you how it happened.

Miss Hewitt was gazing about her and suddenly blew her whistle, just a sec later there was a terrific bang and a whole column of earth shot up, it looked like the waves only much bigger and it was dirt.

I ran up against a wall and a window came out in little bits, I stood there and watched and when the second bang was over I ran up to Olive and began to cry, please don't call me a baby as you would. Tony got a cut round his eye and it bled awful. John got his forehead cut and a titch in the infants got the back of his head cut.

When the bangs were over a Nun came in and began to wash Tony's eye, then a policeman came in followed by two more, then the playground was full or workmen. I then went to sit on the step with Pam who could not walk, her stockings were torn, so I said if Mum would let me she could have mine if they would fit her.

When I came home I had a wash. When I finished, Ralph, Tim and Caroline came to see if we could go to play and Ralph said he was glad that I wasn't crying.

I'll write again soon, excuse scrawl.
Love from Gillian

Note: Gillian was aged ten at the time.

Winifred Huett

I was working in London during the Blitz and staying at a church army hostel in Shepherd's Bush. One day the captain in charge asked if I had any plans for Saturday night. I replied that I hadn't. He explained that the church army, with volunteers, ran a small cafe in Du Cane Road, just a small wooden hut by the railway embankment opposite the gates of Wormwood Scrubs prison. Apparently the hut stayed open 24 hours a day but he couldn't find anyone to fill it on that particular Saturday night.

We were getting raids then every night and before they left they told me that in the event of an air raid getting heavy, arrangements had been made to take shelter in the prison! They left me and promptly the raid started at about 9 p.m.! Nevertheless I carried on making tea and sandwiches for nurses from the nearby hospital and ARP wardens and, in fact, anyone else who dropped in.

As time passed by I could hear the bombs dropping some distance away but slowly getting nearer and nearer until one dropped so near that the cups jumped on the counter!

That was near enough for me! I locked the hut and ran across the road to the prison and banged on the door until it was opened by a warder.

He took me into one of the offices and I spent quite a pleasant night listening to stories of prisoners and escapes.

I never thought I would be begging to be admitted to prison but it took a war to do it!

Bill Pippin

I have lots of memories from the war but one that stands out in particular was the night I decided that my friend Ruth could spend the night in an underground shelter instead of going home from school and into our own shelter, which was the basement of a three-storey house. We were ten years old at the time.

It was dreadful. Everyone had their own spot and we were treading over and around everyone to find somewhere to sit. It was very draughty and noisy. We eventually did find a space and dozed on and off and then I got scared as to what my mum would say and I was hungry!

I was getting really scared. It was all so crowded. Would we get out if we were bombed? Or if there was a fire?

Jo Wells is on the left.

'Ruth, I'm going home.'

'You can't,' she said. 'You're not allowed in the streets during a raid.'

'I'm going anyway.'

She wouldn't come. How I got up all the stairs I don't know. Everyone was settled for the night and I was getting sworn at as I tried not to tread on anyone. I don't know how many stairs there are in the Edgware Road Underground Station but it must be a hundred at least. When I got to the top and out into the air, it was unbelievable. The sky was red and the noise was deafening. I found out later that that night the docks were the main target and it was one of the worst nights of bombing. The air-raid wardens were shouting at me to take cover. It seemed I was the only one out in the middle of the Edgware Road, running for all I was worth to Cuthbert Street and home! All the time there were those awful sounds and flashes and people calling out to me.

As I ran down Campbell Street I saw men trying to put out the fires. All the houses seemed to be burning from the incendiary bombs and one of the men called out to me and I recognised his voice. It was my dad but I didn't recognise him because his face was all black but the picture is still vivid in my mind, although I don't remember what he said to me.

All I do remember is that I rushed on into our shelter until I was home safe and sound and very glad to be back in the comfort of my sisters and brothers as I lay down beside them!

Home sweet home! We did, in fact, get bombed out the following year and we were evacuated to Oxhey but that's another story.

Jo Wells

My memories are of the Blitz in Liverpool where I lived until 1941. I was 15 years of age at that time. My first memory was sad. My second cousin Margaret, her husband and two young children were killed in 1940. She gave birth to a baby under the debris. A gentleman who lived in the house opposite was killed going to see if he could get help for her. His wife said that they could hear Margaret's cries in labour, but the air raid was heavy, and he went over and was just at her front door when the house had a direct hit. When the ARP rescuers got the debris away the only one they found alive was Margaret and when they found her she had already given birth to the baby. They asked the ladies to see to her. They said that she asked for a drink of water, had a sup of it, and then laid back and died. She was just 25 years old.

In contrast, a few weeks after this Margaret's mother was in bed asleep with her daughter when the blast from a bomb blew down the whole of the bedroom wall and blew the mattress out into the street with – would you believe it – both ladies still on it! And the amazing thing was that neither of them had a mark on them. Both these incidents happened in the same area and within a few weeks of each other in the Netherfield Road area of Everton, Liverpool 5.

My other memories are of May 1941 when the raids were heavy night after night. I had taken my younger brother Sonny and my young cousin Joan to Heyworth Street School underground air-raid shelter which was also in Everton. We liked that shelter as there was always a singalong and music from accordions and mouth organs and concertinas. The louder the bomb the louder we used to sing. I remember on one Saturday night in early May we had the worst air raid ever. That night we were all really afraid, and suddenly there was a terrific crash and all the lights went out. The noise was dreadful. The building really shook and people were screaming. We thought the shelter was coming in on top of us, but it was a landmine, which had landed just round the corner where our house was. This was at two o'clock in the morning.

The ARP wardens arrived and soon restored calm and got us candles and torches.

Then I saw my pal Sue coming down the steps of the shelter carrying a big brown handbag which her mother had asked her to carry and which contained insurance policies and birth certificates and such things. I had never known Sue or her mother to go into the shelter before.

She told me her house had caught the blast from a land-mine which had landed in the street where my dad and stepmother and two little babies lived. I knew my dad was out fire-watching but my stepmum never went to a shelter. She used to sit under a table with her mum and the children. By the way, I lived with my grandparents at the top of the street where Dad lived.

When Sue told me where the landmine had landed, I tried to get out of the shelter to go to see my family. I had it in my mind that they would have been killed but nobody was allowed out of the shelter until the 'all clear' at 5.30 a.m. when I could go home. I didn't want to go, afraid of what I might find. I took my little brother's hand and my cousin's, and we were all in tears. But what a sight when we got home. There, sitting on the pavement, were all my family with blankets around them and their faces were dirty with dust from the debris. My dad wasn't there because he had been fire-watching, but to make matters worse a wall had fallen on his legs while he was carrying out that work and he had been taken to hospital. But thank God, he wasn't too badly hurt. When I looked at our house and saw that only the cellar was left I was stunned. But at least our family survived that terrible raid.

My stepmum told me that just before the landmine fell, Dad had insisted that she take the two babies and her mother to the street shelter just outside their house, and if she had stayed in the house they would certainly all have been killed.

Even in the shelter they weren't totally safe. Mag, that's my stepmum, was once sat in the shelter next to a 17-year-old boy, and they were near the entrance. Things were very quiet at the time and so after a little while the boy went out to see what was happening. As he opened the door of the shelter, a landmine fell, and his body was found later on the top of the shelter. Of course, he was dead. There's something else as well. With the door open the blast from the landmine took my stepmum's hair straight up, just like wire. It would not comb down for a week.

When the landmine had fallen, the shelter they were in was blocked at the entrance, so they were helped out of it via the small exit that was available as an alternative. She had to hand her two little babies out first. Little Alec was 14 months old and Albert was six weeks old. She handed them to the rescuers but when she got out she couldn't find the babies. They had been taken very quickly to another shelter where she found them next morning but in the meantime, of course, she was frantic with worry.

During the next week we lived in the schoolroom, as the whole area was just devastated and in ruins. As the weather was good we spent most of the time sitting out on the pavement waiting for the Salvation Army canteen which came round every day to provide us with hot drinks and sandwiches. Then, later on in the day, a Red Cross mobile canteen would come round to give us another meal. Of course, we were very grateful to all those people who gave their time and effort to help look after us.

But we were by now so afraid to stay in Liverpool at night that many people who lived outside of the city area offered to give us shelter for the night in schoolrooms and church halls if we could manage to travel there. So at 5 p.m. every evening hundreds of people, even the old folks, made their way to Scotland Road, where lorries going out of Liverpool would give lifts and we became almost refugees.

When we arrived at the halls, we were given a blanket each and a place on the floor. Hot drinks were also provided. We were lucky as we managed to get a place under cover, but some people had to sleep out in the open. But it was warm weather and we were very grateful to all of the people in the area surrounding Liverpool who gave their time, money and effort to provide us with food and shelter.

However, at 6 a.m. on the following morning we would be on the road again. Back to Liverpool. This went on with my family for over a week and my grandmother didn't think it was right for us children, so she sent off a telegram to my uncle in Redditch, asking if he could find somewhere for us. He did and we arrived in Redditch with just the clothes that we stood up in. I had a siren suit on and I remember I had my best coat with me. Whenever I went into an air-raid shelter I took it with me in a bag! People in Redditch were very kind to us, and gave us clothes and even their own clothing coupons. I didn't go back to Liverpool to live. I got a job in Redditch and settled down here, but at heart I still belong to Liverpool.

Mary Hopcroft

My family and myself lived at a place called St James Lane, Willenhall, at Coventry, when war broke out. I was almost 14 years old at the time and the eldest but one of eight children. In October 1940, my mum had her seventh child, which was a boy. When he was about two weeks old we had the first night of the Blitz.

It was a Tuesday night around six o'clock. The sirens sounded their warning of an air raid and then we heard the dreaded one that we called 'Big Ben' wailing out and we knew that Coventry was in for a bombing if that one sounded.

It started. The guns were banging and the searchlights were shining in the sky and the barrage balloon unit could be heard winding up. That unit was only across the road in the field right near to us.

Incendiary bombs started dropping around us and my dad, who was in the ARP, was outside putting out the fires that they had caused. One came down in our back garden and set alight and that was put out but then one fell in the front garden but that didn't go off. As a matter of fact I have it now as my dad had it made into a moneybox and before he died he gave it to me.

Anyway, the bombing got worse and seemed to be getting closer and closer. There were aircraft factories around us and it was obvious that the bombers were after them.

But the town was bombed also and we had people walking three and a half miles and knocking on our door, asking us to take them in. Their homes had already been bombed and they had lost everything.

On the Thursday night it started again, only much earlier, and people had come from the town before it was dark, because they were afraid. All of us children had been put into the coalhouse under the staircase. Mum had white-washed it and put a mattress in and some bedding for when we wanted to go to sleep. But we were soon out of there and running into the fields and hiding under the hedges. I remember getting wet feet from the ditches.

I remember my dad came looking and found us. I remember him saying that the Chase Cafe had been bombed and had been flattened to the ground. It was burning and all in ruins. Also a landmine had dropped on a row of houses not far away and we found out later that twin boys aged five years were in bed and had been blown over the top of the houses on the other side of the street and into an old Abbey. The beds were still near them when they were found and they were both dead from the blast.

I remember that Mum and I went to town on the Friday morning to get some food but there were no shops around and we had to ask a policeman where we were, because with all the damage that had been caused we were quite lost. The cathedral wasn't far away but it had been bombed and was still burning and everywhere seemed to be nothing but rubble.

The Ritz Cinema had also been bombed flat and people were trapped and killed in it. I remember that at the time it was showing the film *Gone With The Wind*.

Later I went to the shops for my mum and I took the baby in the pram and my six-year-old sister. On the way back home a delayed action bomb went off in a field right near to us and I remember lifting my sister into the pram so that she didn't get hurt and running all the way home, crying, with my sister and the baby and the pram! In fact, I was so frightened that I never went out of the house for the next three days, because it had that effect on me.

My dad got called out to go into the town one day and helped with all the people that were trapped and dead. I remember him coming home that night really upset. He told me that he had heard a lady shouting for help and as he got all the rubble from around her, which was down to her waist, she just fell over as if she had been cut in half. Also he found babies and children and grown-ups' limbs, and had to put them all together to be buried.

Later, and I can't remember exactly how long, I went to the London Road Cemetery and saw 500 coffins ready for burial. We were told afterwards that there was not one whole body between them. Everything had just been a heap of bits and pieces.

Lillian Nixon

I was 16 or 17 years old at the time when the Germans let loose a few bombs in the Widcombe area of Bath. I lived in the area and the main Great Western Railway Line ran along side of Widcombe and so far as I know this was probably the target.

After the bombs had fallen I remember telling my mother that I was off to help the victims. I had a helmet as I was already a member of the ARP, and I wore my only overcoat, which was a sort of green colour. Eventually I found myself along with other people digging and tearing at the rubble with bare hands. It was unbelievable. The heat, dirt, dust and sweat.

The gruesome part of my story is that I came across in the rubble the body of a small child. The awful part is that I almost trod on her. I remember lifting her up and taking the weight of her head and backside in my hands. As I lifted her head my hands became covered in blood. The skull was damaged and it was most likely that the child was already dead. I never did find out, but those horrendous moments one can never blot out. I was literally only a boy myself at the time.

Later on in the evening my cousin came to fetch me home. He was in the Royal Air Force and just arrived home on leave when my mother asked him to fetch me. My mother apparently thought that I should be at home!

The sight of my overcoat covered with blood upset my mother very much. Later, if discussing those long gone days my mother still referred to the blood-stained coat. These recollections you may say were common to many of us who lived through those days.

The twist is this. Like many lads I was called up at 18 years. I served at home and in the Far East. In 1947 I was demobbed and found employment in the Post Office. It must have been around 1960 when I was having lunch with a fellow Post Office employee and our conversation turned to the war years.

It happened that Harry too was an old Widcombe boy and had lived in the very street that was bombed where I had done my stint way back. During our conversation I told Harry about me finding a little girl's body, and the whereabouts of the house and its approximate house number.

He said, 'You know, Pete, that must have been my little niece.'

She had as it turned out been killed. After all those years what a small world.

Peter Hawkins

At the outbreak of war, there were four in our family; Mum, Dad, my younger brother Peter, two years old, and myself, seven years old. Dad was called up straight-away as he had been a regular soldier. He was a sergeant in the East Lancashire Regiment, which had become a Tank Regiment on D-Day.

I remember the first air-raid siren. Everybody was terrified because we didn't know what to expect. All I do remember particularly is that it was a lovely sunny day.

Dad was posted 'somewhere in England', so we followed him to Bungay in Norfolk. Mum got a job as a general help in a large country house, so we kept together for the first months of the war. Then Dad got posted again so we came home to Manor Park. When we got back our house had gone so we lived with my mother's parents.

The air raids became more and more severe, so we got a flat nearby in Ilford as Nan and Granddad wouldn't have an air-raid shelter in their garden because it spoilt the flowerbeds! We moved into this flat in Ilford and as far as I am concerned it was out of the frying pan into the fire! The raids were terrible. They built a large community air-raid shelter and all families moved into these in the evening and slept there until the morning or until the 'all clear'. One night I remember the shelter and the ground shook. The women were crying. Apparently it was a landmine that had landed nearby and it seemed that we were in the middle of an earthquake. To cap it all an air-raid warden came in the shelter in the morning and said then that we couldn't go home because of an unexploded bomb. It did explode later. We couldn't live in that flat any more because the roof had been blown off and all the doors and windows had gone.

Back to grandparents for a short period. We got another house in Parkhurst Road opposite our grandparents but this one had an air-raid shelter! It was called an Anderson shelter. They were quite safe as long as they did not get a direct hit. But they were very damp. The walls ran with condensation. There was no power and the only light came from a candle. Even now when I smell a candle it reminds me of those days in the Anderson shelter. It was at this time that my school friend Steve Dunk and his mother were killed in an air raid when a bomb landed and the explosion killed them both in bed.

Kids being kids, we used to go out in the streets after a raid to collect shrapnel and cannon shells. One morning at school assembly a youth was paraded in front of us. He was there as an example to show what happened. He had lost an arm when a small shell he collected exploded and blew his arm off. That reminds me also of the time when we saw, after a raid, a woman's arm on the roof of the house opposite. Another time I remember we had an incendiary bomb land in our porch and it set the whole of the front door alight in seconds. Fortunately we were able to put it out.

My dad's sister, Aunty Flo, lived at the other end of our road. We used to see her every day without fail. One day a neighbour told us they hadn't seen our aunty about and when we went down to her house, the kitchen wall had been blown down across the entrance to her shelter and she was trapped in there, all alone except for her budgie, but we got her out okay.

I remember that one day a policeman knocked on the door with a message that Dad was seriously ill in hospital. He had been blown up by a phosphorus bomb and badly burnt. He was in hospital in Basingstoke and became one of Sir Archibald McIndoe's patients. He was a world-famous skin-graft specialist. After a year in hospital, Dad was medically discharged from the army and came home. Poor old Mum had to get a job on the buses as a 'Clippie' as Dad couldn't work. When the war came to an end in 1945 we were still a complete family. In my view we got through the war lightly. Some families had no dads coming home any more.

Sidney Knight

I was in the Metropolitan Police and never missed one day of the Blitz. On 29 December 1940, I was in the City of London when what they called the second fire of London occurred. Over 100,000 incendiary bombs rained down on the City in quick succession.

John Jenner on the left, with his brother.

I can remember the heat was licking at St Paul's Cathedral and the whole of the City and Southwark were blazing. The mains water failed. The fire brigade pumps were clogged with mud from the riverbed. The Thames tide was at its lowest, and that night was a full moon.

Everywhere was on fire. In the combination of search-lights and fire, I saw enemy bombers over London, and heard the scream of bombs and the explosions seemingly somehow coming nearer and nearer. I dived for shelter under Southwark Bridge and it seemed almost as if the sky was ablaze and lighting up London. I remember clearly that even though it was night and there were no lights, you could read a newspaper.

The London Docks were ablaze. Miles of dockside ware-houses had gone up in flames which could be seen easily miles and miles away. They were a choking inferno. There were calls for extra pumps to the London Control. The River Emergency Services were at Woolwich, towing burning barges away. All power cables had gone and the only way to get a message anywhere in London was on a bike. By mid-night the whole of the Thames to Woolwich and along through South-East London and to the Docklands was burning.

Dockland was full of little houses, built cheaply for dock-workers, and all of them within a short walking distance of the wharfs. Those houses simply fell down, shattered by the blast of the falling bombs or, if they didn't fall down from that, they were set on fire. Almost the whole of the East End was evacuated and life was at a standstill. Half of Stepney had moved out as everybody fled. Four hundred and thirty were killed in that small area alone and 1,600 badly injured and made homeless.

The next night London was still burning, making it easy for the bombers to find their targets, and again hundreds were killed. This was to be only the beginning for what was an ordeal for the East End in particular. People who were there were in a daze, and did not know what to do or where to go. They put their belongings on prams and carts and wheelbarrows and many of them made for Epping Forest where they slept out because after two nights of intensive bombing the East End was at a standstill and the streets were chaotic. There was no gas, no electricity, no telephones. The shock was numbing.

I remember a visit paid by Winston Churchill to Bethnal Green. It was the early afternoon and people were carrying their beds and belongings and coming in for the night. When they saw the Prime Minister they cheered and he put his hat on his stick and held it high and twirled it round and round. I remember that he shouted out to them 'Are we downhearted?'

'No!' they shouted back. 'Hit 'em back, Winston, hit 'em hard!'

What marvellous people those East Enders were.

John W. Jenner

Although I don't sound it, I can claim to be a genuine cockney, born within the sound of Bow Bells. I was in London when war broke out in September 1939. The first thing my mother decided, along with thousands of other mothers, was that the Germans would bomb London straightaway. So I, as the youngest, had to be got to a place of safety.

She took me to my paternal grandparents in Devon. That was me evacuated. It was all done so quickly I hadn't time to argue. I was deposited like a parcel and my mother returned to London to look after my older sister and brother.

For months I lived in Devon and went to school there. I loved it. My grandparents were wonderful and I took to country life like a duck to water. Their cottage was surrounded by fields and there was a large orchard where I used to climb the trees and sit for hours watching the rabbits playing. I collected the eggs that the hens laid – no easy task when several of them simply wandered about in the hedgerows and deposited their eggs anywhere! But finding them was great fun.

All our drinking water came from a well in one of the fields and rain was collected in a water butt at the side of the cottage.

The one drawback was an outside loo, right at the bottom of the garden, but even this couldn't kill my enthusiasm for my new life. Mind you, there were times when I was desperately homesick. It was during one of these spells that my mother made the fatal mistake of visiting me – and I remember hiding under my grandmother's kitchen table and screaming and screaming until she agreed to take me back with her to London!

I'll swear someone telegrammed Hitler to tell him I had returned. I had been home less than a week when the Blitz started! My mother's first thought was to despatch me back again. I eyed the kitchen table ominously – she decided she'd risk it and keep all the family together!

I trotted backwards and forwards to the nearby school quite happily, carrying my gas mask at all times. We had some air raids during the day. There was one in particular

when, instead of going into the school shelter with the other children, I decided to make a dash for home, which somehow always seemed safer. I was halfway there when I realised that a single German plane was overhead and that it was dropping a stick of bombs! It's the one and only time in my life that I had to throw myself to the ground and I had plenty of bruises to prove it. I never left school again during an air raid!

Most of the raids though came at night. You could practically set your watches by the air-raid siren. Nine o'clock seemed to be the popular time.

Every evening my mother made up sandwiches and cocoa. I was wrapped in an ancient fur coat over my pyjamas and carried down to our Anderson air-raid shelter, half buried at the bottom of our garden. I always carried Panda the cat in his basket and Bruin my teddy bear. We had a hanging lantern, books, magazines, jigsaws, a wireless – all the home comforts. We tucked ourselves up, put in our earplugs and slept the night away. At least I did! I was secure in the knowledge that we were all together and I felt quite safe.

Anderson shelters were terrific and proved time and time again that they could stand anything but a direct hit. Some nights when the bombing was really bad, you could hear the explosions, even with earplugs in. I have to confess that I used to take mine out to hear how bad it was! Even then I don't remember feeling very frightened. Somehow it seemed more like an adventure.

My brother, by this time, had joined the Royal Air Force and was away from home. With two daughters to look after on her own – my father had died when I was two – I realise now that this must have put my mother under tremendous pressure. But at the time I just expected her to cope with all emergencies – and she did.

One night when my brother was at home on leave, we were in the shelter as usual. The sound of explosions outside was worse than ever. Next morning we dreaded opening up for fear of what we might find. A landmine – a deadly thing that came down by parachute – had landed several streets away, completely demolishing an entire row of houses. The explosion had severely damaged our house, blowing out all the windows and, in fact, moving part of the structure.

We went to see the devastation the landmine had caused and I couldn't believe that one bomb could have done so much damage. My mother managed to pick up a piece of the actual parachute to keep as a souvenir. I still remember it. It was a turquoise colour and made of a knitted effect fabric. Although it looked very innocent, it was in fact very strong.

My brother took one look at the chaos and decided, as the man of the house, that he was going to pack us off to Scotland, to my mother's family in Dundee. Once again there was no time to think. Clothes were packed and we struggled through the centre of London, part of which was by now absolutely devastated.

The rest of the war passed much more quietly. We never again had to spend a night in a shelter – indeed, my grandfather didn't even have one, a fact I found quite amazing at first until I realised how peaceful Dundee was compared to London.

I did my small bit for the war effort by collecting waste paper and saving all scraps for pig food. There were huge containers at chosen street corners. You collected your scraps of food daily and took them to the containers. They were then taken away to feed the pigs. If only we were as organised today. I still cringe when I see paper or bottles or food being wasted. It's all a definite hangover from the war!

It's strange but I can't remember the exact moment when I found that the war was over. But I do recall an incredible feeling of relief when the news finally did sink in and the disappointment when rationing did not stop straightaway! Somehow I had expected everything to change overnight. To be able to guzzle sweets to my heart's content! Heavens, I'd almost forgotten what chocolate was! It was to be a long time until the time I had a chance to remember too. The most important thing though was that the danger was past. As I said, I can't remember actually being aware of fear at the time – but the sound of an air-raid siren can still make my blood run cold.

Another bad legacy from the war is my fear of bangs. Anything from a burst balloon to a gunshot can make me break out in a cold sweat. One souvenir I have, which is still very much in demand, is my brother's kitbag. One of my sons slings it over his shoulder and uses it to carry all his belongings around. He's even been stopped in the street by someone asking if the bag is genuine.

Jean Kydd

At the beginning of the Blitz, my dad sent my mum and I to Chesham in Buckinghamshire. We were billeted with an old couple. The old fellow called 'Grampy' sold my mum a dormouse in an old sock for half a crown, but the crafty old sod sold her a dead one!

The local girls were very forward and the local boys thought we were easy targets but we soon sorted that out. My uncle Frank, who lived up on Pond Park Hill, had buried an old Austin Seven in his back garden at Chesham, and one night the siren sounded and my aunt Nance, her two kids and Mum and me went down into the old motor for shelter.

Suddenly there was a droning of bombers overhead and then we heard a swishing noise, and then a thud. The 'all clear' went about an hour later, and we returned to the house. In the morning Uncle Frank ran in to tell us that there was a bomb about 20 feet from the sunken Austin Seven and a bomb hanging by a parachute from the house opposite. Thank God neither of them had gone off!

We returned home because my mum was unhappy away from Dagenham and at home we had an Anderson shelter rigged out with bunks. It contained all sorts of equipment, including the 'Ever Ready' torch and also the 'ever ready' bucket! Oh the misery of peeing in that bucket. The sounds and their variations seemed to vibrate from garden to garden.

My dad, who was a sergeant in the Home Guard, always stood outside the shelter as long as he could and, so far as he could, talked us through the raids. Sometimes you could hear the shrapnel whining and ricocheting off the slate tiles of the roofs. The lads in our street used to go and look for shrapnel and shell cases around the streets but funnily enough my strongest memory isn't of that.

My strongest memory is of the time that the Hippodrome Theatre was bombed and hundreds of people were killed, including all the chorus girls. I remember seeing them brought out and it is something that I will just never forget. It's probably my memory playing tricks with me but to a child like me those poor chorus girls still seemed beautiful.

Sometimes if my dad was on Home Guard duty, my mum would take me to a posh house where they had an indoor shelter, but I didn't like going there as they had a big ginger-headed girl who could fight like a boy and always won! She used to beat me by holding me down and sitting on my head, and I always got a good hiding for hurting *her*. Actually, I always used to do it by biting her bum but she never seemed to cotton on!

When we were in the shelters we would often start singing the music hall songs, especially if my gran was there because she seemed to know them all. I can always remember one in particular and I have written it just as it sounds in cockney:

> *We're living in a bigger 'ouse nah*
> *Living like a bleedin' don*
> *In a great big place five storeys high*
> *Wiv a real barfroom and the gas laid on*
> *Luvly grounds awl round it*
> *No longer do we mooch around the pubs*
> *For it ain't a mansion or a villa what we're livin' in*
> *They call it Wormwood Scrubs!*

The funny thing that I remember is the war games. There were dozens of them. But the one I particularly remember is looking for bus tickets or tram or trolley fare tickets with numbers ending in 7, or all numbers adding up to 21! The best part was that we really believed if you got one of those with three 7s on it, it meant you wouldn't be killed in the war!

Although I seem to remember only the humour, the tragedies and the sadness were certainly there, although they don't seem to come back so easy, but we did feel and we did care.

Jack 'Satch' Lovelock

My recollections of the Blitz are when I was in London with my pal who was in the Royal Army Service Corps. I remember we went up to the West End one day and made our way towards Aldgate and we went into a Lyons shop for a snack. While we were there the sirens went and we found ourselves in the middle of an air raid.

Eventually when we got out and made our way along Aldgate I witnessed a sight that will always remain in my memory. There were hundreds of taxis with trailer pumps attached tearing along to go to the East India Docks, and many returning with fire crews, their faces all blackened by smoke.

My pal had to return to his army Centre which was outside of London, and I left him at Marble Arch at around 8 p.m. Just as he left the sirens went off again, and the AA guns in Hyde Park fired and I nearly jumped out of my skin! I caught a bus for Ilford, but as we passed the Bank of England the conductor stopped the bus and told us that if we wanted to take the risk of going further we could, but if we wanted to get off we could, and take the shelter across the road.

A soldier on leave was next to me and said, 'Let's get off.' We got on the pavement and the next minute he threw me to the ground and said, 'Keep your head down.' Then there was an almighty bang and a bomb dropped near to the Bank of England.

The soldier then said, 'Come on, we'll shelter in the old railway station,' which I believe used to operate the Southend line. Anyway I remember it was next to Strackers, which was a large printing and stationery firm. We had just got to the entrance when there was another almighty bang and a green-

ish kind of colour I remember and then a crowd of screaming people appeared coming toward us. We both pressed ourselves against the wall and managed to avoid being crushed in the stampede.

Throughout the night one could hear the bombs falling. I tried to sleep perched on a huge roll of printing material. My soldier acquaintance must have left before I awoke because I found that he was gone. So I made my way by bus back to Ilford and I saw the wreckage and havoc caused by the bombing along Whitechapel. There was glass strewn everywhere, buildings smouldering and people busily clearing up. Eventually I arrived back at Ilford.

The following weekend there was another raid while I was at Ilford. The landlady where I was lodging had an Anderson shelter at the bottom of the garden. Just imagine, the landlady, her husband, her son, two dogs and myself in this shelter! The condensation was dripping down and one felt that we were going to choke for the lack of air. Eventually, my health gave me trouble and a doctor advised me to leave the area and so I was given a certificate to allow me to move and this I did and went to live with an aunt in Weymouth.

George Bannier

This story is a true account of my experiences of one night during the war. I lived in Acorn Street then and the factory next door was Hartshorn & Jesson Limited, manufacturers of ladies' high-class shoes. I worked at Wolsey Limited at Abbey Park Road.

The air-raid shelter we took refuge in was used for storage after the war. As far as I know it may still be there. Although no bombs were dropped in Leicester that night, it was still a fearful time for most of us, especially the elderly. My father's name was Henry Baxter and he was well known in the locality.

This story is of one night spent in the air-raid shelter. The year was 1940. During the first month of the war, known as the 'phoney war', the government used this valuable respite to build street shelters. Also factory owners were required to build shelters on their premises for their workforce. Consequently a shelter was built in the factory yard, to be opened at night if necessary for the street residents.

Many of our neighbours had no Anderson shelters because they had no back gardens. The Morrison shelters made of steel construction and as large as a double-sized bed weren't popular because of the amount of room that they required.

My father was the caretaker as well as being a skilled worker at the factory, and he had many other jobs besides. He was now appointed shelter warden and was responsible for opening the shelter in the event of an air raid. In every street two neighbours were appointed street wardens. It was their responsibility to see that stirrup pumps were in working order and blackout curtains were efficient so that they showed no light.

In this period of time we were lulled into a false sense of security. Was Hitler playing games with us? Had he bitten off more than he could chew? We hoped so, but it was not to be.

Germany had been preparing for war for many years. After France fell, the German Luftwaffe mercilessly attacked London and southern cities. Then it became Coventry's turn and the air-raid sirens began to be heard in Leicester and all over the Midlands. How weird it used to sound in the dark hours of the night. It used to make me shiver and it still does when I hear a siren.

I remember coming home one night from the hosiery factory where I worked, having my tea and looking forward to a quiet evening listening to the radio or reading. I was 16 at the time. Our dog was restless so I took him out into the backyard. It was moonlight and the dark outlines of the factory and the nearby houses were silhouetted against the star-studded sky. I remember bending down to stroke the dog. His short hair was standing on end and his body was rigid and he seemed to be whining softly. What did he sense that I didn't? A lone plane passed overhead. One of ours on reconnaissance, no doubt.

We went indoors and settled down near the fire. About half an hour afterwards we heard the familiar wail of the

'alert'. Nearly 8 p.m. and we gathered together blankets and cushions. Our flasks of tea were already filled and sandwiches were made in readiness.

Also there were books to read, knitting and gas masks. We were fully prepared to spend the night in the shelter. We became very well organised in order to be as comfortable as possible. The shelter only had hard forms to sit upon.

My father had already left the house to unlock the big gates for our neighbours to enter the shelter next door. Two elderly sisters who lived together were nearly always first to arrive, armed with their blankets and flask and sandwiches. They were anxious, speaking in nervous whispers, but glad to be with others. They were soon followed by other neighbours all trying to reassure each other in their fear.

Another couple came in with their dog. A skirmish followed between their dog and ours! They went to the far end of the shelter so the dogs were kept apart. Families came in with children clutching dolls and teddy bears and picture books to keep them occupied until they went to sleep. Another family, who had recently arrived from London, came in cracking jokes to cover their anxiety. They had already had a taste of enemy action.

The shelter gradually filled up until there were about 50 of us in all. We were all talking at once until eventually our voices became lower and we began listening instead. An hour had passed by then when we heard them. The throbbing drone of their engines. We now could tell the difference between the German planes and our own RAF. From the sound we could tell that they were very high in the sky. Who was their target for tonight? I silently said prayers for Coventry. They had already suffered terrible losses amongst their population. But at the same time we selfishly hoped it wouldn't be us!

The bombers passed over in waves until all was silent. The lights were dimmed so it was easier for the children to go to sleep. It gradually grew colder and colder as the hours passed by. Our limbs ached. We slept fitfully. I thought longingly throughout that night of my own bed! My thoughts wandered again to the people of Coventry – how much longer would they be able to suffer the bombing of their city? How futile war is.

Once more we heard the sound of the bombers overhead. This time they were returning from their target with presumably their mission accomplished, and on their way home. They no doubt had left nothing but havoc and death and destruction in their wake. The street warden called in at our shelter to check if all was well. My father walked back into the street with him to stretch his legs. Soon he would have to go into the factory to stoke the boiler ready for the workers and their work next day. It would soon be daylight. Already people were waking up in the shelter now and stretching their aching limbs.

At long last we heard the long and continuous note of the 'all clear'. The time was 5.45 a.m. The men and women who had to go to work would have just had time to get a warm drink and have breakfast in their own homes before setting out. I myself would have to be at work by 8 a.m.

My father had already disappeared into the factory. I helped my mother gather our things together to take back into the house. Our neighbours took their leave, saying 'good morning' to each other. It *was* a good morning. A beautiful clear sky tinged with pink. I could see at least one last star high in the sky. As we stepped outside into the cold air I remember thinking how lucky we are. There will be no morning for many families again. We had only suffered an uncomfortable night. One amongst many and one amongst thousands as time would tell. Eventually lack of sleep caught up with us as it became a nightly occurrence. Many of us opted to stay in our warm beds come what may! If we had been living in Coventry or London it would have been a very different story.

Joan Lucas

The following are some of my most vivid recollections of the Plymouth Blitz which happened when I was in my teens.

When we emerged from the shelters many strange and terrible sights met our eyes when daylight arrived. Whole streets of houses collapsed like a pack of cards. ARP men digging for survivors or bodies while firemen fought alongside them trying to control the fires. Perhaps a whole front of a house might be blown away and a fragile gas mantle still hanging untouched by the blast. Direct hits were made on cemeteries and communal shelters and yet people who survived just thanked God and continued with their work, walking when no transport was available.

One night I recall the bombing was particularly heavy and when daylight came most of the centre of Plymouth had just been destroyed. There was no power, water or gas and indeed there was very little hope. The electricity was the first service to be restored and tea (which was the thing that kept everybody going) was made in a metal teapot on top of the electric fire.

The following night we had a return visit. We didn't need sirens as most people knew the sound of the German bombers by now. This time the drop was incendiary bombs. What was missed the night before was bombed then. There was very little water to fight the fires, which made the situation even more frightening. I had been visiting friends in the Millbridge area of Plymouth that night. We all cowered in a coalhouse under the stairs for what seemed to be hours, deafened by the roar of aircraft and ack-ack guns and bombs dropping. When at last it was over I walked home and as I came to the top of Eldad Hill the whole of Plymouth centre could be seen as one great fire. No one could describe the horror of what had been done to Plymouth. There was nothing left except piles of rubble and craters and burning ashes.

After this we decided to move to a house in Milehouse further from the centre of Plymouth. This house was handy for the Royal Navy dockyard where I was employed as a sail-maker. I made red sails for life rafts and Carly floats and lagged ships' pipes with asbestos. The house we moved to had a reinforced cellar fitted with bunks. One entrance was through a false pantry bottom. The other entrance (which was a hatch) led into the garden. It was the law to have two separate entrances in case one became blocked. My mother hated the cellar as the main gas pipe ran through it and she often said 'I may as well be bombed as gassed!' For this reason we often in fact shared the Anderson shelter in the garden of our neighbours, Mr and Mrs Skingsley.

By this time I was 18 and engaged to be married, but my husband-to-be was a sailor and only allowed 48 hours' leave for the wedding. My aunt Bertha and sister, Joan, arrived from Cornwall and as many family and friends as could arrived. We had a real wartime wedding, gleaning the various ingredients for cake and buffet from various sources! I made my own dress and hat, and my mother's hat from material bought with scrounged clothing coupons. The dress was a blue Morican, which was a type of heavy crepe, and my hat was an old cut-down pillbox covered with multi-coloured silk anemones with a veil!

My brother-in-law to be, Jack, managed to get a 24-hour pass to be best man, and all went ahead as planned. Around 11 p.m. on the wedding evening my new husband and I walked with Jack to North Road Station. That was where Jack had to catch his train to return to his unit in Kent. It was about one and a half miles to the station. When we returned to the house we found that everyone had retired for the benefit of the newlyweds! How kind!

However, around 2 a.m., we were all awakened by air-raid sirens, gunfire, and the family banging on the door telling us to get to the shelter. Reluctantly we got up and eventually arrived at the cellar. My aunt was the last and she insisted on collecting her wedding attire on which she had spent her last clothing coupons! My sister Joan was most unhappy and frightened, not being used to air raids as we were, and being only eight years old. Having heard my mother's remarks on the gas pipe she begged us to take her into the Anderson shelter next door rather than staying in the cellar! This we promised to do when things quietened down a bit.

Bombs were dropping too close for comfort when my mother decided to go up the steps through the pantry hatch to get another chair. Then there was a terrific whoosh and a thud! The whole place shook and Mother was blown to the bottom of the pantry steps still with the chair in her hand, but now with a curse on her lips! We all said, 'My God that was close.' When we got over the shock we tried to get out. We could hear someone coughing, but of course there were no lights, and we found that the garden entrance was blocked!

Eventually we got out through the pantry hatch to find the edge of the crater and what had been our back door. The whole place was covered by several feet of soil and debris. The house my mother had lovingly cleaned was hardly stand-ing. The bed I had slept in with my new husband had been smashed to the floor. A large concrete block was now lying across our pillows. The lilac trees that were the backdrop of our photographs were on top of what was left of the roof. My aunties' undies were hanging on the hydrangeas in the front garden!

Worse was to come. When the air-raid wardens finally arrived it was to find the Anderson shelter in the Skingsleys' garden had taken a direct hit. The whole family including their 18-year-old son were dead or dying. This was indeed a tragedy for us of enormous proportions. They had been the guests at our wedding only 12 hours before. That night saw almost the last of the raids on Plymouth. We had been all through it and now we were ill-fated enough to get almost the last bomb. But we were so thankful not to have taken my sister into the shelter next door as she had asked.

Pearl Marshall

I was born in Ramsgate and I lived there until 1943 when I was called up. I remember on Sunday 7 September 1940 when myself and a pal Sid were walking home from the cinema. It was then getting dark and then we met another two lads whom we knew, had a chat and went on our way. I lived in Adelaide Gardens, which was a tall block of terraced houses which still exists and is situated close to the seafront. My mother was down the tunnel shelter that runs under the town, almost 60 feet deep, and with about 20 entrances dotted around.

Sid came home with me and Dad was there, and as usual we all went on to the cliff to see if anything was going on over in France. We stood at a place known as the 'Tidal Ball', which was a small building housing the winding gear for raising the ball up a large mast and lowering it according to the state of the tide. A few yards to our right was a sand-bagged gun emplacement which was empty but complete with a roof and an aperture facing the harbour and out to sea, and on the cliff edge and below us, a road leading down to the harbour.

Behind us, on the other side of the road, was the Foy Boat Hotel and next door, facing the sea, another block of large terraced houses, and behind the hotel in Adelaide Gardens some cottages. It was a nice night and some people were sitting outside the big houses chatting. There was Sid and Dad and myself, and the man from the end house of our block whom we had known, and his family, for years.

There wasn't much going on and our neighbour said, 'I'm off, goodnight.' Not long afterwards we heard the sound that we had got to know and we all said, 'Here comes Jerry.' By this time another couple and a policeman had joined us and then one of the planes started diving and so did we! Looking back it was quite hilarious to recall six people trying to get into the narrow doorway of the gun emplacement. I remember knocking the policeman's helmet off! We just made it when the bombs started falling. I was looking through the aperture when one fell into the harbour, and I think another fell outside, and then one onto the road below and to our left. It went right through the road into the buildings underneath.

Then the whole place shook. There was debris falling on our shelter roof and the Foy Boat Hotel had been hit. The cottages behind it had also gone. Some of the larger houses on the seafront, and our neighbour's house and another opposite, had also been hit.

Our neighbour had apparently come out again and was caught in that lot and killed. People in the cottages were killed and many others were seriously injured and I remember that one of our neighbours lost a leg.

When Sid and I made for the tunnel shelter and we came out of the emplacement, we found that the gas mains were alight and there was a terrible mess everywhere. On the way to the shelter we found our neighbour's wife, who was an invalid. She was on all fours in the rubble and we picked her up and managed to carry her to the shelter where one of her sons was. He said, 'Have you seen Dad?' We didn't know at that time that he had been killed.

During the raid another pub, the Westcliff Tavern, was bombed, and the landlord lost a leg and his wife was killed, and some houses opposite were hit and one of the lads we had met coming home from the cinema that night was killed along with his father.

It was a terrible night and it was fortunate that, being Sunday, all the pubs were closed, otherwise it would have been a different story. There certainly would have been hundreds killed.

Stanley Matthews

I have a few memories of the Blitz, as a little girl in Leeds, Yorkshire. I was eight years old at the time. My mother and I were at home at this time. We lived in a terraced house and I remember workmen coming and taking the iron railings off all the garden walls to help the war effort. We children used to watch the workmen building air-raid shelters in the streets. They were long flat buildings. Halfway down each block were toilets. No doors on, just planks of wood with holes cut in and zinc buckets underneath!

We were lucky because all the houses in our street had cellars so it was considered safe for us to shelter down there. Men came and knocked holes about two foot square in all the cellar connecting walls and then put the bricks back with a sandy mixture. The idea was that if any house was bombed and people were trapped in the cellar they could punch through the weak spot in the wall and escape.

I remember my father reinforced our cellar roof with wood supports made from old bedframes. He always said that the safest place for us was on the cellar steps.

When the sirens sounded we went down there with rugs and blankets to keep us warm. I remember my mother made me a siren suit out of a travel rug. It had a flap at the back held up by the belt, so I didn't have to get undressed to go to the toilet! They were certainly very warm and fashionable at the time.

We used to huddle together listening to the planes throughout the night, wondering if they were 'one of ours' and trying to guess how near the bombs were dropping. I know my mother was always worrying where my dad had been sent to with the ARP and praying that they would come home safely. We were lucky that they always came home. They had some narrow escapes.

I think we children didn't realise how dreadful war was. At school we had brown sticky paper criss-crossing the classroom windows or strong mesh-like curtaining stuck to them to prevent the glass splintering. Gas mask practice was a laugh, trying to get them on and often making rude noises through them! On the way to school after raids we used to look for shrapnel as souvenirs, or go down the street and through the park to see where the bombs had dropped.

My friends and I used to put on little concerts for our parents and neighbours in someone's garden, charging coppers to raise funds for different charities. I remember that we also made lavender bags, bookmarks and kettle holders to sell. Later on in the war one charity we supported was Mrs Churchill's 'Aid to Russia' fund. I was very proud when I got a silvery badge like RAF Wings for another fundraising project. Maybe it was 'Wings for Victory', I am not sure.

We all had to take newspapers and jam jars to school. Nothing was wasted. I still have my identity card and also a Stork wartime cookery book issued with Stork cookery leaflets. When the wars in Europe and the Far East came to an end in May and August 1945, we children had wonderful parties each time. We had a fabulous time and goodness knows how our parents managed to provide the food. My strongest memory is still of the big bonfire we had with an effigy of Adolf Hitler on top.

Betty Moore

On 1 September 1939, I was a ten-year-old lad and I remember being evacuated with my younger brother to an Oxfordshire village, which must remain nameless owing to its hostility towards evacuees! After being pushed around from one unwelcome billet to another we were eventually brought home again almost a year later.

At that time we were living in Woodford Bridge, Essex, which was just outside the London boundary but, unfortunately, not far enough to escape the air raids. If my memory is correct 7 September 1940 was the start of the Blitz and it was certainly a night to remember!

The sirens sounded early on that evening and the target for the enemy bombers was the docks which were soon on fire. We could see the flames clearly from our back garden where we had our Anderson shelter! The 'all clear' sounded around 9 p.m. and we thought that that was it.

But no, back came the raiders at about midnight, and this time the bombing was much closer to home! At the bottom of our back garden there was an alleyway and at the same time during the early hours of 8 September, a bomb dropped there about 50 feet from our shelter. This was the closest shave I have ever experienced. The front of our shelter was blown down and there were lumps of brick, concrete and earth everywhere.

When the 'all clear' eventually sounded, we emerged from our shelter, only to be told by my father, who was an air-raid warden, that there were several unexploded bombs in the neighbourhood and that we had to get out of the area as quickly as possible. This we did and stayed with friends until the bombs were dealt with.

Fortunately our house did not suffer much damage apart from a few broken tiles, but the house next door was minus its chimney, which was scattered in pieces in the garden. We were told on good authority that this was caused by the flight of the bomb which had exploded in the alleyway and I did not think much of it at the time. The family who lived next door were away so that they did not know anything about it. When they returned a month later, they discovered an unexploded bomb, which had buried itself under the foundations after passing through the roof, the bedroom, living room and basement! And to think that we were living next door to it for that time! Of course it was the unexploded bomb that had demolished the chimney.

During the daylight, when it was safe, most of us boys would go around seeing who could pick up the largest piece of shrapnel. I remember the largest I found was nine inches long. We did sometimes also find an unexploded incendiary bomb but had the good sense not to touch it!

Going to school was a nightmare in every sense of the word. Our school was a good half-hour cycle ride away, so there was no coming home for lunch, and lessons were constantly interrupted by air raids and we then had to file out to the shelter. At that stage of the war there were not enough shelters to accommodate all the pupils, so we only went to school every other day.

After about two months of this my brother and I were packed off to Oxfordshire again to a different village. However, that didn't solve the problem. It turned out to be equally hostile!

We came home during the summer of 1941, this time for good. The Blitz was over and, except for the spasmodic raids of short duration, nothing much disturbed the peace of Essex for some time.

That is until the flying bombs arrived again at the end of 1944 and after that the rockets. But that really is another story.

John Parrott

I was nine years old at the time and we lived in Hull. When the raids came we spent the nights in the Anderson shelter. My dad went out nearly every night, as an air-raid warden, and to keep him warm my mum used to tell him to wrap a small blanket around his waist, under his big coat. It was made of knitted squares and she used to call it 'Joseph's Coat of Many Colours'!

One day he was in a crowded underground shelter full of people who were all singing and it got a bit warm in there and so he took off his coat. Apparently everyone stopped singing straightaway and started laughing at his 'Joseph's Shawl' which he had forgotten he was wearing! He was very annoyed with my mother!

If we had been up all night we got the next morning off school, so our usual pastime was going out to see who could collect the best pieces of shrapnel. My tin was on a shelf in a sort of conservatory. One night we heard a huge clatter and we said, 'That's it, the house has been damaged this time.' But when we eventually got out of the shelter we found out it was only my shrapnel tin which had fallen off the shelf!

My parents often used to repeat another tale about me. One day my mother had managed to get a large ham shank and it was on the table and we were all sitting around waiting for her to cut it when, without any siren warning, we heard bombs falling.

Apparently I grabbed the shank and in a flash I was under the table with it, saying, 'Hitler's not getting this!'

The last two weeks that we spent in Hull were horrific. We never got undressed for bed and we had to live permanently in the shelter. I slept on a wooden board and my back has never been right since.

Gwen Oakland, centre.

This ended when the shop my dad managed was bombed. Everything was bombed right down to the basement and apparently the only thing left was the key! My dad was offered another branch in Doncaster and things were so bad that Dad told us to pack up on the basis that we would never spend another night in Hull. I remember him saying that he would go and find a house in Doncaster and that we could go to Malton until he found one for us.

I remember that we packed up and found that there was a train running and when we were ready to go we looked for my brother and someone said that he had gone to the pictures with another lad. We couldn't believe it! But we went to the cinema and looked along the rows with a flashlight but we found that it was the wrong cinema and when we did eventually find him we found we had missed the train! We all went to bed again that night in Hull, with the words ringing in our ears from my dad, 'If we all get killed tonight, it will be our Eric's fault!'

I will never forget seeing Hammonds still burning a fortnight after being hit and as we were waiting to leave on the train I can clearly remember tears streaming down my face as I loved that shop.

Gwen Oakland

People usually associated the Blitz with cities like London, Coventry, Portsmouth and so on, but on an autumn night in 1940 the villagers of Tongham, Surrey had good reason to realise otherwise.

The sirens in Aldershot used to sound most nights, only because German planes were on their way to bomb London or on their way back. So on this particular night, 22 August, it didn't seem any different from the rest, except that a short while later, at 10.30 p.m., explosions were heard. My father shouted to my sister and me to get out of bed and downstairs. We had no air-raid shelter but my father had cleared the larder out for such an emergency. In his capacity as the 'expert' on such matters, you stood a better chance of survival in a confined space. I was 11 years old. Probably, if I'd been older, I would have pointed out to him that they were dropping 500-pound bombs and not pork pies! Incidentally, these first explosions were bombs being dropped at the engineering works at Elstead a few miles the other side of the Hog's Back, a well-known beauty spot in Surrey.

All was quiet for a short time and then we heard the drone of aircraft engines.

'They're looking for Aldershot,' said father knowingly.

Then eight huge explosions, one after the other, rocked the house. By this time I was trying to crawl into the concrete floor of the larder. I remember thinking, 'Either that bomb aimer is new to the game or they've moved Aldershot,' because they sounded as though they had gone right through the gardens at the back of the houses.

'This is it!' screamed Father. 'Get down!'

I covered my ears with my hands. Then there was an

explosion. It was bigger but muffled in a way. One had landed in the village about 25 yards from the school and had blown the roof completely off our seat of learning!

Suddenly I knew what war was all about; there was me, my 18-year-old sister, mother and father, crouching in this tiny larder and someone up there was hell-bent on killing us. The war then wasn't a long way off any more. I knew in those few seconds how those people must have felt in faraway places like Poland, Belgium and France. Places I had heard about on the wireless. I also realised now why my father had never talked much about the First World War. It was horrible, and this was only the start.

Once again there was silence for a short while and then one small explosion from the front of the house, followed by another, and then another, then the voice of the 'expert' again.

'That's an anti-aircraft gun,' said Father. 'They'll get 'em.'

I had my doubts about the ack-ack gun though. We had just been on school holiday and been through all the fields and farms in the area and the nearest thing was a single searchlight about a mile away near the Aldershot Gasworks. That was food for thought. The gasholder there was supposed to be the largest in Britain! What if a bomb hit that? No time to think about that, for there was a rat-tat-tat on the front door.

'There's someone at the front door,' said Mother.

No answer from Father.

'Perhaps it's the pilot asking for his bombs back,' said I.

Father grabbed hold of me. 'Children should be seen and not heard,' which was a fair comment as it probably was a stupid remark considering the circumstances.

Rat-tat-tat on the front door again. This time it sounded more urgent. There being no other volunteers, Father decided to go and investigate. The door was opened and then we heard the deep voice of authority.

'I'm sorry, sir, but you and your family may have to

evacuate these premises as there is an ammunition train on fire across the fields. So if you can get a few things together, I'll be back later.'

I rushed through the dining room and looked out of the window round the blackout curtain and sure enough the trucks really were on fire. The gunfire that Father had heard was nothing but ammunition exploding!

I heard Father reply to the voice of authority, 'No, I don't think we'll bother. We're quite safe in the larder.'

This brought a stern reply. 'Well, sir, we may have to insist on it if that lot goes up.'

This was more stupid than my remarks about the pilot! 'If that lot goes up' we might have found ourselves living in Seale (which is a village about half a mile over the Hog's Back), together with house and all!

I slipped back to the larder. Father said to Mother, 'They want us to evacuate but this is our home and I think we'll stay here.'

'You know best,' said Mother.

I couldn't have agreed more! I was getting quite used to that larder floor. By this time the 'all clear' had gone but the explosions from the fire kept on for a while until they finally stopped. The voice of authority didn't return, so Father ventured to the front window and announced that in his opinion it was safe to re-join society!

Mother had just made the customary cup of tea when my future brother-in-law walked in the back door. He was in the army, stationed in Aldershot, and had been trying to get through to us all night. Together with what he told us and what we found out the following day, it appeared that there was a shower of incendiaries and several houses had been hit in the village, including those of two friends of mine, but several other incendiaries had caught the first two trucks of the train and set them on fire. Two railwaymen, George Frederick Keen and George Henry Leach, together with five unknown soldiers, managed to uncouple the untouched trucks and manhandle them to safety. It was said at the time that if they hadn't acted as they did, there would have been such an almighty explosion that probably the best part of Tongham would have been blown away.

The two railwaymen were both awarded the George Medal for their bravery. Unfortunately George Keen, who was our scoutmaster, died before he could receive his. The reasons for his death are rather obscure but, as youngsters, we were told it was lung trouble, which in those days covered a multitude of things. Rather a shame really.

For weeks afterwards villagers were finding live large and small calibre ammunition in their gardens. Notices posted by the police said that all objects had to be reported or handed in but I think quite a few people kept empty 25-pounder shell cases, polished them up and used them as ornaments over the fire! I found a piece of bomb casing in a crater at the back of our house and kept it hidden from Father. It disappeared from my wardrobe when I was away doing my bit in the RAF.

Eventually, after a year, the school roof was repaired and we went back to school full-time, having spent the first three months off school completely and the next time nine months on half days in the village hall. The council did come round some time later and put air-raid shelters in every garden, which did seem to me like shutting the door after the horse had bolted! Anyway, as soon as ours was finished, Father started to use it to store his potato crop! I had enough trouble with that damn larder without having to throw out a dozen sacks of Arran Banner before I could get in it so I decided to give that a miss next time.

Reginald Nash

I was in the Leicestershire Regiment on fire picket duty on the night that Leicester was bombed. The warning sirens went off at about 7.30 p.m. a couple of nights after Coventry was blitzed. At Brentwood Road in the old Knighton area, landmines were dropped by parachute and the blast could be felt as the explosions went off. That raid lasted for about three hours and the funny thing is that I can distinctly remember a dog howling, which is the most ominous sound you can imagine!

Next morning our platoon was sent to Highfield Road which suffered considerable damage and our job entailed digging for bodies. I can remember uncovering the torso of a young blond woman, which particularly upset everyone. One of the remarkable features of the raid was that one building remained intact. It was a Jewish tabernacle, which somehow seemed to shout defiance at the anti-Jewish Nazis.

One other memory of that terrible night was of a double-decker bus, which had been blown halfway up a tree in Clarendon Park Road. Its front wheels were resting amongst the branches! I also remember that an Italian airman, who had bailed out during the raid, was brought in the next morning to Glen Parva Barracks. To try to be civilised we wanted to give him a shave but I have to say that it was most difficult to find a barber who would shave him without taking more drastic steps!

David Black

At the time of the Blitz on Britain, I was a male nurse in London and my fiancée was a nurse in Bristol. My account of the London Blitz is taken from my diary notes at the time, and my wife's accounts, mainly from her letters to me. I have to say that in those days, despite the disruptions of air raids, we seemed to receive each other's letters the day after they had been posted!

The first part of our story concerns the Bristol Blitz, which is set down by my wife, Isabella Norman, who was Isabella Longsdale before we were married. It reads as follows.

At the time of Bristol's first heavy Blitz, I was a third-year student nurse, working in the theatre. It was Sunday, 24 November 1940, just before 6 p.m. Sister was in her office and we staff were in the main theatre, sitting relaxing, staff nurse busy knitting, others chatting, and I swotting surgery in readiness for our final examinations due in February. Half of the staff were due off duty at 6 p.m.

The telephone rang and staff nurse groaned. She hoped it wasn't a 'case'. One of the nurses went to answer it and was back in a few moments to say a patient was coming up to No. 3 Theatre. That was the ear, nose and throat theatre. The surgeon would be there for 6.30 p.m. Sister had said that those who were off duty could go and would the rest of us prepare the theatre.

Sirens went as we hurried along the corridor to No. 3, but we didn't take much notice of them as we had so many false alarms. I was in the Anaesthetic Room when suddenly we heard a bomb coming down and I thought, 'This is going to hit us.' The sister turned and made a run past me. I caught her and said, 'Stand still, Sister, you're all right.' She stopped and said, 'I thought we would be safer in the corridor.' I replied, 'We can't leave the patients, Sister,' and in that split second we heard the bomb hit. We found out later that it had fallen on houses at the top of Guinea Street, which was the street of our main hospital gates.

The patient had swallowed a piece of meat and it was stuck in her throat and so we continued with the operation which did not take long but the bombs seemed to be raining down as the surgeon carried out his work. I remember he made all six of us look down at the instrument, to see the piece of meat before removing it. Looking back I think he was trying to keep our minds on the job and calming us down because the noise outside was increasing.

Our theatres were on the top floor of the hospital and had huge glass windows. The hospital was adjacent to the Bristol Docks and the Sand and Gravel Company's dock ran alongside the lower part. Over to the right and not five minutes' walk away were the large grain docks. With the layout of the area, the hospital was in a triangulation of water and easy to see.

We cleaned up the theatre and were then sent to various wards to help with the evacuation down to the shelter. This shelter had access to the road at the lower level by the Sand and Gravel dock, which helped later in the fire blitz as being the only way out. I was sent to a women's ward and those who were there were either sitting or lying with washing bowls over their heads, to protect them from flying glass. But that danger had already passed as the windows plus blackout blinds and wire netting protection had already been blown in. The ward itself was already completely lit by the fires burning outside.

One old lady was very frightened. I was frightened too and felt like running away somewhere – but where? I went to calm the patient and she asked me if I could sing 'Abide With Me'. So to take their minds off the noise I got all the other patients singing too. We sang more hymns after that, and the time did not seem too long before help came to move them.

We had teams of male stretcher-bearers sent in to help get them down to the shelter. The patient who had recently been in the ENT Theatre was by now in this ward and by now had more or less recovered from the anaesthetic, so Sister asked me to take her along to the lift. Partway along the corridor I remember she wanted to be sick, so I sat her down on a seat outside a ward and dashed inside to get a bowl. When I got back she was gone!

I stood dumbfounded and then I heard the lift round the corner, the gates opening, and I ran. As I got there the gates

were closing and there was my patient sitting on the one and only knee of a man who was in a wheelchair! I had to laugh. It just relieved the tension!

I was next told to report to the theatre. We already had two of the cellar rooms equipped, one with two operating tables and the other to be used as a Reception/Anaesthetic Room. The Casualty Department also had two tables in their small theatre. Outpatients Hall had already been cleared of all seating, etc., and was filled with rows of camp beds in readiness for arriving casualties. Here they were graded as to the seriousness of their wounds, and given the necessary injections against Tetanus and Gas Gangrene. This would all then be charted with names and addresses, where possible, on a form that was pinned to them.

Our first patient arrived about 8.30 p.m. She had been hurt by that first bomb we had heard come down in Guinea Street. She had a shattered shoulder and, would you believe it, she was apologising profusely for not being dressed properly! She explained she had been getting washed to go to church. I looked at her and thought, if only she could have seen herself. She was filthy. Her ears, eyes, nose and mouth were full of dirt and her skin was peppered with grit. It took weeks to come out.

I wiped her mouth and cleaned her eyes and ears as best I could. Her wounds were just ribbons of filthy flesh. Suddenly, the Sister was at the door saying, 'Nurse, we need a tourniquet. It's in the main theatre at the end of the operating table.'

For a split second I stood and looked at her, thinking – Does she mean *me* to go up there in this holocaust?

'Quickly, Nurse, we need it,' and I was gone. I have never ever got up and down four long double flights of stairs so fast in all my life!

I only remember a few of the patients that came in that night. There was a young girl of 18 years with her right arm hanging in dirty ribbons of flesh from her shoulder and lacerated to her waist. The man who, while waiting, could speak of nothing but 'Is my leg broken?' He was so worried in case it was. He was lacerated from the right side of his waist right down to his groin, which was laid fully open. There, to our complete amazement, was the femoral artery quite untouched. He would have been dead in three minutes if that had been severed. The surgeon was so astounded that he had all of us go and look at it.

All the nurses went off duty that morning at 8 a.m., and I was left to assist the last patient. He had a badly damaged leg and I saw for the first and last time of my life a Kirschner wire used. The wire was drilled through the heel and a stirrup was fixed to it. This was used to extend the leg and pull the bones into some sort of alignment. When I went off duty I suddenly realised that I had been on duty since 8 a.m. the previous morning, that is 24 hours without any break at all.

All the patients dealt with had only received emergency treatment. Their wounds had been packed with gauze soaked in Vaseline and boracic acid to clean them, and the patients would all have to receive further treatment. Our matron told some of us later that when she had served in a hospital ship during the First World War, the same treatments had been used then.

Our next raid was on Tuesday, 3 December, a quote from one of my letters being: 'They only managed to land incendiaries. They were soon dealt with.'

In the raid of 6 and 7 December the sirens sounded at 6.40 p.m. Some of us off-duty nurses watched from the

Nurses' Home sitting room as the flares were dropped in the centre of Bristol.

Within five minutes the Blitz had started again and we hurried to the wards to get patients to shelter. At that time we had a 'full house'. As we ran towards the corridor where the lift was, we heard a most peculiar flapping noise, and in the next instant there was the most horrific explosion and we were instantly enveloped in dust, which got into our eyes and choked us. When it cleared, people were already crowded to get into the shelter. Nurses, maids, students, doctors and patients! The next few hours were a nightmare, filling with rumours, tears, laughter and work. Blessed work to keep one's mind and body occupied.

We had three landmines fall on the road near to the hospital. Landmines came down on parachutes, which was the flapping noise we had heard and then they exploded as they touched the ground, causing the most extensive blast damage. They blew the window and door frames clean off the brickwork, bringing everything with them, doors, windows, blinds, etc., all in on top of the patients.

The emergency water tank on the roof was damaged and the water ran down the lift shaft to the basement, where we had a river for some time. The electricity supply failed so that there was neither heat nor light. All the patients had to be moved by hand. One of our nurses, wheeling a patient in a wheelchair, was blown along the corridor with both the chair and the patient, round the corner and came to rest under an overhead window light. As if that wasn't enough, the blackout blind then came down around her head and shoulders, and she arrived in the shelter with her patient and the blind still around her! We had to laugh.

Another nurse was blown against the wall and knocked out for a while. We had two patients die. One an old lady who was dying already and the other, who had an operation that day, got out of bed and ran because of her fear of what was happening. She died later of shock. Apart from that, not

Isabella Norman.

one of us had so much as a scratch. The 'all clear' went at 11.30 p.m.

Those of us who were not needed laid down on our beds fully clothed. We were on duty at 8 a.m. the next morning as usual. Now it only remained for Matron to arrange the evacuation of all patients wherever she could get them. Also to send nurses with them. Other nurses were sent home or anywhere else they could stay until things were more settled. I stayed with a friend, reporting each morning to the hospital, and eventually was sent to a convalescent home at Weston-Super-Mare with a contingent of patients.

To end my story, I did not return to the Bristol General Hospital until Easter 1941, taking my finals at Bristol University in April and being thrilled to pass them. Our matron received the OBE for all the work she had done, which was equally thrilling for all of us.

The story now of Leslie Norman and the London Fire Blitz.

I was a 23-year-old probationer male nurse in Hackney Hospital during the London Blitz. On the day of the first raid, which was Saturday, 7 September 1940, it all started just before 5 p.m. as I was working in the ward. Gunfire broke out almost at once as planes sounded right overhead. For a while all hell seemed let loose and I remember two especially scary moments when what I thought in my inexperience were aeroplanes crash-diving upon us turned out to be bombs quite nearby!

I had been attached until fairly recently to the Friends' Ambulance Unit, and they had a section stationed at London

Hospital in Whitechapel Road. So when I got off duty after six o'clock I made my way there with a vague idea of giving voluntary help. The 'all clear' sounded soon after 6 p.m. and I managed to get part by bus towards Mile End but there were shells of burnt-out trolley buses and huge craters blocking the road. Beyond the Mile End Road the sky was black with smoke and there seemed to be scores of fire engines everywhere. Houses were on fire in all directions and a scene of nothing but total destruction met me in Whitechapel Road. In that road houses were ripped apart, fronts blown out and glass and debris was everywhere. Hundreds of people and cars seemed in one mad rush in a westerly direction.

There seemed to be little chance of doing anything practical to help, so I was in fact reduced to being a spectator. Nowadays so many people are used to such scenes of war damage through the media, but remember that this was an entirely new experience to me. It was happening for real and I was there.

From time to time explosions could be heard as oil tanks or something similar from the nearby docks blew up, and occasionally time bombs went off. As darkness fell the flames lit the sky and all the buildings for miles around us, as far as I could see eastwards, were just one long colossal fire.

Fire engines continued to tear along as reinforcements were brought in. Crowds of people were now coming on foot, with some belongings in bundles or cases, to wait outside the Whitechapel Brewery, where they could shelter in the cellars. I was on the corner of Mile End Gate when the siren warning went off above me. I tried to steady a young woman with a baby in her arms, as there was a mad dash for the shelter. I saw her safely inside but did not go in myself.

Making my way back to Hackney, I looked back from Cambridge Heath Road, and the scene reminded me of two pictures I had seen somewhere in books. The first picture was *The Great Fire of London* and the second picture was of the crowd fleeing from the destruction of Sodom and Gomorrah.

It was a long walk back with many detours due to streets blocked off. There were unexploded bomb areas and fires everywhere and all the time the continual roar of planes above, ack-ack guns, and bombs dropping, some not so far away. By the time I got back to my lodgings near Hackney Hospital, it was late but the air raid continued for several hours more and at times again it still seemed to be overhead.

In the years that followed, I had some closer encounters, but the one I shall never forget was that first night when I saw the London Docks ablaze.

Leslie G. Norman

I was born on 7 October 1934, so I was five years old at the outbreak of war. Firstly, let me say that all during the war I never felt any fear. I just seemed to accept that all that was going on around me was part of the everyday life that one could expect because I had never known any different.

My first recollection was that my mother, Dolly, and I went to live with my aunt Martha. She lived a few streets away. This was because my dad and my uncle were both in the army and so my mother and her sister lived together, so that they were company for one another.

Inside my aunt's living room was a table shelter, which was called a Morrison shelter. I remember it was made of steel and had a mesh front so that during the day it was a table and at night it could be used as a shelter. However, we always used next door's Anderson, which was an outside shelter sunk in the garden.

Next door to my aunt was an old lady who we used to call 'Old Mother Riley'. I can only think she got this name from the celebrity film star at the time. I remember that all these local children used to sing a song that went as follows:

Old Mother Riley's dead
She died last night in bed
They put her in a coffin, and she fell through the
*   bottom*
Old Mother Riley's dead.

'Mrs Riley' had an Anderson shelter in her back garden and when the sirens sounded I remember being passed over the fence to spend time in the shelter, until we heard the 'all clear'.

One night as I was waiting to be passed over the fence to take refuge in the shelter, I happened to look into the dark night sky and saw there three searchlights criss-crossed. In the centre of that web of light was a silver speck trapped like a fly in a web. It was a German plane on one of the raids over the River Tyne.

At school I always carried a gas mask. Now and again we had practice runs into the dark dingy shelters and then we were made to sit on the lattice seating. However, we didn't have many daylight raids in our area and so we did not use the school shelters much.

South Shields is a seaside town with beautiful beaches but there were no happy sandcastle-making days for me as a youngster. All the beaches were out of bounds during the war and apart from that it was all just too dangerous.

I did have one particularly happy memory. That was the street party when the war ended. It was held in a cul-de-sac where my aunt Annie lived. I remember the tables seemed to stretch miles down the street and it was covered in the best white cloths that we could get hold of. It was set out with all types of goodies and I don't know how many ration books were emptied of coupons that day to put on that spread!

It went on into the dark. In the darkness there was singing and dancing in the streets and in the trees there were jam jars suspended by string and each painted a different colour, and lit by a candle, bringing light at the end of those dark days.

Talking of light, a song which was always sung during the war was 'When the Lights Go On Again All Over the World'. I really did not grasp the meaning of this song until that party night when the lights did go on again.

Jim Page

At the time of the Blitz we were living at Elstree, and my son had been admitted to the Ear, Nose & Throat Hospital in Gray's Inn Road, London, for a mastoid operation. I was visiting him every day because he was a private patient, but the nights were a nightmare. From our home at Elstree we could see the sky over London 18 miles away. It was aglow and it looked like the whole of London was one solid sheet of fire. Every few seconds there would be a flash as more incendiary bombs lit up the sky and we could only stand there and cry. Our little boy was seven and he was in the middle of it and there was absolutely nothing we could do about it.

I remember one particular morning, for some reason, that after the 'all clear' had sounded and dawn approached, we phoned the hospital hoping of course that it was still there, to enquire how our little boy was and we were so thankful to be told that day that he was quite satisfactory and comfort-able. Despite all the emotions that we felt, the funny thing is that I can remember only being able to say, 'Oh thank you!'

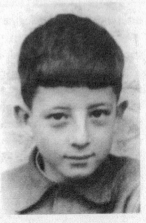

When I visited him that day at midday he asked me to bring him an orange. When I said that there weren't any oranges, he said, 'Well, that man in the next bed had one.'

I went all over London, including Covent Garden, trying in vain to buy an orange for my lad.

One market trader told me, 'You see that man over there in Windmill Street. His name is Jimmy Kirkham. He is a barrow boy and he's got some oranges.'

I approached the man and asked if he was Jimmy Kirkham and told him that I was trying to buy a couple of oranges for my little boy who was in hospital.

He was a scruffy-looking character but he said 'Wait there' and disappeared down an alley. A few minutes later he came back with *five* oranges and handed them over to me.

'Put these in your pocket,' he said. 'They're like liquid gold.' He wouldn't take anything.

Over the next few weeks I saw a lot of Jimmy Kirkham and I bought oranges and cherries and all sorts from him! I was still working in the hosiery trade at the time and was fortunate enough to be able to buy fully fashioned nylons for five shillings a pair (25p) plus three clothing coupons!

So I decided to take two or three pairs into London one Saturday night to see if Jimmy was interested in any.

'No problem,' he said. 'Can you get any more?'

I said, 'Yes, but I need some coupons.'

Instantly he called over another scruffy-looking character and in front of me told him to fix me up with some coupons!

'How many do you want?' he asked.

'About 12 or 20,' I said.

'Oh, that's no use,' he said. 'I thought you wanted two or three thousand!'

Apparently he wasn't interested in 12 or 20!

There were two contrasts. The first was that all this was going on in London at a time of shortage and then during the raid I had to go down on to the Underground stations. Men and women and children were sleeping on the platform with just a few precious belongings. But despite the fact that it was all going on there was that generosity of Jimmy Kirkham in letting me have the oranges for a little boy in hospital who wanted one.

Walter Shaw

In August 1940, we moved to Dagenham. I remember we had an Anderson shelter in the back garden and when the bombing started I remember that my nephew and my daughter had diphtheria and there was an epidemic. My baby got scabies in hospital from other children because there wasn't enough linen towels to go around.

While my baby was in hospital I remember one night when there was a barrage of bombs. I was sitting sewing by the fire, with a little puppy. The first bombs fell without any warning and all the soot came down the chimney and there was soot everywhere. The puppy and I were all alone.

My husband was fire-watching in town and I was petrified. Suddenly I wanted another life with me and I remember that I prayed and hugged the puppy close to me and I can remember even now the feel of its heart beating against mine. It was almost like a miracle and it is something I shall never forget.

I remember another time when I was queuing for a bus and the air-raid sirens went and I remember that I was the first in the queue and that I was pregnant at the time. With the sound of the air-raid siren when the first bus came along, everyone, including men, rushed in front of me and I let them get on because in my condition there was nothing I could do. When they were all on I remember the conductor putting his hand up in front of me and saying, 'No more.' I had to walk one and a half miles until I got to a friend's house, praying that she would be in. Thank God she was. She made me rest and gave me a cup of tea and I was relieved to get somewhere safe and out of the raids that were going on overhead. After a long rest there I finished my journey home, which was another two miles.

I remember that it was when the bombs were falling that I gave birth to a baby daughter. The midwife was called Nurse Bishop and she asked if I had got anyone to look after me. I said that my sister lived across the road and the nurse asked why she couldn't come to see to me. I remember that I said she couldn't because she must have her sleep in the afternoon, ever since she was 16.

I remember the nurse said that we could all do with sleep. The result was that my husband arranged for a neighbour to give me meals and generally look after, me, but she only stayed for a few days. She said that she wouldn't be coming any more because she was too frightened of the bombs. So I was left all alone with my baby after ten days.

I remember that one night my husband was fire-watching in London and I was asleep with my baby in the Anderson shelter in the garden, and I had a dream which I still remember as if it was yesterday. It is still so vivid.

In it I saw my two-year-old nephew get on a chair. He was stretching for some jam which was on a high shelf. I went to catch him and simultaneously, in my dream, a landmine came down and at that time I woke up with a start. I was terrified, I could still hear all the crumbling around me and I said to myself, 'It's all on the shelter.'

I knew I had to get out but I fully expected our house to be down. I was surprised to find that I could open the shelter door but I was frightened to open my eyes and look up but what a shock I received to find that my house was still standing but it took me a while to gather myself together and then I made sure the baby was all right. She hadn't even woken up!

Then I thought of the dream. So I quickly ran over all the rubble that was lying in the street to my sister's house, and when I got there I saw that half of it was gone. In the upstairs the wardrobe was hanging dangerously over the half side of the house outside.

Clutching my baby to me, I rushed through the rubble and saw my sister and her brother-in-law and his wife on the floor. I looked across the room to a wall which wasn't there any more but should have been. Amazingly in that scene of destruction was my nephew, with his eyes popping out of his head, sitting bolt upright in his cot!

There wasn't a sound from him. But there on his blanket that was covering him was parts of the broken wall and ceiling and glass.

I had to think quickly what to do. Gingerly gathering the blanket with one hand, while I held my baby with the other, I pulled it off him so that he wasn't hurt. Having done that I gathered him in my free arm and took him back to my shelter.

My sister and her brother-in-law and his wife were killed. How my nephew survived I don't know. Why I had that particular dream that drove me to go to make sure they were all right, I don't know. But the raid continued throughout that night and I am sure to this day that my nephew doesn't know that that night I saved his life.

Hannah Smith

I came to England from Scotland in 1938 to live with my father and stepmother in Essex. I was full of romantic ideas about seeing London with its history and streets paved with gold! The reality for me was to be a bit different as, by the time I got to visiting or living in London, the lights had gone out and the full blackout was in force!

I worked with John Lewis Stores and it was bombed.

Later with the Great Western Railway on the buffet at No. 8 Platform, Paddington. It too was hit. But the saddest part of all was when I worked with Handley Page in Cricklewood. While I was there I got married and my wedding photographs were spoiled, so a fortnight after the wedding we had to go to a studio and dress up in all our wedding clothes,

to be retaken, with only my maid of honour, as my little bridesmaid was down with a child's infectious complaint.

Before the photographs came through my maid of honour was killed by a direct hit on her house, and never saw her photograph. I came through all of the Blitz unscathed physically but who says that fate does not take a hand?

Alice Keller

My first memory of the war is being on the beach at Freshwater East in West Wales with my older cousin John. A small plane was flying over and he suddenly shouted 'Get down! It's one of theirs!' He pushed me flat behind a sand dune! I peeped out, looking for a swastika but didn't see one. If it *was* German it was well out to sea, and if returning from a bombing mission to the oil tanks at Milford Haven would have no bombs to drop on US!

John's father lived in Somerset and was in the Home Guard. Apparently one of his duties was to paint the local Westbury White Horse green so even enemy pilots would not be able to use it as a landmark. His wife and John, aged 12,

had a contingency plan to ride on horseback across country to our house in Wales if the Germans ever invaded southern England! Civilians had been warned that our troops, rushing to meet the foe, would run right over you on the roads if you got in their way.

My memories are chiefly happy ones of time spent on the local farm where Mother and I were given refuge when there was warning of a bombing raid at Pembroke Dock. Pembroke Dock was hard hit and I enclose a picture of our house after the bombing and one of me with Daddy just before the bombing. The plaster repair can be seen in both pictures. He and the housekeeper, sheltering under the stairs, were uninjured. But it was the war which cost him his life. He was so fully stretched with so many casualties to care for when he lost his partner in a drowning accident. The extra

The distinctive repair as a circle can be seen in both photos.

work proved to be just too much, and he died in 1945 at the age of only 47. The other tragedy was the loss of our local shop and the much-loved couple who ran it, the Kintons. They always seemed able to manage to stretch the rations to find little treats for us children!

When Daddy died we left the area. Four years ago I was eating alone in a Cardiff restaurant when a lady at a nearby table came over and asked, 'Are you by any chance Sheila Stewart?'

'Yes,' I said, 'but I am sorry, I have no idea who *you* are!'

When she said Dorothy Uphill it all came back to me. It was her parents' farm we used to go to, and the last time we had met I was four and she was seven! I still find it hard to believe she recognised me. It is not as though I have any physical peculiarities, only a very ordinary sort of face!

Ironically the 'safety' of the farm nearly did for me. A farm worker happened to see a child's feet sticking out of a rain barrel, and pulled me out just in time. I had climbed up to look inside and toppled in, and was wedged head down and rapidly drowning. I have no memory of that; they say you blot out distressing recollections.

I do remember once the whole family went off to gather firewood but I was 'too young', so I was left behind. I sneaked out and followed the foraging party and tried to climb a crumbling stone wall but fell and cut my head. Daddy was enjoying a rare break from his duties. He picked me up and dried the blood and comforted me and carried me back to the farm. Finally, another memory. From a very early age I was entrusted with the task of cutting the family butter ration into equal shares; it has left me with a VERY strong sense of fair play!

Sheila Stewart

Prior to the big Blitz period I lived exactly eight minutes' walk or five minutes on my bike from the factory where I worked. For a while we had what we called 'nuisance bombs' but nothing particularly serious, although we did notice that they seemed to be getting closer and closer night after night!

On 11 October 1940, I left work at 7.45 p.m. I was unable to ride my bike because the battery had gone in the lamp and as I didn't want to be caught and fined five shillings (25 pence), which was half a day's pay, I didn't get home until near eight o'clock. Anyway, my wife had a cup of tea ready but the sirens had just gone so she insisted that I take it with us to the shelter. After a bit of nagging and argy-bargy I eventually went!

After a few minutes the bombs began to fall rather close. We counted five that seemed to creep progressively closer, the last giving quite a bang. Then there was a sound like an express train rushing through a station and I remember thinking, 'Oh blimey, this is it.' I shouted to my wife, folding myself around her and our seven-year-old son.

There was no bang, just a terrific rush of air and the floor lifted and the shelter physically tipped over sideways. There was mortar and dust, and mixed with it was an acrid choking smell that filled the shelter. It was all followed in an instant by the sound of crashing bricks and rubble which collected around the doorway and blocked our way out.

I suppose we were blast-deafened. For a few moments there was deathly silence and it certainly took a few minutes to shake off the shock. Then, a little panicky, I tried what was supposed to be the emergency plate at the back of the shelter. You were supposed to simply knock down two brackets, although with what I am not quite sure! But anyhow, despite all my kicking and cussing, I didn't seem to be able to make any headway with the emergency door so I decided to try the normal entrance. Pushing and cursing again didn't produce anything. There was just a solid wall of rubble. But we decided that this could be our only way out, so working a loose brick, then another, we worked away at the rubble, stacking the bricks behind us in the shelter as we moved forward.

What joy when we pulled one in and clear air rushed in through the gap. But the thing that struck me most was the moon shining brightly in a cloudless sky. The only trouble was it was shining where our house should have been! Turning to my wife, I can distinctly remember the precise words I said: 'Bloody hell, the house has gone!'

Making a hole big enough to get through, I told my wife to stay put until I found out whether it was safe to go out or not. The house was completely demolished, just a big hole along with five others that had gone with it. The Anderson shelter was on its side, with the remains of our house piled up on top of it. Hearing squeals and shouting from the next-door garden, I saw that shelter was also totally blocked with rubble and so, despite everything, I rushed over to start to clear it away. Eventually I got a clear access to the entrance and out popped the lady and her teenage daughter like grey-hounds out of a trap! Up and away, not a word. Would you believe it! I never saw them again!

The house next to ours was also down and as I stood there in the darkness I heard moaning and cries coming from the rubble. The two old people who lived there were 72 years old and I immediately ran to that house and started pulling aside all the bricks and timber to try to locate the moaning sound. Fortunately, after a short while, I was able to get through to them. They had taken shelter in the pantry rather than the Anderson shelter because of the cold. That was supposed to be the strongest part of the house, but the floor and roof above had collapsed on them. Fortunately they were not too badly injured and I managed to get them both on to the roadway.

A widow, who was a neighbour of ours, had been caught in one of the side entries and I saw that she needed some assistance. So I left the elderly couple on the roadway while I went to help. She was shaken up and bruised and scraped all over but otherwise she seemed to be all right. An ARP warden, who had been standing a few yards down the road, took the full blast and was blown over and over until he finished up against the wall. When they took him to the first aid post his clothing was in shreds and the only solid clothing that he was wearing was his shoes and his tin hat. Otherwise his clothing, for what it was worth, had practically gone.

Unfortunately five of our neighbours did not make it and I had the grim job of identifying three of them later on.

When all the dust had settled, as usually and inevitably happens, you get a silly jumped-up bugger coming along to take charge! This one was an ARP warden who had kept well away sheltering until then but when things had quietened down suddenly took charge, shouting orders like 'Keep clear' and 'Leave it to me'. The usual palaver. He had to make a report and I can guess what a report it must have been. Giving himself a right build-up no doubt! Later on I read about him getting the George Medal for rescue work. Ironic, ain't it!

The plans for personal aid after being bombed out were really poor. After being cleaned up and scrapes and bruises tended, a cup of tea (well, warm water) was given to us. At 2.30 a.m. the 'all clear' sounded and so they turfed us out into a public shelter in the park so they could get their heads down! Now, the middle of October, at 2.30 a.m. in the morning, is not the time to send people like that 72-year-old couple out into concrete shelters. It was bloody cold and they were still suffering shock. I had to slip back and 'nick' a grey army blanket for them. But the Sally Army were very good in the way they came round with tea and biscuits every couple of hours, doing the best they could to help everybody out.

A Roman Catholic priest came round, asking what help he could give to anyone, and I asked him to help the 'oldsters' but either he couldn't or he wouldn't because they weren't Roman Catholics! But I remember that he took away a big brawny Irishman who was more canned than sober and I remember him saying, 'I can find you a night's shelter, my son.' For a moment then I could have committed GBH.

My wife, incidentally, was three months pregnant at the time and so apart from trying to look after our 72-year-old neighbours, it was not a happy situation.

We were recommended to go to the bomb victims' relief centre at a local church. We were told that there they would fix us up with reasonable clothes, etc. I still had a few clothes on me but they were in tatters and not decent at all!

But the old reverend at the church hall was very sorry. He had been designated as the 'relief officer' but had not yet received a single thing! He could see the mess I was in and found me a pair of flannel trousers but they must have been, I think, pre-1914! Certainly they were made to fit someone about four stone heavier than me and what a right Charlie I felt when I got them on. But they were certainly better than the ones I had been wearing. When all you have is what you stand up in, and all your life's possessions have gone up in a puff, I can tell you that you are very grateful because you realise that you are still alive and you shake yourself and have another go!

The next thing was finding some kind of money relief. I remember having to travel way across Birmingham and having to wait for hours without even a cup of tea and then when your turn came, seeing some jumped-up, ten-a-penny clerk, who made you feel like a thief or a beggar. Filling forms and answering daft questions. He then handed me ten pounds to be paid back out of our war damages payments in the far distant future!

Then the damage assessor. Another one who thought he was God-appointed! Every working man's household chattels were valued at £120. This was a hide-bound ruling. It was based on the theory that no working man had more than one suit and a pair of shoes. This I would not accept and after a hard session I managed to get £145 to be paid as near the end of hostilities as possible – less the £10 I had already had. Incidentally, that money came out of the blue in October 1947! By then everything was going sky high, making it worth a lot less than when it had been awarded. Blessed is he who expects nothing, for he shall not be disappointed!

Trying to find somewhere to live was a nightmare. Days wandering, looking at the most appalling places. One, a council house with a bomb crater like a huge mole hole in the back garden. Another smelling like a tripe shop. Then one expected us to sleep three in a wooden shed.

Poverty has no friends. A couple of weeks' lodgings at Ruberry and then we had to move out at a moment's notice because the woman's sister was afraid of Birmingham being bombed. She was a big, fat, useless lump. I don't think a bomb would have moved her! It might have made the fat ripple a bit!

We spent nearly a week in public shelters before a council house became available to us in the Acock Green area of Shirley. It meant sharing with my in-laws who were also homeless. What a shambles! I, trying to stay sociable on top of everything. Wanting to get my wife settled. We ordered a replacement bedroom suite because we had nothing but in the waiting time we had a raid. Loads of incendiaries and one went through the roof and stuck itself in the wall where our wardrobe would have been had it arrived!

The bomb set fire to the house but it wasn't so bad and we soon put it out. But I can tell you that the order for the bedroom furniture was quickly cancelled after that episode!

Every night the routine warning time was the same. Me trotting up the road to the park's public shelter. Ours was always full of water. A small fireside chair. My wife with the young one. You still had to turn in for work at 8 a.m. Without seats, you made your own comfort!

Suddenly I have remembered a funny incident concerning my father-in-law. He was fed up going to the shelter because sometimes you had to go for nothing. So one night he decided he would stay put. About two hours later he shot down to the shelter steps, all shaking and gasping. He said, 'They've got one down the chimney.' Nobody dared move. Later we found that we had left some baked potatoes in the oven and they had all exploded while he was asleep in bed, and that there was no bomb down the chimney. But then he never was known for his heroics!

Going back a little, two days after our bombing, we visited the ruins to see if we could salvage anything. It had been picked clean – so much for friends, who needs enemies! But there was one thing that gave me a chuckle. The trousers to my best grey pinstriped suit were hanging on the phone wires on the main Stratford road, just as if they had been hung out to dry!

Going to work in the mornings was like an obstacle race, with frequent re-routings. Going to and fro through 'Brum' centre, High Street, New Street. The lovely arcades, etc., were all home to me and there they were, the '50 Shilling Tailors', Samuels Jewellery, C & A, all wiped out in one great ball of fire. The old Market Hall also burned out. Fish could be smelled for miles. It smelled like one gigantic fish and chip shop.

Having to walk partway to work because there was an unexploded bomb embedded in the main road. Five bomb disposal soldiers trying to get it out. On arriving at work the end of the factory had been blown off and we couldn't work for three days. Walking back on the main road, there was the most awful bang nearby. An unexploded bomb had gone off. Diving into a doorway and waiting until it had cleared. I started to run towards the site and I remember running across the Mermaid Pub car park. I kicked what I took to be an old shoe and part of a foot fell out. There was nothing left, just an awful mess.

But we always seemed to attract the action wherever we went. No matter where we tried to settle, it seemed to follow us! At one time we got spare rooms in a place that was also let to a homeless couple. I don't know how they became homeless but he apparently hadn't seen anything of the war and thought it was a bloody great adventure. I remember he used to walk up and down the garden with his tin hat on, wishing for action! Then a bomb dropped nearby and scared him legless. Me, being a confirmed coward, was in the shelter at the first sound of a siren. Such a scuffle as he fell in head first, gasping, 'Oh blimey I thought they'd got me!' I don't think he got his colour back for two days. After all, courage is the art of being the only one who knows you're scared to death!

One thing that struck me as really gruesome was when my second son was born. We had to get a baby gas mask for him and it was the most ghastly-looking thing I have ever seen. It was a round rubberised container that wrapped entirely round him, with a plastic window in it. Apparently you bunged your child into this outfit, sealed it in, and then proceeded to keep the poor little sod alive by pumping a concertina-like bellows while the baby was screaming blue murder inside it all!

Funny little things caused difficulties. Getting your hair cut was a problem because nearly all the barbers had been called up or were on war production. In desperation, my wife cut mine. Made a nice job of it too. In fact I've not had a proper barber's cut since.

But there were many gruesome incidents which still stick in my mind. Like the Carlton Cinema at Sparkhill. It was bombed on a Friday evening when it was full and I can leave the rest to your imagination. Alfred Road Square when about 200 houses were wiped out in an instant. The devastation was massive. Balsall Heath, where the old houses were back-to-back and they were also wiped out and the victims stacked like firewood; and then the oddments. The lodging house that was blown away but a bottle of milk and a packet of eggs were left undamaged on the front step. Stories, stories, stories, enough.

Harry R. Vokes

How well I remember the war and the Blitz. I was just seven years old at the time and I was terrified of the air raids and at night when my mum used to tuck me up in bed I used to lie awake listening for the drone of the aeroplanes. I used to shout down to my mother, 'Mum, whose aeroplane is that?'

Ever-patient Mum used to go to the front door, and stand there a few minutes humming a tune loud enough for me to hear and so reassure me, bless her. And although it was blackout time and I realise now she couldn't see a thing, up would come the reply, 'Oh yes, I can see it now, it's okay, it's one of ours. You can go to sleep now.' So one reassured little girl fell asleep because oh what trust I had in my mum! All was well for that night anyway.

I remember however one day when the goods station was bombed in Newcastle. All of my family ran out of the shelter as the bombs exploded all around, and watched in horror as the flames leapt into the sky. We lived about five miles away from the actual Goods Stations, but the margarine and sugar that were kept there made the fire that much bigger and that much fiercer.

Eventually my sister and I were evacuated to Brampton during the heaviest period of the bombing. Ah! What memories that brings back. I must be getting old!

Ruth Luke

I was nine years old when the Blitz on Greenock took place. On the first night when the sweeping searchlights and noise of anti-aircraft guns in shore batteries and on naval ships in the port made it clear that this was no false alarm, we left the house to take shelter in our small shop alongside. We lived on the second floor and felt safer at ground level in the little store, although it had large windows. There were six of us: my parents, two older brothers, a baby sister only a few weeks old, and myself.

The noise was almost deafening, and the interior was lit intermittently by the flashes of gunfire and exploding bombs and landmines, and by parachute flares dropped by the raiding planes. Assorted goods from the shelves above us fell on us as we lay on the floor, wrapped in coats and blankets. There was one advantage – we were not short of food and drink. Any of the boys could have found his way to the lemonade and confectionery even in total darkness!

We waited long after the 'all clear' sounded, until daylight, and went out then to a changed world. There was quite a bit of damage in the area. Some houses had totally collapsed, and others were burning. We stayed near home as police and air-raid wardens warned of unexploded bombs. There was a lot of broken glass to be cleared up in both house and shop, but fortunately the shop windows had fallen out rather than in. I think we still had gas, and we were able to prepare a meal, but certainly we had no electricity. After our meal, however, it was business almost as usual in the shops after the windows had been roughly boarded up.

Some neighbours offered us a place in their Anderson shelter should there be another raid. When the sirens sounded the alert that night we were much quicker in getting out of the house! As we ran up the road the greatest danger was from falling shrapnel from exploding anti-aircraft shells, but we were not aware of this until later. As we reached the neighbours' gate there was a huge explosion not very far off. We threw ourselves into the narrow front pathway, the baby in my mother's arms, and then made our way down to the shelter and the rear of the house! My father had stayed in the shop, but that still made five of us to squeeze in beside the family of five already in the shelter, and Anderson shelters were not very spacious!

The shelter had no door, so we heard all the din around us. The sound of crackling flames being very close, although the nearest burning houses we found later were some hundreds of yards away. Although the noise gradually died until we could only hear the crackling of flames and the occasional sound of a fire

brigade or rescue vehicle, the 'all clear' was not sounded until daylight. We staggered out of the shelter bleary-eyed and stretched our cramped limbs. Out on the road again we looked at a tenement block along the lane by the school playground.

Three houses were missing from the middle of the block and had been replaced by mounds of rubble and shattered timber. Beyond that there were gaps in Brown Street where single-storey houses had collapsed or been blown apart. The school was intact and was crowded with homeless people and voluntary helpers. We went home happily to find our shop intact.

My father had come looking for us before the 'all clear' sounded. Now we had a close look at our house. It was built of steel plates covered on the outside with roughcast. This whole block of four family houses had been planned to keep shipyard workers in employment in the thirties – hence the steel walls. The roofs were covered with heavy tiles. Ours had partly collapsed. We went up the stairs. In the boys' bedroom the beds were buried in tiles. There was now neither gas nor electricity.

Our parents decided we should now make our way to the

house of my mother's aunt, which was about three miles away, in the hope that her house would still be intact. While they packed the bags we went exploring the much-altered neighbourhood. We collected incendiary bomb tails as souvenirs, and pieces of shrapnel from the streets. We thought we had pieces of German bombs, but in fact the fragments were from anti-aircraft shells!

In Brown Street we found what had been the home of people we knew. Now there was a huge crater with a child's toy, a scooter I think, lying halfway down. There was also a howling dog. That was all. We moved towards the dock area.

In a half-demolished tenement some rescue workers were working with spades in what had been called the tile-lined 'close' or entrance passageway. We thought they might be digging people out. As we went closer one of the men angrily ordered us away.

My older brother sneaked round to the other side of the work party. He looked very serious. The men were not digging people out. They were scraping parts of people from the walls and floor of the 'close' where they had been sheltering, and placing the pieces they found into big wooden boxes. We left in a hurry and went round Carwood Street on our way home.

The little library at the corner had burned out, and houses in nearby Sinclair Street were still burning with survivors raking about looking for anything of value in the debris. Every now and then we would find a house with one side or more sliced off, while the furniture and fittings seemed quite untouched. Or there would be a solitary gable end with mantlepiece ornaments and pictures still in place on some of the 'floors', but there were no floors or ceilings or roofs or walls.

People we met were usually silent, although some children we knew would come across and tell us of their story. When we reached home the baby's pram was loaded with as much as it could hold. My brothers and I were allowed only to take a few essentials. Peter, aged 12, insisted on taking a set of bagpipes formerly owned by my grandfather! We packed our school bags and took a suitcase or a carrier bag each. My father was staying to look after the house and shop, because there were rumours of looting.

We made our way along streets we could now hardly recognise. We looked like a family of old-fashioned tinkers on the move. My mother carried the baby. My school, Hill End, was still intact, but there were many gaps in East Crawford Street and Baxter Street. We reached Belleville Street, to find it now almost totally destroyed with piles of rubble blocking the streets in places. Firemen, rescue workers and air-raid wardens were very sympathetic, and helped carry the pram over or round the piles of rubble. When they heard we were heading for Dempster Street one said, 'There's no use trying to go down and along Ingleston Street; it's even worse than this. There's not a house left standing. You'll have to go over the hill.'

We took a narrow lane past the bowling green, which was now minus its clubhouse, until the lane joined another which led past a blazing distillery a safe distance below. From there it climbed a bit to pass Walker's Sugar Refinery, which was also burning. We found out much later that a relative of ours had been fatally burned by malt and sugar in the refinery.

Suddenly there was a huge explosion. We looked back. A great flare of flame and black smoke rose from the distillery. I never did discover whether this was a delayed action bomb or a whisky vat exploding, but at the time we assumed it was a bomb. Passing the refinery at a safe distance we bumped the pram over several fire hoses and we reached the road again.

This part of Greenock was less badly damaged, and Dempster Street, at this end at least, looked reasonably intact. There was a tearful reunion with my grand-aunt, who was also a shopkeeper, and whose customers and friends had brought horrifying tales of the total destruction of our end of town. Holmscroft School, just across the road, had been prepared as an Evacuation Centre, and my mother decided that since it was then late afternoon, we would report next morning for evacuation to the country. She assumed that we would survive another night of the Blitz. Fortunately there was none. Next day still without my father we would be documented, ticked and despatched on a bus for Beith in Ayrshire where a much happier episode in my life was to begin.

One of the saddest tales was about our neighbours, which we heard much later, a family of three who were our good friends. They lived in Brown Street close to where a land-mine had taken out the centre of the tenement block. The father had carefully dug a pit in the garden for their Anderson shelter, turfed over the roof, and since he worked at a ship-yard had managed to get a heavy steel plate to cover the door. This was not recommended practice. But he did it and bored ventilation holes near the top and covered these with mesh. As a final touch he built a 'baffle wall' of bricks to defect any blast a few feet from the door.

When the landmine fell his house was flattened. Other people in nearby Anderson shelters survived, but in his the bricks were punched through the steel door as if it were tinfoil. The only survivor was the family pet dog, which was protected by the deep entry sill.

Just two other small points when I eventually returned from the evacuation to Greenock to begin secondary school, a boy I met had a very impressive souvenir. His older brother had found a complete incendiary bomb which had failed to ignite, and they kept it in the coal bunker!

The other thing I remember is a solitary gable end wall a few 'floors' up with clear evidence of a family's divided loyal-ties. Hanging on one side of the mantlepiece was a picture of King Billie (William of Orange), and on the other side a picture of the Pope. They were still hanging there even though the rest of the house had gone, and each was framed in a nicely polished wooden toilet seat!

Kenneth Stewart

My wife and I will never forget the night before our wedding which was to take place on Sunday, 20 April 1941. I came home on leave from my RAF Station in Norfolk on Saturday and went round to see my wife-to-be that evening, but soon the siren went and heavy bombing and barrage started. The wedding dress, etc., went under the kitchen table! Then we all dashed off to the Anderson shelter.

Thankfully we came through that night safely, but feeling very stiff and sore with sitting around down the shelter and with corrugated iron marks down our backs! We came out at about 4.30 a.m. when the 'all clear' went and having spent the last night of my bachelorhood with my wife-to-be (almost an unheard thing in those days!) I went off back to my parents' house to get ready for the wedding.

This took place at 12.20 at St John's Church, Leytonstone after a violent thunderstorm. My brother turned up with soot in his hair having been bombed out in Bushwood. After a short reception we left for a three-day honeymoon in Morecambe, where there were 12 RAF men billeted in the boarding house where we stayed!

After reporting back for RAF duty I found myself with an overseas posting, and within a few days it was off to the Middle East so I did not see my wife again for three and a half years!

Some wedding eve! Some wedding day! Some honeymoon!

Geoffrey Maynard

When I was ten in 1940 I kept a diary of events in old school exercise books. They have long since disintegrated but not before I had committed them to paper and had them typed up. This is the part that I wrote about the Blitz in 1940. It opens in the Anderson shelter at Plumstead near the Woolwich Arsenal in South London. My father had survived four years of the First World War and was in the Home Guard. The date is 8 September 1940, which is the day after the Germans had switched their attack from the fighter stations and radar sites to London. I remember that my dad was a great organiser and that comes out in my notes taken at the time.

We were sat in the Anderson shelter – 'Was it as bad as this in the First World War?'

'Aeh?' he said, taking his pipe out of his mouth. I repeated the question.

'Much worse, son. This is nothing.' He used the interruption as an excuse to fit another plug of Rubican Spun Cut Tobacco into the bowl of his pipe. 'We used to have a creeping barrage. A shell every ten yards. When one fell near enough you ran and jumped in it because the next one would be where you were. If you see what I mean. We had "whizbangs", too. Very frightening they were. My mate had his head blown right off. He was standing right alongside me when it happened.'

'Sid, stop that talk,' said my mum. 'Ugh, that pipe is foul.'

My dad winked at me.

The drone of the engines faded and the gunfire became intermittent. We went out into the garden and surveyed the scene. No doubt about it, the fires in the Arsenal were raging fiercely again. Then my dad pointed. 'The wind has changed. Look, those clouds of smoke are just drifting over this way now.'

I did not see the significance until my dad said thoughtfully, 'The next lot to come over will think we are in the middle of the Arsenal. Come on.'

We went out to the Anderson shelter. The time was 9.30 p.m. I feel asleep.

I was awake as the shrill rushing screech was in the air. The explosion seemed to lift the shelter. I heard the patter of stones and rubble falling, accompanied by the sound of crashing glass.

My dad had fixed a periscope in the shelter and was looking out through it.

'The house is still there,' he said disbelievingly.

The drone of the bombers filled the air. It was a deep sound that I would never ever forget. The guns were blasting away. I had slept through it all on the lower bunk, the cat across my legs, until the bomb fell.

I thought it must be within 50 yards. More bombs fell then there was a whizzing sound followed by a plop, then another, then another.

'Incendiaries,' my dad said.

He opened the shelter door and rushed out. I pulled on my tin hat and followed. The gates of hell must have looked like this. A bright flickering glow over everything and the sound enough to numb your mind. An incendiary was burning in the middle of our small lawn and another one against the side of the house. The flames were already reaching out towards the wooden lavatory door.

My dad rushed for that one and I grabbed the shovel. I dug deep into the flower border and lifted a good shovel of earth. The bomb was glowing as the phosphorus ignited. It was about 12 inches long with a tail fin made of aluminium. I covered it with the earth and then added another shovelful. I watched. It seemed to be dead.

More whizzes. I looked up. Mr Wright was dealing with one in his garden as another one hit his roof. It dislodged some slates, which slid off, but the bomb stuck, half in and half out.

'Sid, there's one in my roof!' he called.

My mum was outside working the stirrup pump and the

one outside the toilet was out. My dad kicked it away from the blackened door and picked up the hose.

'Turn on the tap.'

My mum rushed into the scullery. A jet of water streaked up to the roof and played around the fins clearly sticking out. The glow seemed to die down and then the tail of the bomb disappeared.

'It's gone through!' shouted Mr Wright.

My dad threw me the hose. 'Keep it going on the roof,' he shouted and leapt over the low wooden fence, taking the stirrup pump with him. By now I could see a glow in their upstairs bedroom.

A large piece of shrapnel clanged on the corrugated iron shed and I flinched instinctively. A 'whoosh' and another bomb landed on Conway Road near the Catholic Church. I had thrown myself down.

The guns banged out their message of death. I could not help feeling that they were doing more harm down here than they were up there!

Then whizz, whizz, whizz, plop, I saw an incendiary land on Mr Wright's chimney stack and bounce across to our roof. It held there for a second and then like some nightmar-ish pinball game it turned, fins downward, and rolled in a parabola down the roof, stopping at the opposite end for a moment and then down and back again. It hit the gutter and lodged firmly and squarely.

My mum was back in the shelter. I ran to the coalshed. I grabbed my dad's garden rake and tore up three flights of stairs then up the ladder, throwing open the lookout.

The bomb and I were within eight feet of one another. It was below me to my right and by leaning out and holding on with one hand I could just touch it with the rake. It was glowing and the phosphorus smell I was to know so well was making me cough.

In nightmares things sometimes happen in slow motion. In real life it can be the same. I have experienced the feeling twice and this was one of them. It was as if there was only me and the rake and the bomb left in the world. In my mind everything was still and quiet.

I tilted it then lost it. I tilted it again and this time it stood up, tail first, the molten metal already sticking to the iron gutter. If I tilted it over again it would be out of my reach. I concentrated hard and gently swung the rake in an arc with my right hand. It was heavy and I knew I would only get one try. The metal head of the rake hit the bomb at its base and it toppled free of the guttering to the concrete yard below with a great shower of sparks. The rake followed it!

I rushed down and out into the garden, tearing my knees again and blistering my palms. My mum was out of the shelter now and had the hose going on it. It rolled away from the brick wall and having manoeuvred it into the dustbin lid with the rake, we put it in the metal dustbin with the lid on top. At this moment my dad came out of next door's scullery with their bomb still glowing and threw it on the garden, covering it with earth.

Theirs had gone through to the ground floor. It must have been quite hilarious in a sick sort of way. The bomb had burnt its way through the roof and three floors with them chasing after it with a stirrup pump, and Mrs Wright shrieking, 'Mind my carpet' and 'Mind that lino', until they caught it on the shovel as it was about to go through the ground-floor floorboards.

Within the year the Germans had added anti-personnel explosives to their incendiaries. If they had invented them before 8 September 1940, we would all have been dead and most of Griffin Road would have been a burnt-out shell.

Peter Walder

I was in an RAF Balloon Section in 1940 when I was posted to Hull. I was an LAC and billeted in Pearson Park on Beverley Road in Hull, in charge of a section. We had our orders to fly the balloons at different heights, varying from 1,000 feet to 6,000 feet when air raids were due. I don't think the public ever did understand the protection that the barrage balloons gave to them during that time.

My wife was home with our baby son at that time and I remember I decided to go home on a 24-hour pass. On the way back to Hull, the train pulled up at Brough for two hours, with lights out, during a raid, and then crawled into Parragon Station and we could see that the city of Hull was burning badly.

I made my way up Beverley Road but I had to take shelter owing to falling shrapnel from the bombs. I can remember going into a nearby public house where everyone was already in a state of panic. It was 4 a.m. when that raid ended and when it was finished we all drank like hell. I have never been a heavy drinker but in a situation like that who cares! It was a very frightening experience.

It was after that that I was posted to Manchester and on to the Bowlee Balloon at Middleton. That was the worst experience of my life. Everyone knew that Manchester would be a target sooner or later, so we dug underground shelters made of metal but covered with soil and stones. Near our site was a 16-room house that was managed by a married couple with two children. They used to provide treatment for anyone who needed it, even though they had two children themselves and were fully occupied.

I remember it was on 21 December [1940] that the sirens went. It was about 9 p.m. and down came hundreds of firebombs which set fire to warehouses and a tar factory. I remember the tar ran down the nearest road like a river with the heat. At the time all we had was buckets of sand to drop on it and that was quite useless.

About 70 firebombs fell on our site but we were soon able to deal with them. The lady from the house and her children came to our underground shelter and I asked her where her husband was. 'He's in the house and he won't come out,' she answered.

After a lull we could hear the bombers coming back so she decided to go back to fetch her husband, despite our appeals to her to stay put. Within a short time the house received a direct hit from a landmine attached to a parachute and the house and everyone in it was killed. Our shelter, of course, stood the blast. If only she had stayed a little longer.

It seemed ages before the dust settled and when we ventured out, we helped to dig amongst the rubble with the Local Civil Defence people to try to find the family. It was heart-breaking because as we dug we came across the toys the parents had bought for Christmas for the children.

After about four to five hours we came across the family halfway down the cellar steps. The mother had the two children under her. The blast had killed the whole family. We never did find her husband. He must have been somewhere in the centre of the house.

The second night was bad but didn't affect Salford so much as Manchester. The following week 500 people were buried in Southern Cemetery, Manchester. To think of all those innocent people cut down for ever. After that it was goodbye to balloon sites. I was re-mustered and sent on an engine-fitter's course to Glamorgan. But although I didn't have any further contact with balloons, I still think that the public really didn't appreciate the balloon crews and all that they did to try to protect them.

Horace Birkin

I was living in London during the war. My husband was abroad in the Fleet Air Arm. I had taken my four-year-old son to stay with an aunt in Scotland. I was a welfare adviser in a rest centre service. We were stationed in those strong old red-brick schools.

After a night's bombing the wardens brought the homeless to us and we cared for them with beds in the basement and endless cups of tea, until we could re-house them. I remember no panic, no tears and no quarrels! Helped perhaps by the fact that there were no children!

One day I arrived for duty at Canonbury School, to find it had been bombed and that the welfare adviser on the other team had been killed. She had been asleep in a camp bed in the basement. When the bomb fell the force had sucked out all the air from the building, collapsing the lungs of the people inside. In retrospect, my almost callous reaction to the death of a colleague amazes me and I am sure it was not due to the slightly ironic fact that the dead girl's husband was a German! The bomb had destroyed the nurses' quarters. We stood silent, my group and I, looking down a crater, at the bottom of which was the medicine cupboard, spilling out an unsavoury mixture of medicines and tablets. Then on the window ledge I noticed a milk bottle, unbelievably intact and three-quarters full of unspilled milk!

Another sad memory. A young soldier came to the centre one day. He had arrived home to find his house had been bombed and he was looking for his wife, mother and father.

We had no record of them coming to us. The soldier looked so weary and so worried but he refused even a cup of tea before he continued his search. We were all sickened by the horrors of war but that soldier walking sadly away was somehow symbolic of the whole 'behind the scenes' misery.

There is another picture I will never forget. My colleagues and I were in Whittington School on Highgate Hill. From a top window we could see the centre of London being bombed. There were fires everywhere. Whenever they faded a bit, bombs would fall out of the black sky and we could see them falling by the light of the flames below and the fires would flare up anew. We felt helpless and angry. Next day when I was home in 'safe' Winchmore Hill, a couple I knew arrived. They had been in the West End on the previous evening but had found safety in the cellar of a pub, which they owned. It seemed impossible that anyone could have survived that inferno but fortunately many did.

We chatted a great deal in the centre, trying to ignore the maddening drone of planes overhead. The old people were most interesting. Most had had hard lives but their stoic calm had to be admired, especially when talking about their children. Saying, for example, 'Had seven, buried three', or 'Had five, buried one'. One evening an elderly couple were brought in and after a cup of tea, Rose told her story. 'I awoke in bed when the siren went and pushed Tom, telling him to get up.'

'Bloody hell!' he said 'I'm not getting up.'

'But I made him. Good job too. My name? Rose Brown – no, he's not Tom Brown, he's Tom Smith! We never got married – meant to, of course, but I wanted a nice dress and he wanted a nice suit, but whenever we had the money the kids needed shoes or something and after a while we stopped bothering! He's a good man is Tom, always puts his pay envelope on the table on Friday!'

There were peaceful periods, of course, when much of our work was the normal social welfare type. Sometimes we

even went to the theatre. Once to The Windmill, the theatre that never closed!

We went by Tube train and all the Tube stations were filled with people quite early in the evening. Metal bunk beds had been erected so that the maximum number of people could sleep there. Food and drink and even entertainment was provided by various groups of voluntary workers.

You may be interested to know that my husband came home unscathed. My son was unaffected by his experiences and I had a daughter in 1946, who herself has two gorgeous children. So we count our blessings!

Hilda Watts

I have many memories of the war and not all sad by any means. I worked in a cotton mill at that time called the Derker Mill or as we used to call it 'Old Darby's'. I had to go to work as I had a young baby and my husband was in the RAF and I used to take my baby to the mill nursery and so this entailed me getting up before 5 a.m. to get everything ready.

One day the ARP wardens came to the mill to show us how to put out incendiary bombs if they should fall on the mill! I got into trouble right away because I couldn't pick up a huge bucket of sand! I was supposed to pick the bucket up and throw the sand over the bomb. However, as I was only seven stone I found this impossible and all my workmates had the same trouble and we all had quite a giggle at the time. That is until the ARP warden went berserk! I think he had visions of leading a commando squad! But we had our own back when he got stuck trying to climb through the manhole leading on to the roof!

I often wonder if anyone else had all the trouble we had at our house when the air-raid sirens went? First of all we had to find the cat! All dogs, cats and kids had to be rounded up and taken to the shelter. We lived in a row of six houses. We only had one big shelter, which was in our yard. Incidentally, our tortoise was the first war casualty. The builders didn't know he was in hibernation and they built the shelter on top of him!

Then we had to wait for my mother. She always said if she was 'going' she wasn't 'going' not properly dressed, so we had to wait until she put on her corsets and combed her hair!

I can tell you, it wasn't something we looked forward to, going into the shelter. The rain came in, it was dark and cold and full of kids and dogs and cats fighting. Definitely not the place to be!

We had some excitement one night. We all heard someone trying to get over our yard gate and my mother, all five foot ten inches of her, was ready. No German was going to harm her kids, or her house!

Picking up a huge piece of wood she went outside to meet the 'enemy'. All she could see was a man in uniform coming over the gate. She wasn't to know it was my husband coming home on a 48-hour pass, and knowing we would be in the shelter he came round the back. It was a good thing he shouted to my mother or maybe he would have been the second casualty!

He always said that that was the most dangerous time of the whole war as far as he was concerned!

Ivy Scott

I was only three years old when the war started but I remember my mother, who was a widow with six children, donning a pair of wellie boots and scrubbing out an unused cesspit in our backyard for an air-raid shelter! Everyone else in our road had Anderson shelters or went across the road to sleep in above ground brick-built shelters, but I think we were unique in *our* shelter, full of mosquitoes and lizards! Also the odd toad!

To get into it you climbed down through the manhole (no other way out) and to this day I get uncomfortable in lifts or any small space. I used to have nightmares about the little entrance getting blocked (by Hitler personally marching over our garden with soldiers in line). Sounds daft now but to a three-, four- or five-year-old, all things are real, and Hitler was a very real man to me – on a par with the devil!

My elder sister was working in Vickers-Armstrong at Weybridge when it was bombed and she came home in an ambulance, shocked but unhurt.

Later we graduated to an indoor Morrison shelter and as there wasn't room for us all in it I slept in the larder, which was under the stairs. Incidentally, I used to bump my head on the sloping ceiling regularly when I woke up in the mornings!

My brother, who was 17, revelled in all the excitement. He used to go outside in the garden, even later on in the war when the V2 doodlebugs were going over, and when they cut out, he used to rush in shouting, 'All in the shelter, this one's for *us*!'

I remember my mother grabbing me and trembling with fright and *me* comforting *her*, not the other way round!

My brother couldn't wait to join up and slipped away and volunteered for the Fleet Air Arm without waiting for call-up, and he saw active service.

We lived in Shepperton and after the 'all clear' one night we all looked out of the front window and watched fires all around us. That was the night a lot of the shops in Walton caught it – including Blake's and Greenberg's, etc. Another night we had an incendiary bomb outside our gate which broke all our windows and covered all my mum's lovely front garden flowers with oil!

At five years old I had to walk a mile and a bit to school in Shepperton – back home for lunch – then back to school and home again at four o'clock. We couldn't afford school dinners!

Sometimes we would be halfway home when the siren went and I *never ever* ran back to school but always ran for home, however far away it was! Only once was I not allowed to leave as a raid was on at twelve o'clock, so I had to have a school dinner. It was served in the air-raid shelters in the playground. But do you know I remember that I had to take the money the next day to pay for it!

When I was eight, my mother remarried and the only casualty my family suffered from the Blitz was a little still-born sister in 1944. That was due, the doctor said, to the state my mother used to get herself into during the raids.

The memories are endless but what I remember most is the abject *fear* which went on for years every hour of the day and the *learned* hatred of the Germans, which I still have even if it is totally unreasonable. That is what it all did to you. It is nothing personal but it all happened to us – and it's still there!

Sheila Inwood

Though I was only two and a half years old at the outbreak of the war, I do have some vivid recollections, perhaps the most vivid being the night that Coventry was bombed.

We lived in a detached house in Lichfield, with a large garden, at the bottom of which was a small orchard of fruit trees. Amongst these, buried beneath the ground, was our Anderson shelter. It had a dank, earthy smell which hung in the damp air as the door opened. Amidst wailing sirens and roaring aeroplane engines, I distinctly remember that the Anderson to me was frighteningly safe as I was wrapped in my mother's fur coat and bundled down the steps!

My father was a gunner in the Royal Artillery and on the particular night that I remember, we had staying with us a dear friend of my father's from London, known to me as Uncle Laurie Gray. Once Uncle had installed my mother, grandmother and myself in the shelter, I recall that he found it impossible to keep the door shut and stay inside with us, despite my mother's pleas.

The planes droned over and I remember Laurie calling from outside to my mother to see the 'sky of fire' and Grandmother crying about 'which poor people were getting it tonight'.

Following on much later came the 'all clear' siren. But I still recall a coloured sky that then I didn't understand, but later was told by my mother that it had been Coventry burning. Even now I do not fully comprehend how this could be so but in fact it was.

My mother's family lived in Devon and Cornwall. Her brother and his family lived in Plymouth, which became my second home. As a child I seemed to spend half the year in Plymouth and half in Lichfield, and I can distinctly remember my own disbelief when first I saw my uncle's bungalow with a holed roof and secondly the devastating sight of the heaps of rubble amidst the ruins that had once been the houses and shops at Plymouth.

The ruins of Charles Church in Exeter Street had a startling impact upon me and indeed these church ruins have been retained in the same condition today as a memorial to the many civilians of Plymouth who died during the war.

I was in Plymouth at the end of the war and vividly remember the excitement and atmosphere of the lights again being switched on upon the Hoe. Corrugated green tin huts, reminding me of large Anderson shelters, sprang up along the streets and housed the shops that had been flattened.

Gradually the mounds of rubble that had been all over the city disappeared, and ruined buildings, to me ghostly with their exposed rooms open to the sky, were demolished and a new Plymouth was eventually built.

Then there was the pride when my older cousin, Barbara, visited. Barbara was a Petty Officer in the WRNS and when our grandmother was taken in hospital in Lichfield, Barbara came to visit her in her uniform. I well remember my grandmother's pride in answering the doctor's query as to 'Who was that young WRN who came in yesterday?'

'That's my granddaughter – she's a petty officer!'

And how the heads turned to look when we walked through the narrow city streets of Lichfield with her in that uniform. I too was so proud that this was my cousin Barbara.

Jean Bird

My memory of the Blitz period is one morning lying in bed with my mum and younger brother Peter having our cups of tea. My dad was out in the back garden. Suddenly we heard him shouting that a plane was coming across the sea.

We still stayed in bed because there had been no siren sounding, but a few minutes later we heard some bombs going off. Instantly we jumped out of bed and rushed downstairs.

As we got there Dad came in from the garden to say that he had seen the bombs leave the plane somewhere he thought

*Betty Candy
extreme right.*

over Bishopstone. My brother and I had our breakfast and got ready for school. Off we went along Steyne Road on our bikes.

We turned up Saxon Lane and when we got to the other end a policeman stopped us and asked where we were going. I answered, 'We're leaving our bikes at my father's garage in Broad Street before we go to school.'

The policeman asked me my father's name. I told him it was Mr Turrell and he told us, 'Go back home. There's no school today. There's an unexploded bomb in the Plough Inn yard, and tell your dad to get up here quick. His garage was hit by a bomb this morning.'

Peter and I could not get home quick enough. Being a child of 11 years I didn't think or know about giving people heart attacks! I just burst in the door shouting, 'Dad! Dad! Your garage has been bombed!'

I remember he was shaving. I also remember he didn't really believe me at first and made me sit down and tell him slowly what had happened. Then he wiped the soap off his face and got his coat on and called my older brother, Les, and off they went.

Much later when they arrived home we heard how much damage had been done.

The Manor House, I believe it was Mr Bruce who had that, and a shoe shop had been destroyed and there were lots of slippers and shoes on the garage roof. I remember that my father was amazed because some were still in pairs as though someone had put them there.

One of the bombs had gone through the wall of the garage, through a car which was inside, and then out of the other end of the garage. It had shot across the churchyard, chipping a tombstone and finally landed in the Plough Inn yard outside the back door. Apparently the landlord's wife was decidedly frightened when she went outside and found it!

I think everyone thought it was a new German weapon because it did not have any fins and had not exploded. After three days I remember that my father and brother were still trying to sort the mess out.

Les was inside the garage examining the car which the bomb had gone through when suddenly he got a nasty shock because he could see some fins sticking out from underneath! The bomb disposal squad obviously had to be called for. It turned out that the fins came from the bomb that had landed in the Plough Inn! We had those fins in our front garden at White Lodge for years. Some people there might remember them.

That is my particular memory of wartime in Seaford.

Betty Candy

I was about 22 at the time and worked as a building machinist making hydraulic pumps to operate the various parts of our fighting aircraft. During this period Acton suffered severe bombing at night, especially in Park Royal. On one occasion, hundreds of incendiaries were dropped, causing considerable damage, with a wall of fire 600 yards long. Acton was a densely populated area of small factories involved in engineering and electrical components.

One night I was staying at the home of a friend of mine called Frank. It was a Saturday night. A stick of four bombs landed in Horn Lane, Acton. One at the bottom of his road about 200 yards away. Frank told me later that when that first one landed I stirred! The second roused me a bit more and on the third I rose horizontally out of the bed and as the fourth exploded I remember putting my hand out to feel if the wall was still there!

Realising that the house was still safe, we got up and walked down the road to see where the bomb had landed but it was too dark. We went down again in the morning to find it had landed in the middle of Horn Lane, leaving a crater 30 foot wide and 15 foot deep, which was by now full of water. It took months to repair the road due to an underground spring which fed Acton Wells. Across this period numerous bombs and a landmine fell in South Acton and one of my workmates was actually bombed out three times.

I cannot remember the exact date but my parents woke me one night to say that we had to evacuate as an unexploded bomb had landed in our garden. I collected a few things and went up to Frank's house. I don't remember where my parents went.

The next day I decided to go back home to have a look and collect a few more items I wanted. On my arrival a policeman stopped me and said, 'You can't go in there, there's an unexploded bomb.' I said I knew that but I had some things to collect. Anyhow, I went in through the back gate, collected my things, and had a good look down the hole.

It was a 500-pound bomb which had entered the galvanised steel coalbunker of our neighbours. We lived in a block of flats and the bomb was at an angle pointing towards our flat! In going through the bunker it had taken with it five hundredweight of coal that our neighbours had had delivered the previous day! When I looked down the bomb was plain to see about 15 foot down. I didn't hang about! I went off to Frank's for several days until the bomb was made safe.

Moving on from the Blitz, I remember that later on when I was in the Forces and was on embarkation leave, and sitting on a fireside fender box at my parents' home, polishing my army boots; suddenly there was the loudest bang from a bomb that I had ever heard. My mother and father came dashing past me and I remember saying, 'Where are you going?' It seems a daft question now and I remember he replied, 'Back to the air-raid shelter.'

I said, 'It's too late now it's landed.'

He replied, 'Never mind there might be another one.'

As it happened there wasn't and we found out later it was the first V2 rocket which had landed not far away in Chiswick. At the time it was rumoured that there had been a gas explosion! That can give you some idea perhaps of the strength of the explosion. I presume everyone believed that it was a gas explosion because no one knew what else it could be and certainly no one had any idea of a bomb with that strength.

Bertram Wedlake

I was fortunate to be almost 11 years old when World War Two began. Fortunate by being old enough to appreciate and understand the major events that took place during those fateful years, and at the same time too young to be called up for National Service.

From the many dramatic and exciting memories I have, the most vivid one concerns an incident during the Blitz, of which Grantham, for its size, had more than its fair share! All these years afterwards I still remember it as though it was yesterday.

It was just before ten o'clock on the Saturday night of 24 October when the air-raid siren sounded. It seemed to be almost a nightly occurrence during that year. My father worked for the local main line LNER shed as a blacksmith, but was also a member of the breakdown gang being the steam crane driver. This particular night he was called out about 45 minutes before the siren sounded to attend a derailment in the goods yard. So my mother was left in charge of my two younger brothers and myself.

She dutifully tucked the three of us into our steel table shelter, known as a Morrison shelter, and went out to the front of the house which is in Bridge Street, to take my father's place on the fire-watching party.

On this occasion I do not recall hearing the sound of aircraft, but after what seemed only a few minutes there was an almighty bang and choking dust and total darkness except for a few glowing embers of the fire which had somehow disintegrated in the grate. The three of us were unharmed apart from being shaken, and my youngest brother, who was only eight, was I remember frightened and crying. We just did not know what had happened to us and more worrying what had happened to Mother!

Eventually a squad of soldiers who were billeted in some nearby lodging houses came to take part in the rescue work, and two of them released us from our shelter and guided us through the rubble and smashed furniture of the two downstairs rooms. The lower part of the house was partly shielded by a street surface shelter, one end of which had taken the full force of the 1,000-pound bomb.

Now came the sight which I shall never forget as long as I live. As we emerged from the remains of our house an elderly man, who was obviously severely shocked, stumbled and staggered along the debris-strewn pavement. He was completely covered from head to foot in white plaster dust, and his head and face were streaming with blood and the whole scene was brilliantly lit by the silvery light of an almost full moon.

As this poor man, who I recognised as a neighbour from two doors away, passed by, he was repeating over and over to himself, 'Which is my house, where is my house.' The combination of white dust and red blood bathed in a silvery light and the injured man's pathetic groaning reminded me of a scene from some Boris Karloff horror film.

But thanks to that same street shelter my mother escaped serious injury, being knocked unconscious and suffering broken fingers and facial cuts. Incidentally, since that night I have ceased to regard 13 as an unlucky number. I was born in No. 11 Bridge Street, Grantham, which was a two-bedroomed house, but as our family increased my parents wanted a bigger house and we eventually moved two doors away to No. 13, which has an extra bedroom. No. 11 was completely destroyed in that raid, and we escaped unharmed from No. 13!

Alan Church

During the Liverpool Blitz I lived in the town of Warrington which was directly on the bombers' route. We had all the air-raid warnings and heard the drones of planes overhead.

At work we lost a lot of production time during the day in air-raid shelters, and finally an 'Imminent Danger' warning sign was devised. We took it in turns to watch for the flag on the high tower of the brewery, which was clearly visible from the rear windows of the factory.

One evening there was a blaze at a paint warehouse which lit up the whole town, and the whole town appeared to be ringed with incendiaries with the planes dropping several explosives in the middle for good measure. The following week they narrowly missed the parish church and demolished a row of old cottages of great historical interest. Next but one to us was a furniture shop which was completely gutted.

The Saturday following was a lovely sunny day and I left the house to play tennis with a friend. After tennis I went home with my friend who lived at the other side of town. When we got there her brother told me of an unexploded bomb in the park nearby which the police had cordoned off. As we finished our tea there was a terrific bang, and all the windows rattled violently and everything on the table seemed to shoot in the air! When we had recovered enough to mop up the spills and put things in order again, we found out that the unexploded bomb in the park had gone off!

Dorothy Hodkinson far right.

We walked into the town to the cinema, and I remember vividly the film was about Stephen Foster who wrote the song 'Camptown Races' and 'I Dream of Jeannie with the Light Brown Hair'. Before the picture started a message was flashed on to the screen. It read 'Would any doctors, nurses or persons with knowledge of first aid or firemen or auxiliary works of any kind go at once to Thames Board Mills and would the rest of the public keep away.'

It was some time before we learned what had happened. Apparently a plane had dropped several bombs in the midst of a crowd of people at a Gala Day at the Thames Board Mills. The mayor had previously begged them to cancel the event, and of course it was presumed that the works which stood on the banks of the River Mersey was the real target and that the bombers had missed it.

But there was sheer devastation. People were buried beneath marquees and blown across the meadow and there were many dead and several went to the Winwick Mental Hospital. I remember that a baby blown from her pram survived, but her mother was killed and her aunt never did come out of the mental hospital.

When I arrived home my father had already gone to bed, and my mother said that he couldn't speak or tell her what was wrong. We learned later that he had seen the plane diving down and the bombs falling and out of that lovely blue sky had come more damage than the town received for the rest of the war.

My friend died the following year. I went into the Women's Land Army and served for four years. It was very hard work, and very eventful, but nothing made such an impression as the horror of the events of that bright sunny day. Certainly my father never really recovered and died in 1947.

Dorothy Hodkinson

I was only a young schoolboy at the time but I would like to tell you a true story of what happened to me on the night of 21/22 April 1941 during the height of the Plymouth Blitz.

With my father away working in the north and my older sister staying with friends, the remaining family members in the house that night were my mother, my maternal grandfather – a truly wonderful fellow in his early seventies – and myself.

The air-raid warning had been sounded some time before my folks decided to go to the public shelter situated by the edge of Plymouth's Central Park. The air-raid shelter was only 300 or 400 yards from our house, but by the time we set off bombs were dropping from German aeroplanes and there

Brian Searle with his grandfather.

were tremendous bangs as anti-aircraft guns opened up. With shrapnel raining down and ARP wardens yelling at us to take cover, the three of us cautiously made our way to the shelter.

It was a reasonably spacious shelter set underground with two entrances. Quite a large number of local residents had gone to the shelter on hearing the wail of the siren, and were comfortably seated by the time we arrived in a somewhat dishevelled state. My grandfather decided to remain by the entrance with his pipe-smoking pals and my mother and I went just inside where we sat with a neighbour named Mr Turner.

After some time a neighbour called Mrs Hawkins with her two children, David and Pat, who were two of my playmates, came from the inner area of the shelter and asked my mother if she would exchange places as she needed some air. My mother agreed and together with Mr Turner, she and I moved towards the inner chamber of the shelter.

More time elapsed and then there was an enormous explosion. The lights went out and screams rent the air and the choking dust permeated everywhere. We appeared to be trapped. The shelter had received a direct hit on what was later established to be the entrance area where we had been sitting, probably less than an hour before. Sadly, my grandfather and a number of friends and neighbours died that night including Mrs Hawkins and her two children who had been sitting in the seats previously occupied by us.

The vast majority of the people in the shelter were saved that night, but all those who were sitting towards the end that received the direct hit perished. The last three persons to be dragged out of an escape hatch alive were Mr Turner, my mother and myself, and I remember spending the rest of the night being very sick.

Months later after my father had returned home from his detached duty in Newcastle he too had a lucky escape when minutes after using the upstairs toilet in our house, a large bomb dropped in close proximity and a huge rock hurtled through our roof and smashed the toilet pan into a thousand pieces.

On another occasion an incendiary device pierced our roof while we were all in the public shelter, and the house was only saved from destruction by the brave intervention of neighbours who were on duty locally as wardens.

As you can see it was pretty hectic in Plymouth during the Blitz, and indeed throughout the war.

Brian C. Searle

I was 12 years old when the war began and lived in Birkenhead on Merseyside. I had two younger brothers and my father had been badly wounded in World War One on the Somme, so he was not called up, thank goodness!

The Blitz on Merseyside was really terrible. Night after night after night we spent terrified under the stairs! The sirens would sound their warning of a forthcoming air raid any time from about 5.30 p.m. or sometimes we were lucky and nothing started until about 8 p.m.! But once the raid began it never stopped until the early hours of the morning.

To make matters worse they had positioned their mobile anti-aircraft gun on the road behind us, so what with *that* firing and the bombs dropping, it was all very very frightening! Then there were the incendiary bombs to contend with and I must say that the firefighters did a marvellous job of putting them out and dealing with any small fires they had started.

Three times in 1940, a landmine fell on the houses at the back of us and caused a great deal of damage to our house as well as to many others. All our windows were blown out and soot from the chimney fell out and covered everything and the cistern burst so that there was water everywhere as well! So you can imagine how my parents felt!

I must tell you that in the middle of all this terrible mess the time came for me to be confirmed at the Anglican Church. So there I was in white dress and veil, picking my way through all the mess before going to church!

It was one whole year before they put new windows in again for us and, believe it or not, they were blown out once again in a raid that very night! So yet again we had to live in electric light for many months. After all the damage to the house, my father applied to the council for another house. In due course, at the start of 1941, we were offered the choice of two houses. One was in the north end of Birkenhead and the other was in Bebington on the outskirts.

We accepted the latter but sadly the family who took the other one were all killed when a bomb hit the house. How simple decisions can change your lives! What dreadful days they were!

We had friends who lived in Burnley in Lancashire and they were continually begging us to go and live there and get away from the bombings. They only had one air raid all the length of the war and only one bomb dropped and that fell into the park and hurt no one, thank goodness!

However, my parents decided to make the move in March 1941 and my father, who worked in the Town Hall, asked for a transfer to Burnley Town Hall! Luckily he was granted his request and so we moved to Burnley.

We had only been there for six months when one day my youngest brother, Peter, who was aged four, became very poorly and we had to send for the doctor. After his

examination, the doctor said that he should go to hospital as soon as possible. Peter was admitted about 6 p.m. that day and sadly he died about midnight. It was such a terrible tragedy, especially as we had decided to move to Burnley to escape possible death or injury from the Blitz and then this tragic occurrence had to happen. He was a lovely little boy, with blond curly hair and big blue eyes. The doctor eventually told us that he had died of acute chorea and it had been caused by shock due to the bombing.

So we, like many other people, had little or no love for the Nazis who were responsible for his death. I don't think I have much more to tell you I am afraid, except that, of course, once the Blitz began I had little and eventually no schooling whatsoever until the war ended!

There are lots of small points that I can remember that might be of interest. Like the first pair of nylons I was lucky enough to get from a friend of the family who had a relative in America. Did I think I was a real swank! I sure did! I can remember the first banana I was given and when eggs and sweets became readily available!

Ironically, when we were settled down in Burnley, it became an area to which women and children were evacuated. Quite suddenly my father was asked if he would take on the job of billeting those who were sent up to Burnley. It was not a very popular job for him but he managed to get them all settled comfortably and became very friendly with quite a lot of them. They were so grateful for all he did for them, and when it was all over and they were due to go back home, many of them told him, 'You must come and stay with us for a holiday soon!'

Patricia Tottey

I was living in London all through the Blitz. I was six years old when the war started, and I have scribbled out what I remember of being bombed out. I never did hear any warning of the bomb that destroyed most of our street. I remember my brother crying and my mum's friend from the next street saying, 'Here, I have brought you some tea,' to my mum.

There were nine of us in the air-raid shelter. It was an Anderson shelter in the back garden. There was Dad and Mum and my brother aged six and my five sisters and me by that time aged eight. We used to sleep in there during the worst of the Blitz, and it was cold and damp and lit with just candles and torches. I remember that the corrugated iron used to be dripping wet, and everything about the whole place was damp. The night we were bombed out when we got out of the shelter there was just grey dust everywhere, and glass as well, but our house was still just standing. It was my sister's birthday, and somehow Mum had scraped together everything that she could to make a cake. It was now decorated with dusty bits of glass!

We made our way through the rubble to the front of the house. Was this Adamsrill Road? Most of the houses were gone. Certainly all the windows were gone, and all over everything was dust, just clouds of it.

Of course, whether there was a Blitz going on or not, we kids were still hungry! Up the road was the WRVS van doling out hot tea and sandwiches, so off we went for a feast! Later on I learned that in that raid two people were killed, one of whom was a young lad who was in the cellar of a house. He was not injured in the explosion, but gassed when a pipe was broken and he was not aware of it.

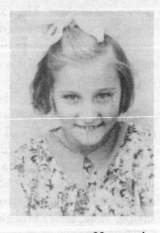

When the extent of the damage was sorted out we had to find somewhere else to live. I remember trailing round London with Mum who tried estate agents and finally the council requisitioned a big empty house not far away.

We salvaged what we could and moved in there. But we still went back to our old shelter during the worst of the air raids as we didn't have one in the new house! We also had to go over to get Hector the cat. He steadfastly refused to move and stayed precisely where he was at our old premises. The important thing is that I am certain that Mum would have done the same if she could!

Joan Gilbert

We lived in Dagenham when the Blitz started. I was only a child but I remember that as it got dark the sirens and the guns would start almost simultaneously. We used Mrs Stoh's shelter, which was two doors up. Mrs Stoh was afraid of going down the shelter so she and her son, Siddy, would huddle under the stairs all night. She would scream continuously when there was a lull in the bombs. We could all hear her all the time.

At first there was only my mother, my brother, Maurice, and myself. Then the people from Wapping came. They were some sort of relation of the Sullivans where we were lodging. There was the mother, her young sister, Rosy, and brother, Johnny, and her two young children, Raymond and Rodney. They had been sheltering down a wharf when the entrance to it had been hit by a bomb. There had been an escape of ammonia, so they had all peed on their clothing and held it to their faces and so saved their lives. When they got back to where they lived their house was completely demolished. When they arrived in Dagenham all they had were the clothes they stood up in.

Rosy and Johnny shared Mrs Stoh's shelter with us. Maurice would lay across the back. I lay down the right side and Rosy lay down the bottom right, so we were like sardines! My mother lay on a sort of bedchair in the middle. Johnny was on the left. He was 16 and a very nice boy. Rosy was 18 and I liked her too.

Every night as the sirens and guns started we would take candles and coats and water and a bucket to wee in. We would play noughts and crosses and dots until we settled down to sleep. But the Anderson shelter had a condensation problem. The droplets would soon begin to run down the sides. And as we laid on sand with only a coconut mat between us and the sand it wasn't comfortable. We soon became very lousy people. Not only head lice, but almost every variation on that theme! I had big mauve lumps all over my body. What with them and scabies and other rashes we seemed to have everything that was unnamable!

In spite of all this and Maurice's snoring because he needed his adenoids out, I can never remember being kept awake by the barrage! And mobile anti-aircraft guns are deafening when they are near.

One night my mother spent the night down Mrs Jeffrey's shelter. Mrs Jeffrey was nervous when her husband was on night work. That night we had our nearest miss. The scream of the bomb filled the shelter. There only seemed to be the scream and as the candle went out my head went under the coats.

Everything rocked and the shelter was suddenly full of dust. Maurice was crying and saying, 'I've lost my tooth.' We thought we were buried. The coconut mat that covered the entrance would not move. Someone had lit a candle and Johnny took off his shoe saying he would undo the bolt at the back of the shelter. We knew that this was the way out. As Johnny bashed at the bolt with his shoe a voice suddenly said, 'You kids all right down there?'

A warden's face appeared at the entrance. We were not buried after all! There was a lull and then I heard my mother crying and saying, 'Where are my kids?' Then dear Mr Hume saying, 'It's all right, Mrs Virrels. I can see the shelter.' And as far as I can remember we settled down to go to sleep!

It all became a way of life to us. It was as though sleeping down a dugout was normal. We would come up the next morning as the 'all clear' sounded and someone was always heard to say, 'Well, that's another night we have lived through. We'll have a tale to tell when all this is over.' Often there was no water because the mains had been hit. We would collect our buckets and get water from the point where it was available. Other times there was no gas for the same reason. Us kids would go to where the worst damage was. We would gaze at the huge hole and the half rooms that were left. As far as I can remember we quite enjoyed it! When Campden Crescent was partly demolished by a land-mine it was really interesting. We would talk in terms of how big the bomb was. If it was judged to be less than a 1,000 pounder it was really not very big or interesting!

Then my father turned up on his white bike. He said there were plenty of houses at Rainham. There was, but there was a reason. Hubert Road was five minutes' walk from Hornchurch Aerodrome. When the planes went over it seemed they would surely take the chimney off! When we first went to see the house at Rainham there was almost a whole road of empty houses. When we moved in a week later there were all taken by families bombed out from Canning Town, Stepney and Bow. The whole of the East End seemed to have moved at the same time!

At first we shared a shelter with the people next door, but they were a very large family and crude in a way that we were not used to. They only seemed to use four-letter words, and all the conversation seemed sexual! Also they were nervous wrecks!

There were always rumours when people were killed. They were always supposed to be doing something they shouldn't have been, such as having a bath or making a cup of tea, thereby showing a light that had been seen and acted upon! But as the winter closed in we took to sleeping in the house. It was a bit silly because if anyone had thumped our table it would have collapsed! But the state of our bodies and the cold weather combined with unpleasant neighbours all seemed a good argument for taking up residence under the table!

We would lay a sheet on the coconut matting, then the top sheet down, then covered with coats. What we would have done without all those coats I cannot imagine! They were the same coats that covered us in the Anderson shelter, the same that used to cover us in our beds, for we had no blankets. Where did they all come from? I don't know and my mother is dead now, so I shall never know!

One night all the back windows were shattered and the back door was blown off. As I swept up the glass the next morning I realised that if we had been sleeping in that room we would have been horribly cut. The glass was everywhere. In every nook and cranny, even the smallest crack was full of glass. It seemed far in excess of the windows broken! I am told that the Blitz lasted 70 consecutive nights. Certainly our worst was when we were still in Dagenham.

Then there was a frightening experience concerning a visit to the pictures. Usually we would get back just in time to adjust the blackout and settle ourselves under the table. This time we must have been later than usual. Since we had failed to get on the bus we ran attempting to get on several lorries. At that time every vehicle would stop to pick up men leaving Ford's and Brigg's, so getting them home before the raid started. Before we knew where we were the sirens and guns started and we knew there would be no more transport. So we decided to walk home as neither my mother or us kids liked public shelters, and we knew if we stopped now we would be stranded for the night.

As we walked the sky was aglow with planes and search-lights. The guns were going and screaming bombs were dropping one after the other. But what really frightened me was the shrapnel. Maurice used to collect the shrapnel every day with the other boys. They thought it was for the 'war effort'. There were great jagged lumps, and you could hear it falling and it always frightened me when I was outside. But this time was the only time we were well and truly caught out. We walked close together and after a while we were joined by a security man from Fords who said he walked home through it every night! I remember thinking that he must be very brave. He told my mother off 'having those kids out in this', and wanted us to stop and take shelter. But after what seemed hours we eventually got home.

There are times that stand out in memory when these years are recalled. The most vivid concerned the surprising Sullivans. At the outset of the war Mrs Sullivan seemed a real baby, crying at the least little thing. But when the Blitz started she took to driving ambulances! Her five children hardly ever saw her. Mr Sullivan was a thin weedy man seemingly nondescript. But when the Blitz started somehow he was in the Auxiliary Fire Service. One morning he came back from Silvertown. He was soaking wet and looked so pale and worn that I thought he would stay home for a week. He said he had been on his ladder high above a burning building. His mate was on the ladder next to him. Then a piece of shrapnel 'that big' (and he cupped his hands) hit his mate in the stomach and he fell into the fire.

Later the pumps dried up and they moved their position and then his ladder was hit and he fell into the Thames. He went back to the East End that very night, and if I did not know that this was true I wouldn't have believed it.

There was another time. The worst of the Blitz was over but this was a particularly bad night. Mr Collinson from across the road came over saying, 'You should not be alone with those children,' and he gave my mother a tin hat before escorting us to his house. My mother gave the tin hat to me and I gave it to my brother who gave it back to my mother who in turn gave it back to Mr Collinson. Obviously unthinkingly he put it back on as he escorted us across the road! And so we joined the Collinsons under their table!

Another time Mrs Storey next door came in saying we should go to her house as the raid was 'heavy'. We groped our way in complete darkness. When there was no danger in showing a light someone lit a candle. The entire Storey family were coal black. The soot in the chimney had been brought down by the barrage! Mr and Mrs Thorogood who lived in a room upstairs screamed their way through the raid just as Mrs Stoh used to. They had been bombed out from Canning Town. By that time we were only having occasional raids or bouts of raids.

About 4.30 p.m. one day I went to get a bag of chips and as I walked back, dreaming as usual, a German plane glided out of the low cloud. I ran for the nearest door. As I got through it I slid on their polished lino right under the table where the family already were sheltering. In the years that followed when I see any member of that family they howl with laughter at the memory of me sliding for cover across their lino straight into their table/shelter. But it had its serious side. As I crashed into them the machine guns from the plane opened up.

Another time Lill who lived next door and Nellie who lived up the street and myself were at a dance in Rainham

Village. The sirens went and we all wanted to get home. So we ran for a bus. It seems that most of my childhood was spent running! The conductor cracked jokes about how lucky we were but warned us that the minute bombs started to fall the bus would be stopping! We got off at the top of Cherry Tree Lane, and as we did all hell was let loose. Guns were sending up shells that whistled, bombs were dropping and the whole area was as light as day with flares. Lill, who was a very fast runner, took off saying she was going home. Nellie who had wanted to shelter panicked and ran after her crying! I was afraid of being alone so I followed Nellie! As we came into Cherry Tree Lane incendiaries had set alight the cornfields on the right. So everything seemed ablaze. As I was not such a good runner as the other two and saw a door open at the top of Hubert Road, I went in and joined the family under the table. When there was a lull I ran home as fast as I could.

The later doodlebugs and rockets were never in my opinion in the same league as the bona fide air raids. But by that time I had learned to fear. A short spell in the country had declimatised me and I didn't think it was funny working in a shop without windows. It was just cold! Also, I was a responsible wage earner who recognised my mother relied on my money. We were in Rainham and the rough family next door had moved.

A middle-aged couple took their place. Mrs Bell had been a nurse and had resumed her duties at the outset of the war. They too came from the East End. Mrs Bell told my mother when the Blitz was at its worst she had been on duty and there were so many people brought in dying that they were just placed in the corridors and left to die there. By the morning the self-same corridors had been stacked with bodies and they had come to hold a fascination for her and she could not resist keep going back to look at them, unable to believe her eyes. That was the horror of the Blitz.

When the doodlebugs started I was working at Brigg's canteen. It was in an attic which was inaccessible to light and air. The first night of the doodlebugs was a puzzle to people who had experienced air raids. 'Now you listen,' said my mother. 'Every time the engine stops a bomb drops,' and so it went on all night. No thought of shelters now, we had had enough of that.

At work the next day the 'funny' air raids continued. The whole factory was down the shelter 27 times I remember, because I counted. Not that I minded that much. I hated my job in the canteen!

After a while the papers told us what was happening. It was a secret weapon. Tales of secret weapons were popular in those years, so the powers that be decided that the factory would only take shelter if the doodlebug was coming in our direction! The warning was a quick beep-beep. None of us girls in the canteen were over 16 and we were at a great disadvantage in as much as we were in the most inaccessible part of the building. So when the danger warning went we ran! I can never remember actually getting as far as the shelter before the inevitable explosion! But I can remember being trapped in the Drawing Office more than once. As the Drawing Office was almost completely glass, it was quite frightening.

The rockets were frightening too. Again there was no warning. I can remember leisurely walking down Cherry Tree Lane when one went off. I started to run, even though I knew that the explosion had already happened! I knew that the second explosion was only some sort of reflex thing, but nevertheless I ran and my legs would not stop. There was nothing I could do about it.

One evening a rocket dropped on a house in Ford Lane. Myself and friends ran to it as we had in the beginning. I can remember that in the light of the fire, I saw a fat, headless woman brought out. I ran home full of horror. The time of childish glee in what was happening had long passed but that sight had made it even worse. That in a way summed up my memories of the Blitz.

Betty O'Callaghan

Here are my few snippets by way of recollections of the Blitz.

1. A north of England evacuation officer told me this story personally. She was so disappointed to see a Newcastle family who had been evacuated back home from the countryside. Why? The answer was very simple. 'We can't stand the awful 'ush!'

2. When I was in Northants I was asking directions to a farm I had to visit. The answer I got was quite straightforward.

'Go along past the bomb hole on your left and just past the bomb hole on your right. The bomb hole on the left is *their* bomb hole, *ours* is the bomb hole on the right.'

While those are my snippets of the Blitz, I do also have another recollection of a little incident later on in the war. I was visiting a farm on the Essex coast and I first met the farmer's wife and their son, aged six, but before I could say anything the boy said excitedly, 'Do you know, a V2 can fly faster than sound?'

Going along with him of course I said, '*Really*, how wonderful.'

But my heart was saying sadly, 'And you would know nothing if one came your way!'

Constance H. Burton

My father died when I was seven years old and just after the war started our mum died leaving we four sisters and one brother orphans. My younger sister and I were taken by my brother and put into domestic work at St Thomas's Hospital in London. My other sisters were already married and my brother waiting to be called up.

We were bombed pretty badly, and we were under a bomb, which we were lucky to get out of alive. I remember the smell of cordite and the blackness and the screams and trying to get out of the door. One maid was hysterical when we found we couldn't get the door open, and then someone socked her one and the medical students of St Thomas's carried us out! We lost all our belongings and our bedrooms were gone and absolutely wrecked so that we were not allowed to go back to them.

We were given clothes and I remember we were only given one vest and one pair of knickers! As we returned along the main corridor I remember seeing awful injuries and civilian injured coming in all the time. There seemed to be ambulances coming and going without stopping.

We had mobile canteens outside the hospital to get tea and something to eat. Thankfully my sister and I were not hurt. We had to go back home to my sister's flat but we were left alone a lot and so we would wander round the streets looking at all the awful damage and when the siren went we would quickly go into a shelter until it was all over. Strange, I was never afraid of the bombs themselves, only scared of being trapped in a shelter at night.

I remember one Saturday and it was dinnertime and my sister was cooking the dinner. The siren went, and somehow we knew it was going to be a bad raid, but my sister said, 'You go with the kids and get into the shelter. I'll finish off the dinner.' I didn't want to leave her, but she didn't want the dinner spoiled and so I had to go to the kiddies as they were calling.

I kept calling, 'Mary, come on, leave the dinner.' But

she just kept shouting that she was all right, and then suddenly the bombs were falling and I remember my sister came running out with the colander in her hand and as she got to the entrance to the shelter the blast of a bomb pushed her half in! She had the cabbage in the colander but her backside was still sticking out of the shelter and we had to pull her in, and she was swearing about the 'bloody bombs'. Although we were in a dreadfully dangerous situation we couldn't stop laughing it was so funny. I don't suppose it is funny to anyone reading it, but we've laughed about it for years.

We had a bad experience one night. We were all in the shelter one night and my other sister had come with her little girl. She had not long given birth to twin boys. We were very cramped in the shelter and then a warden came and told us that we all had to get out as an unexploded bomb was in the garden a few doors away. We had to go to another shelter and I remember holding one of the twins and the little girl running along the road ducking down every time the bombs came down. We were lucky and got in a shelter. While we were there we thought about the bomb and whether it would go off and that would have been another home gone. But it was dismantled and so the home and other homes in Albany Road were safe. We were told

Rose Holden (centre) with her brother on the right.

later it was a 500-pound bomb, but whether that was true or not I never knew.

I should say now that St Thomas's Hospital had not forgotten us. We were now classed as being in 'reserved work' and my sister and I were sent to St Martin's and St Nicholas' Hospital at Pyrford in Surrey. We only had one case between us and a railway ticket to West Byfleet. We started out at eleven o'clock in the morning and finally got to the hospital very late at night. The train was held up for hours because of the raids, and also we lost our way. No one helped us, which was understandable. Everyone seemed to be in a frantic panic, and the funny thing about being moved to Pyrford was that I would keep coming back to London as soon as I got paid my monthly wages. Quite frankly it was too quiet for me in the country, and I was forever 'on the carpet' in the matron's office for going off, but she was very kind to me and I grew quite fond of her.

Gradually I came to love the country and I remember hearing one night a nightingale singing in Pyrford Woods. I have never forgotten that, it was breathtaking.

I eventually got into the Land Army and it was the making of me. It was hard work working for a grumpy farmer who didn't like 'bloody Londoners' but then he couldn't do much about it! I was billeted with two other girls and we would cycle miles to go to a dance. We were in fact near an RAF station in Cambridgeshire, and I started to spend a lot of my time with an RAF officer observer of 'F' for Freddy Lancasters. I lost my virginity to him at 20 years of age and thought foolishly that he would marry me, but I found out after the war that he was married all the time.

Finally, I remember the day that the war was over. I was working on the land when the news came, and I flew down the road on my bike because as far as I was concerned I was heading back again to London! I remember I met the farmer. He said, 'Where the hell are you going?' and I remember saying that the war was over. He shouted and raved at me saying he didn't care if it was, get back to work!

I told him where to go and headed off back to London all the same!

Rose Holden

I was 13 years old and living in London when war was declared. After six months' quiet, it was frightening to hear the anti-aircraft guns blazing away during the nightly bombing raids.

The beautiful church across from us had an incendiary bomb dropped on it. It was lodged between the tiles and the false roof and burned unchecked. All the fire engines were out fighting house fires and the fire just burned on until the whole church was on fire. I will never forget the wonderful glow through the stained-glass windows. I went to bed but in the morning the church was a ruin. It stayed like that for ten years before it was rebuilt.

We lived on Muswell Hill and during the daylight raids we could see bombs dropping out of the planes and exploding on the houses. I remember that one evening I was cycling home during a raid and I actually thought that the sun was setting in the *east*. It wasn't until later that I realised that it was the docks on the Thames, all burning.

My dad was a part-time fireman and he spent over 24 hours helping to fight that fire. I remember he came home exhausted and filthy in a corporation dustcart because that was the only transport available. They had to leave the pumps and all the equipment with other firefighters still trying to put out the flames all those hours later.

I could go on quite a lot as I was in London the whole time and saw all the Blitz. But there are good things in life and one little thing always makes me smile. I travelled up to Sheffield in 1945 to see my fiancé and the train was so crowded and I was so small that a soldier lifted me on to the luggage rack in the train at London and a sailor lifted me down when we got to Sheffield!

Rita Van Beuren

There was no sign to warn us of the approach of enemy aircraft. Our first intimation that something was wrong came from Miss Bentley who was our class teacher.

'I want two strong boys to help me,' I remember her saying. 'Quickly now! The rest of you get down under your desks.'

Trestle boards were rushed from the corner and laid over the desktops to provide some sort of emergency shelter. There we all huddled, unaware of the real danger outside.

I was eight years old and living in a part of Lancashire which was considered to be so safe from attack that we 'took in' evacuees from Manchester. This Monday morning, however, saw the random unloading of a stick of bombs over Darwen as the pilot hot-tailed it back to Germany after his mission elsewhere.

We had practised bomb drill at regular intervals for months. The long crocodile up the road to the air-raid shelter. 'Don't run! File in orderly fashion, please.'

On arrival the bricks swallowed us up in a dank void as we bumped into each other, waiting for our eyes to become accustomed to the dark. Once acclimatised we were encouraged to wear our gas masks. First we had an India rubber stitched onto a hanky which had to go between the teeth to protect them from impact. The hanky end was left protruding so that it could be tugged should we swallow the rubber. The cambric blotted the tongue dry on impact. Next came our golden-syrup-coloured ear plugs, tied together with a yard of retaining string which could be worn to the front or back of the head once the plugs were in place. Our teacher must have thought our heads very empty indeed! The plugs produced further disorientation. Then came the hateful rubber-smelling mask itself.

The baby class had Mickey Mouse designs, but as we were big boys and girls our masks were merely functional with a green metal grill at the end of each black concertina of trunk. We carried these instruments of torture to school regularly under threats of dire punishment should we forget! Each one with its own cardboard box with a string handle.

At the count of one we placed our thumbs into the webbing straps which were meant to go over the back of the head. At the count of two we pushed our chins into the suffocating snout, at the count of three the thumbs were slipped down securing the straps to the head before checking along the rubber sides of the mask to ensure a good seal around the face. The celluloid visor steamed up immediately in the cold, even when we had licked it first. Instant panic!

On this particular Monday there hadn't been time for these frivolities. We waited in limbo, maskless. The teachers were in the dark as to how long we should remain beneath the desks! I later learned that the bombs had landed in the area where many of the children, including myself lived. Two bombs had exploded. Another one had fallen down a well remaining an unknown quantity! Another two bombs had landed where my father worked as manager of a co-op store.

'When the coach arrives,' Miss Bentley said cheerily, 'we are going down to the canteen for lunch.' I was dumbfounded, for I had never been to the canteen. Only 'free dinner' children went there!

My hand shot up as I explained that my granny always came to collect me at dinnertime. But I was promptly put into my place.

'We are all going to the canteen today!'

So it was with relief that I saw my grandpa standing in the doorway. He had come to take me with him to share a corned beef sandwich at the home of his elderly chum who lived outside the present disaster area. I remember that the radio blared away as I tried to eat, but I was too upset about the whereabouts of my mother whom I suspected I might never see again.

She was weaving khaki for the war effort and was in the mill when my granny rushed over to inform her that 'Your house is down to the ground.'

A bit of an overstatement, but understandable because she had been bending down to reach another potato ready for peeling when the kitchen window exploded over the top of her! She was imprisoned in the kitchen by a twisted back door until the police rescued her. My mother on arrival home found that the situation was nothing like so cataclysmic, but the policeman would not allow her into the house at first. There were cordons around the road where we lived. He said that the bomb might explode at any moment. However, all our worldly goods were inside, and she told him that she was 'no good without money'. So she was allowed two minutes to collect the deed box, her money and the jewellery box containing two gold watches which had been 'in the family' and were going to stay that way!

She and Granny then went up to the vicarage expecting to find Grandpa and myself there, after discovering that I had been moved from school. Disappointed, they were persuaded to stay for a cup of tea with most of our neighbours who were encircling the vicar's drawing room. My mother described the scene.

Herself clutching Granny and the deed box! One neighbour nursing her baby grandson swathed in the towel she had thrown round him as he lay gurgling in his bath until suddenly covered in soot from the chimney! He was lovingly stroking his granny's face and spreading soot liberally! A dog whimpered at the knee of his master. They were both shaking with shock. Subsequently they all had to smile at the picture they must have made, taking tea out of the vicar's wife's best china and many of them not even knowing her before that day. Generosity indeed!

Grandpa and I meanwhile roamed the streets in distress looking for my mother and Granny until we bumped into them looking for us! What a reunion! Next we had to search for Dad for we were not to know that he was standing guard outside his shop where all the windows had been blown out. He was on the lookout for looters because food was on ration, of course. Another joyful reunion! We relieved him of his vigil while he went off to get some tarpaulin and wood so that he could secure the windows for the night. Those commodities were difficult to come by due to sudden demand.

That night we stayed with an aunt until the bomb had been defused. Next morning we returned home to find broken glass everywhere in spite of Dad's efforts at putting 'leaded lights' into the panes which was supposed to strengthen the glass against shock waves. Narrow strips of lead were criss-crossed over the panes and stuck down with a colourless fixative. The resultant patterns were enlivened by painting the infills with transparent coloured varnishes. Mondrianesque but futile! I had to stay put in order to avoid splinters.

My parents got the downstairs looking fine by evening and exhausted we were ready for bed. But when my mother went upstairs with me, we found the same conditions up there. Broken glass everywhere, including all over the beds.

In all the panic and in all the work nobody had thought about the upstairs!

Yet we were the lucky ones. There were six people killed in that raid. One a coalman, who had died while he carried a sack of coal on his back, unable to get underneath the lorry with his mate who had not been so encumbered at the time. Other places were far worse off. At night the sky glowed orange where the bombs had fallen in Manchester and Liverpool. Our Blitz was a one-off affair, and we were thankful for that!

Edna Vidler (née Leach)

I was born and lived in Grimsby in Lincolnshire and in 1941 and 1943 the town suffered a series of heavy raids in which 196 people were killed. On the nights of 13 and 14 July 1943 the heaviest raid of all killed 99 people in one night. My mother and sister were two of them.

I have memories previous to that and I remember watching the bombers and was witness to other raids while I with my mother and two sisters and brother were going to the Anderson shelter. Also I remember hiding in the basement of the school when a raid was taking place over Hull across the Humber. The school that I attended was I would think unique insomuch as it had a playground at the top of the school and it was there that I witnessed a Spitfire shooting down a German aeroplane. I could clearly see the flashes of the guns. Even at that age I knew what a Spitfire looked like as they flew over almost every day.

Another time I was witness to a blazing factory when we were heading to the communal shelter which, incidentally, was hit later on by a bomb but nobody was seriously hurt. On the way to the Anderson shelter somebody pointed to the sky, and there in the night were three German bombers coned by a searchlight. They looked as if they were made of silver. But my most vivid memory is that of the night of 13 and 14 July.

Tony Eaton standing forward, far right.

Anderson shelters were prone to flooding and as things go, on that particular night it was flooded! When the siren sounded, with me being the youngest, my mother held me close and ushered my brother and two sisters under the stairs of the house. That is when what was described as a parachute mine exploded. The house along with many in the street was completely flattened.

My elder sister, Betty, was killed and my mother, who was still holding me, was killed and I could feel her cold face against my hand. The hand of death is indiscriminate, and myself and my brother, Lawrence, and my other sister, Sylvia, were unscathed apart from a bit of bruising. After being pulled out of the rubble and put on a stretcher I distinctly recall thinking how bright the sky and stars looked.

Eight people in our street were killed that night. My father died a couple of weeks later of cancer, after being invalided out of the navy. From there we were put into Brigagate Home where the occasional raid took place, but by Christmas I had been evacuated to Patley Bridge in the West Riding to the Sailors' Orphan Home where I stayed until the end of the war and then from there I went to Hull, which was the true home of the orphanage.

There was a lovely development to this story . Much later, I received a letter from a Mrs Brenda Archer asking if I was the Tony Eaton she had been searching for for almost 50 years. Of course I was and we arranged to meet along with my brother and sister. It was a lovely reunion and Brenda Archer was one of the children of the street who was also bombed out but nobody else being hurt. Her mother, Mrs Wilson, who was 85 and who was my mother's best friend, was overjoyed to see us for the first time since that dreadful night. It was a lovely meeting and I still can't stop telling people about it!

Tony Eaton

I lived at Langley near Birmingham at the time of the Blitz having only moved to St Helens on my marriage. We were a family of seven. There was my mother and father and two boys and three girls. My two brothers had joined the army early on so it was 'all girls' at home apart from my father!

My sister's first memory of the Blitz was that when the first air-raid warning sounded her only thought was to run upstairs to rescue her new coat which had a squirrel collar. It was her most treasured possession and had only just been bought. Money had always been short in our family so none of us were the least bit surprised when our Kath thought the coat should go down the air-raid shelter with us! However, when we found that we were continually having to stay in the air-raid shelter because of the severity of the German attacks, her coat was eventually left to its fate in the bedroom! Happily for all of us it remained intact!

As far as I was concerned I remember coming home from the office at about 5 p.m. and going to bed to get a couple of hours' sleep and then we all repaired to the air-raid shelter for the rest of the night. When anyone saw me in my grey slacks there were hoots of laughter as they were quite bow-legged from being sat in for so many hours. Sometimes I almost felt that it would be preferable to stay in the house and risk the bombs than have to sit down in that dark dreary Anderson shelter with beetles and all other manner of insects crawling over me.

My sister, Joan, was courting and as her boyfriend was in a 'protected' job, i.e. his job was so important to the war effort that he was kept out of the Forces, he sometimes came down the air-raid shelter with us. More often than not he would stay for just a few hours until he could wait for a break in the enemy action to make a dash for it to his own home. But of course on some occasions the activity never ceased so perforce he had to stay all night. I can remember one particular night when to my sister Joan's chagrin and enormous embarrassment it was one of those occasions when I was unfortunately suffering from wind. It was partly through fear; although I was dozing this didn't prevent me from any 'noises off' session!

Of course in those days all bodily functions were kept well under wraps, and so I certainly blotted my copybook! After that I dreaded her boyfriend having to stay as it usually meant I had to try and keep awake and not embarrass her again!

My father was a man who I am sure didn't know what a kettle was for! I was surprised that he even knew it had to be filled with water to make a drink! But he showed me that I was quite wrong because I remember that although he would never come down the air-raid shelter with us, when the raid started he always used to come to bring us a jug of cocoa when things were quiet, and check that we were all okay. Of course inevitably after the war he never made a jug of cocoa again!

Josie M. Fairclough

Early in the war my husband and I and our children were living in Middleton Junction, which is a fairly small community about six miles from Manchester. Then we decided to move house to a larger one about half a mile away and our next-door neighbour, I remember, was a little upset and begged us not to leave as we had been very good friends.

However, we moved on and I can remember one Sunday night in October that the German bombers came over our locality. We were quite close to an aeroplane factory which was probably the real target. My husband and I were out visiting friends that evening and came home when we heard the sirens to make sure that our children had gone into the air-raid shelter.

The next morning, which was a Monday, I had done my washing and then went to a local for something I needed. The shop manager greeted me with, 'My goodness you were certainly born under a lucky star.'

When I asked him why he told me that the house we had left previously had been practically destroyed the night before, together with most of the other houses nearby. My friend and former neighbour was now homeless and she and her husband had been lucky to escape with their lives.

I rushed off to look for my friends. They were sitting in one of the houses that was still untouched, looking shocked and bewildered and even at that time of day still in their night clothes. I arranged to bring them both to our house, together with their small dog which had been rescued with them.

My two girls willingly gave up their comfortable double bed and settled for two borrowed camp beds. We turned our front sitting room into a bedsitter for our friends to give them some privacy when they wanted it and they stayed with us for three months. Luckily we were then able to arrange for them to rent a small cottage nearby until their old home was rebuilt. We also managed to recover some of their furniture and possessions.

I remember when they were thanking us I said to them, 'You didn't want us to leave next door to you, but we had to make a home for you here!'

On another occasion I remember a whole stick of bombs was dropped on Middleton Junction, and a lot of people had to evacuate it but not one of the bombs exploded! This for a time earned us the nickname of 'The Holy City'! All the bombs were located and removed safely and no damage was done to property, unless you counted the holes in several gardens and backyards.

My strongest memories of the war are of the caring sharing people when neighbours were in distress and of being able to go out and about in the blackout whether on business or pleasure without the fear of being mugged or robbed.

Alice M. Fish

I had just arrived home on embarkation leave in January 1941. It was about 8.30 p.m. Not too cold for that time of the year. I was dressed in the usual khaki uniform, including tin hat, rifle, bayonet, small pack, water bottle, etc., plus the standard 50 rounds of .303 ammunition. Not really encumbered as dress went in those days!

I left the Midland Station after a train ride from South Wales, about three hours late, due to enemy activity. An air raid was in progress and the sky was filled with flying fragments from our ack-ack. I was quite used to such conditions as I had been on search and rescue in Cardiff during the raids in that part of the kingdom. There was the usual thrum of enemy bombers and I put on my steel helmet and adjusted my gas mask in the unlikely event of a gas attack. All this was in the pitch darkness of a built-up area.

I knew my way blindfold into my home about a mile away but there was suddenly an almighty bang about 300 yards ahead. I really thought that a blockbuster had landed on the gasworks. The flash had also taken away what night-sight I had acquired and I ran slap bang into what I thought was a dustbin, which someone had carelessly left on the pavement. The bin toppled over and I fell with it and into it! I leave you to imagine the type of language I used!

Finally I got out and continued to grope my way home. When I was a few hundred yards short of my house I saw that the door to my pre-war drinking house was slightly open, which was surprising as I knew Harry, the landlord, usually kept it tightly closed during air raids. By this time it was about 9 p.m. and at least one hour of drinking time left so I went in!

There was the usual dim glow of the night-light in the bar, which was deserted, not a soul about. It was eerie.

I shouted 'Hello' rather in the manner of Alf Garnet in later TV shows. No reply. Right, thinks I, a free pint for Albert, and went behind the bar to draw one myself. I heard a kind of mumbling from under my feet and went to the top of the cellar stairs and shouted, 'Is anybody there?'

A thick curtain was suddenly thrown aside and Harry came up the steps.

'Bloody hell, it's Albert Wood! And where the dickens have you been? Come down and join us, Albert.'

I descended the stairs and there were half a dozen of my pre-war boozing pals sitting on upturned beer crates playing cards on top of a barrel. As I went down into the light there was a roar of laughter.

Albert Wood, centre.

'Just come back from a raid, Albert?' said one.

I couldn't understand the reason for their hilarity until I looked down and saw the awful mess I was in. Then it dawned on me. I had stumbled into a fog bin on Station Street. These bins were a very short-lived idea. They were filled with old oily rags and when the raids started they were set to smoulder, giving off an oily smoke, which was supposed to hide the outlines of the city from the air. They weren't very successful! They were certainly very dirty!

We didn't have a bathroom in the terrace-type house I lived in with my father and mother and the public baths would have been closed long hours ago. Hot water was at a premium in our house before the war, never mind in wartime with fuel rationing, so I was at a loss to see how I could get myself cleaned up. I really was in a mess. My hands and face were covered in black charred oily goo and my uniform was a disgrace! I had soap and towel, etc., in my bag so there was no problem, but water and hot water especially would be hard to come by.

When the laughter had subsided I was told to 'get some ale down you lad' which I did. All buckshee. After the fourth pint we all started to figure out how I could get cleaned up. Harry said the water main had been blown out and so there was no water at all available. He went upstairs but came back down shaking his head at the bad manners of his missus, who would not let him use any of the household water supply which was needed for emergency purposes!

'Oh yes,' said old Fred, 'and we all know what that emergency is. Water in the bloody ale at a bob a pint!'

It must have been about midnight and we were all very merry indeed. Many and varied were the suggestions I received on how to make myself presentable to my father and mother when I eventually did reach home. At the rate we were supping that would be just about when my ten-day leave was up!

It was Harry who came up with what he thought was an ideal solution and revenge on the brewery who had been curtailing his supplies. He said he had a barrel of beer which was 'off' and due to be returned to the brewery. How about if we heated it up on the stove and I had a bath in it! Quickly the idea was unanimously upheld and we set about draining a large metal bucket of beer to set on the stove. The remainder of the barrel was slowly drained into a tin bath and we sat supping ale until the beer on the stove was nearly boiling when it was poured into the tin bath and I was persuaded to strip and sit in it!

Soap was rationed so I thought it only fair that I used my own but by this time we were all drunk I think and they threw beer over me as they dipped their glasses into the bath. No way could I make a lather with my soap and Harry fetched a tin of soft soap which did the job quite well.

Old Fred suddenly said, 'Here, Harry, won't the brewery test the beer when they get it back.'

'What's the difference?' answered Harry. 'That beer will be well off after Albert's dunked his black arse in it! In any case, they will only draw a pint off to test it.'

'They had better!' said old Fred again.

By dint of borrowing I managed to dress sufficient to make my way home without arising the ire of the constabulary, but before that we put a funnel in the bunghole of the barrel and with our pint pots poured all the beer out of the tin bath back into it! Soft soap and all! I have often wondered since if people realised just how sticky beer is!

Two weeks later I sailed to the Middle East, after a hair-raising double crossing of the Atlantic. I did not return home until June 1945, by which time the tenancy of the Sir Garnet Wolsey had changed. So I never did find out what happened to that barrel of beer! I was just 22 years old at the time. What an experience!

Albert Wood

I was in the London Blitz living in Hither Green near Lewisham. I was 14 at the time and my school was evacuated but I didn't go. My mother was a widow so I wanted to stay with her and my sister.

We slept in the Anderson shelter at the bottom of the garden every night. It was very cold and we took hot water bottles and food and Thermos flasks with us. Sometimes the rain would run down into it and we had to bail it out.

The bombing was severe, but we were very lucky not to get even a pane of glass broken. My father had died and I was just one week old so I did not even know him. All I knew was a very large photograph of him hanging on the wall and we were brought up by my mother to kiss him every night when we were small before we went to bed.

So imagine my surprise when one night in the air-raid shelter there he was as plain as could be sitting beside me! He was wearing his army uniform the same as in the photograph so that I could recognise him. It was such a surprise that I remember saying 'Oh' and my mother who was sitting opposite under the blanket said, 'Whatever is the matter, Joyce?'

I didn't want to frighten her so I said it was nothing. My vision only lasted for a brief second and he was gone, but the next morning my mother tackled me about it and she said

that she knew I was really frightened by something. She wanted to know what it was. So I told her and she was quite excited by it and said 'It's your daddy coming to protect us as we are in such danger. He has come to keep us safe.'

Sure enough, a couple of nights after, the bombs were falling all around and the anti-aircraft guns were firing at the bombers and the noise was deafening and then all of a sudden a bomb screamed down louder than the rest and the earth shook and we could hear debris falling.

My mother was shouting, 'We've had a direct hit on our house, I am sure.'

We all crawled out of the shelter and there was thick smoke everywhere. It was dust really and as it cleared we could see the house in the next road that backed onto our garden was gone. There was a deadly hush. The guns were silent. The German planes had passed over.

We rushed round the corner but there was nobody about. We were worried about the occupants as we knew them so well. We wondered who could have survived under that lot.

But soon the fire engines and the ARP were there and I remember seeing them pulling at the rubble. None of the family had been in their shelter. The father was killed. A heavy mantelpiece had struck his head but his wife, his son and his 80-year-old mother were injured but okay.

My mother said later, 'I told you your dad had come to look after us!' She said it with such pride. I have often told people of my vision but many were sceptical. I am not really bothered about them because I know what I saw.

Joyce Manley

I remember the Blitz. I was living in Silverton, London. It interrupted our social life to the extent that we daren't go out in the evenings. Being teenagers, of course, we got a little fed up with that so I remember that my friends and I decided to go to the Woolwich Granada one Saturday afternoon in September. The idea of going in the afternoon was that we would be able to get home before the German planes came.

While we were in the cinema, at about five o'clock a notice came up on the screen to say that an air raid was on and advising everyone to leave and to go to the public air-raid shelters outside. We stayed for a while until all of a sudden, without any warning, the cinema shook so we thought it was about time we left!

Everywhere outside was chaotic. By then bombs were literally raining down and we went into the shelter. But people are funny. After a while some of them began to get impatient and started leaving in between each bombing and eventually an air-raid warden had to come in and advise everybody to stay there until the 'all clear' had been sounded. Apparently a lot of those who had left between raids had been injured or killed while they were out on the streets.

When the 'all clear' went we came out of the shelter to catch the train home from Woolwich to Silverton. We had to trample over rubble, glass and fires everywhere. Apart from that there weren't any trains running so we had to walk, although we weren't quite sure of the way. It was bad enough normally but with the chaos that was around us we were really confused. Then we met one of our neighbours who was coming home from work at the Woolwich Arsenal

and he guided us through all the rubble and made a number of detours until we finally reached Silverton.

When we got there we found we couldn't get to our street because houses had been flattened everywhere, including ours. The neighbour who had so kindly guided us through all the rubble was told that his wife and son had been killed. In fact, she had been coming to the pictures with us but had changed her mind at the last minute. The same fate would have happened to us if we had stayed at home.

My brother Bill was home on leave from the army at the time. He and my other brother, Charlie, had reinforced the shelter in our garden with sand during the morning and when the raid had come, my mother and baby sister, Pat, and my two brothers had been able to lie flat in the shelter. If my sister Olive and myself and my father had been there, we would have had to sit up in the shelter and caught the blast.

The neighbours on either side of us were killed through the blast. The houses had direct hits but it was the blast that caught the shelters. One end of our shelter was torn off and when we eventually got there my sister and I had a job to find my mother and young sister. We really believed that they were dead. But fortunately Bill had taken them to a school for safety. Charlie stayed behind to help get people out of their dugouts. Dad, at the time, was working in the Woolwich Arsenal and so he didn't find us till next day. Believe me, it was a relief when we all got together again.

We lived in a church hall until they found us living accommodation and then it was a question of furniture and clothing, because all that was left was what we literally stood up in. We had no furniture or clothing because everything had been destroyed in that one raid while we had been at the pictures.

Daphne Deakin

I lived with my family in a flat over my father's place of work, which was a combination of Post Office and Way's

Glassworks. One August day I remember my two sisters and I were preparing our clothes and washing our hair and waiting for our turn for a bath in a tin tub! That evening we were intending going to a 'grand gala' at the Wellington Shilling Hop.

Suddenly the air-raid siren went off! But we totally ignored this as we were becoming quite blasé because we had heard it all before!

However, my father shouted up the stairs, 'Get your behinds down here fast, the bombers are coming.' We certainly moved fast because of the way he shouted but by the time we reached the cellar the ack-ack guns were going and the barrage balloons were up and bombs were dropping. I perhaps should mention that we were close to Portsmouth main railway and the dockyard. The noise was horrific.

It's funny what one does think of under the strain and I remember that I said to my sister, 'My God, I've left my one and only pair of decent stockings on the line.'

Then my mother began to sing a hymn, 'Oh God Our Help in Ages Past'. I had never in my 19 years heard her sing before. We shared the cellars with others and the children started to cry in their fright and we could only keep repeating that it would all be over soon. Then to pass the time away we started to play 'I Spy'!

Eventually the 'all clear' sounded and I remember my father bounding up the stairs from the cellar to street level. He was initially blown straight back down by the blast.

When we did get out the sight which met our eyes was quite unbelievable. Our place was standing but minus every bit of glass and, being a glassworks, you could imagine that there was plenty of that about!

A shop a few yards away had suffered a direct hit and everyone had been killed. The street scene of all services trying to do their work is unforgettable. In our place we picked our way through glass, timber and dust. Our stairs were intact and so up we went.

No one cried. But the mess! Everything was covered in soot. I said to Mum, 'Well, Mum, you can cancel the chimney-sweep!'

But we set about clearing up and to my amazement I found that my stockings were still intact with not even a speck of soot on them. But everyone was very subdued and quiet. It seems daft to me now but we decided we would still go to the dance if it was still on because we had paid for a ticket and our clothes seemed all right and it wasn't far away!

Strangely, the Wellington had escaped. Considering the decor consisted of mirrored walls, they were very lucky indeed! Many others turned up as well out of bravado but there was a strange atmosphere nevertheless.

Announcements were made, our dance teacher and friend looked lovely, the evening began, but only just. The siren went off again and as the place wasn't big enough to accommodate us all and as we were only a short distance away from the cellar we had occupied earlier, my sisters and I fled to it!

Nothing was ever to be the same again. That's my memory of my first air raid in Portsmouth in 1940.

Doris Gunn

18 November 1940. This is the day that my father died. My father worked at the Austin Works, as it was then known, at Longbridge. He died suddenly at work after being involved in a raid by German bomber planes some two or three days previous to his death. He then died of shock and pneumonia. At that time I was 15 years old and even at that age was working in a factory on war work.

We learned that the Austin Works had been attacked in

the late afternoon but the news said 'no casualties'. I hurried home from work to my mother and three very young sisters who I found to be very agitated, waiting for my father's return, and when he returned home we learned from him that at the time of the raid warning, he was outside of the building passing from one office to another when the attack happened very suddenly and the planes were diving low and using machine guns.

My father dived under a truck to take shelter but he was caught by machine-gun bullets all down one side of him but, fortunately, he received no damage apart from holes in his clothing and boot, all on the one side. After being treated for shock he then returned to work, dying at work a few days later from shock and pneumonia. His name was Tim Pagett and he was well known and respected.

18 November was one of the worst bombing attacks on Birmingham. We were bombed for most of the night. When my mother received the news of my father's death, my elder married sister was called for. She decided to go to my father's parents' house to break the news to them. I volunteered to go with her and we had to walk from Ladywood, where we were living, to Winson Green, which was quite a long way. We set out soon after the air-raid warnings were given and all transport was taken off the roads and everyone more or less took shelter except for the patrolling air-raid wardens keeping watch for fires.

The bombing started very quickly and it seemed that the whole of Birmingham was alight with fires and flares and bombs dropping and buildings collapsing and it was very frightening and a noisy experience and one of many so vivid in my memory.

The air-raid wardens kept asking us along the way to take cover but my sister kept repeating, 'No, we must keep going.' Eventually we arrived at my grandparents' house, feeling tired and nervous and we stayed with them until the worst of the raid was over.

Kathleen Simkiss, second from right.

Walking back home we experienced the sight of glass everywhere from windows blown out, and roofs blown off buildings, and a huge number of houses and shops burnt to the ground.

We arrived home to see our humble little house still standing but several houses nearby had been bombed to the ground and there were wardens and firemen digging for the bodies of people whom we had known for years. Dozens of people were killed near us that night, a number of whom were our school pals.

Kathleen Simkiss

In 1940, at the age of 18, I lived in the East End of London. On the Sunday evening of 8 September, the air-raid siren sounded.

I knew my family would make their way to their shelter so I went to join them. The shelter was pretty full when we arrived but I found my mother, my 28-year-old brother, his wife and their two-year-old girl. Also my 20-year-old brother and his girlfriend, along with some of our neighbours whose children had been evacuated.

Frank Targett, two weeks after the incident described.

We had just settled down when my father looked in on his way to work. He said that he was going to call in at his local! The important things in life carried on, even in an air raid. He worked at St Peter's Hospital in the East End and was required to do shifts, and this particular night he was due to start at 10 p.m.

At that time, being 18 years of age, I did not drink but for some unknown reason I wanted to go out with him. My mother begged me to stay in the shelter but I went and promised to hurry back. I waited inside the public house while Dad had his pint and as we left the publican, who had just been outside, warned us that he had heard a German plane searching overhead and told us to be careful when we left.

On the way back we had to pass a large warehouse and as we reached the corner we heard a loud whistling sound followed by a blinding flash and then a crashing of glass. Instinctively I left my dad and went running as fast as I could down the street towards our shelter. It was now a heap of rubble with only one corner standing.

There were clothes still hanging on the doors and people's possessions strewn around. It is a sight I have never forgotten. My first thought was to start moving the rubble. Suddenly I felt a hand on my shoulder and it was my dad and he was shaking his head and telling me it was no use. But I, being young, did not want to accept it. He was right. We never saw any of our family again.

Our flat in the same street was also unfit to live in, so my dad took me with him to the hospital and stayed the night there while he went to work, despite all that had happened.

Next day I too went to work. I was an electrician's mate. I spent the next few days at the home of my maiden aunt down in Surrey. I had previously volunteered for the RAF and during that week I received notification to report for enlisting.

My father advised me that it was best that I enrolled. This I did and served six years in the Royal Air Force, the last year being in the Far East.

I have nothing left belonging to my family except a few photographs and my mother's death certificate, stating the day that her body was recovered. That was the same day that I left to join the services.

I believe the bodies were taken away in bags and piled on refuse carts, but what happened to them we never knew. Nothing was organised at this time in 1940.

It was a trying time for my father with all of us gone and I don't think he ever got over it. He had a certificate for war wounds from the First World War and it seems as if some families got more than their fair share in wartime. He died in London in 1955.

As told to Brenda Targett, by her husband Frank

We had many heavy air raids in Birmingham in 1940. We used to shelter under the stairs and I can remember even having baths during air raids and listening to the anti-aircraft guns while in the bath!

In early October one night we had a stick of incendiary bombs fall and one fell at the top of our garden. It made a loud hissing noise and burned with a whitish-blue flame and lots of smoke. I remember we kept a bucket of sand in the house and I carried the sand up the garden, which was no easy task because it was heavy and awkward to carry in the complete blackout conditions. I remember that I got to the bomb at the same time as another man and he was wearing a cloth cap and a raincoat and I remember that he carried a spade.

I poured on the sand and he dug the bomb into the ground. I can remember it clearly. His breath was coming in loud sobs with his efforts. We never exchanged a word and then he disappeared into the night. To this day I don't know who he was. That's how things were in those days.

On 19 November 1940, we experienced a very heavy raid from 7 p.m. until 3 a.m., and several times we had to go under the stairs. About midnight I remember that I was sitting in the hall on the stairs, reading a novel, when we heard it coming! More of a hissing and whizzing noise and coming very close. We all fell flat – no time to get under the stairs – I went down on top of Teddy, our dog. Funnily enough I remember thinking, 'Why should he get killed in a war!' Everything shook and heaved with a roar as tiles cascaded off the roof. Amazingly, in the noise and the shambles, we managed to get under the stairs!

Shortly afterwards, footsteps sounded outside and then there was a pounding at the door.

'Are you all right in there? Is anyone hurt?'

I opened the door to a police sergeant and some other people.

'A bomb has fallen here,' he said.

'I know,' I said. 'We heard it!'

My 78-year-old grandfather was under the stairs with us and on hearing this he started to laugh and chuckle. Apparently he found my answer extremely funny.

'Good old Brian,' he said. He kept on chuckling and laughing throughout the raid, to the extent that he eventually set us all off into fits of laughter. It may sound strange but that's how it was. Looking back it was all probably a nervous reaction by everybody.

During a lull in the raid I went outside to see the damage. The bomb had fallen about 25 feet from our front door but fortunately on soft ground, which was our salvation. In a ring all around the crater was the most finely sieved earth imaginable. It was as fine as a lady's face powder. I remember that as I approached it I sank well above my ankles in the earth. Light rain at dawn compressed the earth somewhat but I have never seen earth so fine. It was literally pulverised.

We had two cats. They used to live in our garden shed. This night they would not go near the shed and spent the night four houses away. They would certainly have been killed as the shed was blown to pieces. Strangely, although we heard the bomb descending, none of us heard the bomb detonate. They say that you don't hear the one that gets you. What I do remember is that when the bomb was coming down it was nothing like the whistle that one hears on TV and cinema.

Much damage was done to our roof and to our shed! Amazingly not a single pane of glass was broken. Our roof had been wrecked but it was covered soon with a large tarpaulin sheet as a temporary measure pending repairs. It may sound funny to be laughing in the middle of a severe air raid but, looking back again, my grandfather certainly had the most infectious chuckle.

People did not spend the whole time cowering in shelters. It only happened if the action was local. That is how it was in our area anyway. I remember that later on there was another hefty air raid with many planes circling and diving and dropping their bombs.

Suddenly the sound of an aircraft diving louder and louder until it became a scream and the whole house seemed to be shaking with the noise and the engines seemed to be in some sort of torment. There were two short bursts of machine-gun fire and the sound of bullets thudding, and the aircraft must have passed very close overhead because it crashed a few hundred yards away, unfortunately into a row of houses with a loss of life.

I tore outside and flames were already leaping up and the red and green flares were exploding. I set off in the direction of the crash but realised that I could be of little use. The police, the rescue and ambulance services were on the scene in seconds, as they always seemed to be.

Later we experienced more heavy raids and, in particular, a stick of incendiary bombs fell again at the top of our garden but these were completely different. They had bright red flares, three or four feet high and they exploded as they came down. They were real horrors.

Another night we had to hurriedly evacuate our house as an 'object' had hit the road. We went to friends about half a mile away. I remember taking the dustbin lid for protection for my mother, holding it over her back and neck because shrapnel was still falling.

When it got light I returned to our house. The whole area was barricaded off but as no one was about I sneaked through to feed and water our poor old Teddy, who was a rather fierce dog with strangers and we had had to leave him behind in the house.

On the way back I looked at the hole in the road. Amazingly, someone had placed a little tea table over it and put a vase of flowers on that! Many shops had their windows blown out but they used to clear up rapidly and get back into business, often with a large notice 'Open as Usual'. I can particularly remember one shop with a hole in the roof. They cleared up the debris and then put up another notice. 'More Open Than Usual'!

People reacted very well on the whole. I never saw any panic or hysteria or lack of resolve. We all tried to carry on as normal as possible. The 'More Open Than Usual' and vase of flowers is the type of reaction which I imagine is uniquely British. We tried to behave as normal as possible. We must be mad!

That reminds me. The plane that crashed near to us was a Junkers JU88 with a crew of four. Two were killed in the crash and two made parachute descents, one landing near to us. The one who landed near to us was a young lad in a state of severe shock. The other man came down about two miles away. As I remember that plane coming down, I can only say it was impossible to describe the tormented agony of sound of the crashing aircraft. Why the pilot fired the two short bursts of machine-gun fire I cannot imagine. Was it a last act of defiance? Or the result of sheer fear? Probably it was a soul in extremis.

In mid-November 1940 was the infamous Blitz on Coventry. That was a peculiar night for us. The air-raid sirens sounded at about 7 p.m. and we took cover. The bombers came overhead. We were getting used to this by now and waited in awesome expectation. The bombers came roaring overhead, revving their engines and in a fine pitch, and we awaited what appeared to be the inevitable. It didn't come!

They usually seemed to bomb on a north-to-south line, and yet they went thundering overhead away from us and into the distance. Only the noise of their engines. No bombs. No anti-aircraft gunfire. Nothing!

After some time we emerged and looked outside. We were safe but the sky to the south was aglow with the fires of Coventry's martyrdom.

But for us on that night there was only the growl and howl of their engines on their bombing runs. But our turn came the following week!

Brian Williams

I had made my usual once-a-week evening visit to my mother-in-law after work, arriving at about 7.30 p.m. and back home at 9 p.m. My sister and her husband were staying with us, us being my single sister and my father. My mother had died of cancer about six months earlier. My sister and her husband had lost their home and all their belongings in the bombing of the previous week.

We had all decided on many occasions during family talks

that we would not go into the air-raid shelter in the garden for the simple reason that it was mostly full of water!

This particular evening, although the air-raid warning had gone, we were sitting around a large oval dining table, having a bite to eat, when suddenly we heard a plane overhead and someone said, 'This one's for us – under the table!' Little were we to know that the table was to save our lives, as the bomb hit the air-raid shelter where we would have all died.

I remember seeing a huge flash of blue light and then nothing, just pitch black and eerie silence. After what seemed like an age but was perhaps a few moments, I heard my father's voice asking, 'What's happened and can we open the door?'

My married sister was crying and calling for her husband.

My single sister, and the one I always loved most, was calling out, 'Where are you, Rita?'

'Well, I'm here somewhere but I can't move,' I replied.

In fact, none of us could see or move as it was as black and silent as a grave. Although I was only 21 years of age at the time, I really did think it was indeed a grave for all of us.

We all lay in pitch-blackness for what seemed hours and I was thinking that no one would ever find us alive. We were able to talk to each other but we couldn't see anything at all. I could not move my head or my left arm. They were totally trapped. We all seemed very quiet, no doubt busy with our own thoughts but nobody said that they were badly hurt.

I tried to make myself as comfortable as possible, for I was in no doubt that I was going to die where I lay. My past life did indeed keep going through my mind! The strange thing was that I really did not feel frightened. None of us were now crying, only every so often someone would ask, 'Are you all right?'

Having been married only four months my mind went back to my wedding day, and the thought of not seeing my husband again seemed to trigger off something in my brain. I called to my sister, 'Perhaps if we all started shouting, someone might hear and help.'

After a while we started to hear a faint tapping noise but loud enough to break the deadly silence around us. Dust then started to fall on our faces, which was a little unnerving in the darkness to say the least! Someone said, 'Maybe someone above is digging around.'

Then we heard a man's voice, faint but certain. Once more we shouted, 'Help us please!' Suddenly a pinhead of light appeared. Then more and more light appeared, although we still could not see each other. Then more men's voices asking, 'How many of you are there, and don't move, we will find you, but it will take time.' Of course we had no idea of the time of day or night.

Slowly the pinhead of light got large enough for us to see a huge spotlight almost blinding us, and we were now able to talk back to the unknown faces above. Dust was everywhere, in our eyes and mouths, making us cough, but I could not touch my face.

Now the hole was large enough for one of the ARP men to crawl down. One by one we were set free but my head was trapped under a dining room chair so someone was sawing away at the cross piece between the chair legs. In doing so he cut my ear, and for the first time that night tears ran down my face. To release my arm a timber beam was moved and I was lifted out of the hole.

'What time is it please?' I asked. Two-thirty p.m. was the reply. My poor father was the last out at 3 p.m.

I was put on a stretcher and remember little else from then on until I came to in a hospital bed in the children's ward of the hospital. My head was bandaged, there were pieces of plaster on my face, and no feeling in my left arm, which was in a plaster cast. But for the moment the fact that I was in the children's ward worried me more! I called out to one of the nurses and said very proudly but maybe a little timidly, 'I'm married.' In those days, being only five feet tall and seven and a half stone, the mistake in hindsight was forgivable!

But the most marvellous thing I remember is that when I said that, the nurse cuddled me and said, 'Sorry, darling, we didn't realise.' Aren't people marvellous. Later that day four men visited me with flowers, saying, 'We just had to come and see you in the daylight.' They thought I was a blonde when they rescued me, my hair being covered in white dust. I think that when they arrived they were disappointed to find that they had a brunette!

Subsequently, of course, I was able to leave hospital with my left arm in plaster, but I was oh so happy to be alive and, of course, swore never again to moan. The family were all eventually reunited with tears of joy all round.

That experience has helped me throughout my life since, and I still have regular laughs at my indignant protest at being placed in the children's ward but worst of all not being recognised as *married*!

Rita Cooper

I lived at Reading during the war, where bombing was really unheard of apart, of course, from hearing about London being bombed every night. Reading itself saw about four bombs, I believe, throughout the war, but here is my little story.

At the time I was at school and every Wednesday I used to leave school to visit a friend in the town centre. My father always told me to take shelter under the Arcade if the sirens sounded.

Well that afternoon the sirens sounded just as I got off the trolley bus, but instead of doing what my father told me I raced through the Arcade and straight to the home of my friend, which was only about 300 yards away. No sooner had I got there than machine-gun bullets crashed through the window next to where I was looking out and the bombs dropped on the Arcade where several people were killed.

I was not allowed home for a while but before I got there my mother had heard about the Arcade being bombed and she was worried stiff. I remember distinctly the look of relief on her face when she saw me running down the road towards her and when Dad got back home he told me how pleased he was for me not doing as I was told! I reckon that was the only time I got thanked for going against his word!

The next day, Dad and I went back to see the damage, and it was dreadful. Everything was in a shambles and I can clearly remember him turning to me and saying what a lucky lad I was.

Charles Wheeler

I spent my childhood at Swansea, and I can remember the air raids very well, especially two nights when my father had miraculous escapes.

I remember the day that a loaded lorry stopped on our road. Men descended from it and began to carry some unusual shapes of metal into each house. The juvenile population were curious but the adults regarded the pieces with trepidation. The men delivered four corrugated sheets, which curved at one end, together with some smaller pieces, iron bars, nuts and bolts. My father answered our eager query by telling us that these strange parts were to be made into an air-raid shelter, which he would have to build.

Soon we knew why the air-raid shelter had been erected. Whenever the wailing sound of the siren was heard, we had to go into the shelter.

My father put in some wooden steps to make it easier for us to descend, but once in my haste I fell against the metal edge, cutting my legs badly, the scar of which I have to this day.

We had chairs and games and books, etc., in the shelter, but we hated the enforced stay and were always delighted to hear the long continuous sound of the 'all clear' when we would run back to school or return to whatever else we had been doing.

Winter set in and night air raids. It was dreadful being woken up and taken from a warm comfortable bed into the cold dank air-raid shelter. I became ill. The doctor diagnosed jaundice. In fact, he said that I was the worst case he had ever known and on no account was I to be taken to the air-raid shelter. Instead my bed was brought downstairs and I didn't leave it for weeks.

Mrs Cowley's father is second from the left.

The family, of course, stayed with me and so the air-raid shelter was abandoned. We never went in it again! Frogs took over. There was heavy rain and the shelter became half full of water. One day when I was better, we were delighted to discover ducks swimming in it! We found out that they had come from a smallholding about half a mile away.

My father was a telephone engineer who worked at the exchange in Swansea. Throughout the war he worked in shifts, and I remember that it was in February when he had gone to work in the afternoon on two till eleven o'clock shift.

That evening there was an air raid. We woke up. It was impossible to sleep because of the noise of guns and bombs. My mother had not gone to bed and was walking around the house anxiously in her overcoat. Our next-door neighbour came in and we heard her say that the town was ablaze.

We were too young to realise what it meant, and that my father was probably in the middle of that inferno. Subsequently, my mother spoke many times of the horror she felt when she looked from the house towards the red, glowing sky three miles from where we lived. She thought that she would never see my dear father again.

The 'all clear' sounded and we, not comprehending the full horror of it all, promptly went back to sleep again! My mother sat in a chair all night until my father arrived home at about four o'clock in the morning. He had walked that three miles home, taking so long because all the roads were blocked by fires and falling buildings. He had walked that distance throughout all that terrible sight, having already worked a nine-hour shift, and he was exhausted.

My mother went through the same terrifying experience a second time and it was a living nightmare. Again my father returned worn out but unscathed in the early hours of the morning.

Later he told us how he was working in the telephone exchange in Swansea when a bomb came through the roof.

It went through various floors, taking one of the workers with it. Miraculously it did not explode.

Some time afterwards, the man who had taken a ride with the bomb was given a medal. We were pleased to hear of the award but I always will believe that my father certainly deserved one for all he went through.

Elizabeth Cowley

Although I now live in Derby I am a Londoner by birth. I was 15 years old on the outbreak of war and entered the ATS just before my 17th birthday. During those first two years I can recall many things during the onslaught of the Blitz. One story comes to mind, which on looking back was funny.

I lived in Kennington in South-East London in a tenement house during the height of the bombing. We lived in the basement and at night we made a bed up under the table for my father and mother and my brother and myself.

On this occasion my father had a huge carbuncle on his head. As we were trying to settle down the raid that night was very bad, and all of a sudden there was an almighty bang and the floor shook and I can remember that the table vibrated.

We all bounced up in shock, and, yes you've guessed it, Dad banged his head and burst his carbuncle. Although I can laugh about it now, we didn't laugh about it at the time and the language was unprintable.

There was another occasion when another raid was on which again was very bad and we decided to stay in the Anderson shelter. I might add that it was the one and only time we used it! I remember distinctly that there were dry twigs on top of the shelter.

Anyway, Dad being very deaf did not hear the raid as much as the rest of us. So we settled down and tried to get some sleep. Suddenly I called to my brother, 'Bill, I can smell

WE REMEMBER THE BLITZ

burning.' No reply. I shouted again, 'Bill, wake up, something is burning.'

Bill got up and after trying to remember where he was, poked his head out of the shelter and came back, and I can always remember his exact words.

'Wake the old man up quick. The bloody shelter's on fire.'

A bomb had landed in the garden two houses past us, and the result had been that all the dried twigs on top of the shelter had been set alight!

After I joined the ATS I was at one time in Knowle Park at Sevenoaks in Kent. When I was there we had a direct hit on the cookhouse, and many of my comrades were killed. As a result I was chosen to go in attendance to a military funeral for them, and it was a very memorable and moving experience. But I was also very proud to be there and show one last remembrance and affection for them.

Dot Carey

I was at York in the ATS when the Germans bombed the cathedral town. At the time I was 17 or 18, living temporarily with my girlfriend at the YWCA, when after retiring for the night, we were awakened by the sirens, which was a very common occurrence in York, and we were ushered down to the basement. The bombs were already dropping close by. It was very frightening and we felt sure, and we were right, that this was going to be 'a big one'.

The constant bombing went on for two and a half hours with no let up. It seemed impossible that we could escape being killed. The planes were flying in so low to drop their bombs that we thought each time 'this one' was for us. Then we would hear the scream and thud of the bomb and know that it had missed us once again. We heard glass shattering and people shouting and screaming. One very young civilian girl with us had a weak heart, and was very ill with fright and kept fainting. We didn't think that she would survive the night. Another young woman resident was an air-raid warden and very brave. She went out immediately the sirens sounded, with her tin helmet and gas mask, and each hour or so she came back to tell us what was happening. Many people were killed and injured that night.

When after about four hours the bombing tailed off and then stopped, we heard the 'all clear' and we made our way up the stairs, only to find that a very large floor-to-ceiling window on the landing was smashed and the glass strewn all over the staircase. Of course we had no lights, and we were all very cold from being in the basement. On arriving at our bedrooms most of us found that the windows there were shattered and there was plaster and debris everywhere. The building was very close to the railway station, which had been one of the main targets.

Some time later a WAAF was shown up to our room. She had been sitting in a train outside the station for the duration of the raid with the bombs dropping around her. She was in a terrible state of shock, and told us the next day that she had been in London in the 'Silver Slipper' nightclub the night before. That night it had been bombed and many couples had died as they danced.

The next morning when we went to our offices in the Fulford Road, a roll call was taken and it was discovered that one of our ATS girls who, in fact, sat at my desk, was missing. She had been staying with friends in a private billet, and they said that when there was a lull in the bombing, Dorothy had opened the lounge door to look out of the hall window. At that moment a bomb dropped and they did not see her again. She had been blasted up the stairs and blown through the landing window.

The soldiers in our offices were the Northern Command Pay Offices. These men were in the pay corp because they were not physically fit for more active units, and they started a shift system to go digging in the craters outside the house where Dorothy Thompson had been. They dug with spades every day for what I think was about nine days before they found her body. That was the first time I had seen men cry. Some of us from the offices went to Harrogate to Dorothy's funeral, where we met her grief-stricken father and fiancé. It was a terrible time. The amazing thing about this raid was that York Minster which was in the centre of damage and devastation, was untouched. Seventy-two people were killed and over 200 injured. Nearly 10,000 houses were destroyed or damaged.

Before all this I remember that I was in a shop in the main street of my hometown of Skegness, just opposite the cinema, where the children had just left the Saturday afternoon matinee. It was about 4 p.m. and almost dark, when a German bomber came in from the sea and flew low down the length of Lumley Road. It then turned and dropped a string of bombs, with a direct hit on the cinema, which the children had just vacated. My friend and I came to on the other side of the shop. We had not felt a thing but we had been thrown by the blast right across the shop and the front of the shop was blown out. It remained closed for the duration of the war.

Ros Davis

In 1940 I was living in Upper Edmonton, North London. My husband was in the army and I was helping my father-in-law in his business. Most weekends after work I travelled

to Surrey to visit my parents. The journey involved travelling from Turnpike Lane Underground Station on the Tube
train to Waterloo. The following happened one Saturday in
September.

I left home as usual at 6.30 but when the train arrived at
Leicester Square it was 'all change'. We were told by the
station staff that the siren warnings had been sounded and
so the flood doors had to be closed. Buses were waiting
outside to take anyone on to Waterloo. When on the bus I
could not see anything but I remember the bus ride very well.
The driver went at speed and going over Blackfriars Bridge
the bus swayed about a lot but nevertheless we reached
Waterloo safely.

I walked into the station and made my way to Platform 7.
I was still standing there waiting when the bombs began to
fall and incendiary bombs in particular began falling
through the roof. I remember the railway staff putting them
out with stirrup pumps and buckets of sand. All the people
waiting for trains were told to go down the escalator to the
Underground entrance and wait there. We would then be
told when the raid was over or it was safe and the trains were
leaving.

It seemed a long time before a porter came and called out,
'All stations to Woking.' A gentleman waiting for a train to
Chessington escorted me to the train and into a carriage.
Just as the train began moving out slowly, two soldiers
jumped on and I remember
one asked if I would mind if
the blue lightbulb was removed
and the blackout blinds lifted.
Of course I didn't object.

What a sight met our eyes.
London was burning, or at
least a part of it was, and the
flames lit up everywhere and
the buildings stood out in the

glow. It was frightening. As we passed along the track I noticed a hut built of sleepers and wood, used by the railway workers (and remembered from my childhood), and which was blazing and even on the train we could feel the heat on the glass of the train windows.

We went through Vauxhall before the lightbulb was replaced and the blinds lowered. We did not speak about what we had seen until we had passed Clapham Junction.

I left the train at Hershem and walked down the steps into the darkness. A strange feeling of fear and realisation that there was worse to come came over me and I remember that as I looked back towards London I could still see a glow in the sky.

Helen Hall

When the war started in 1939, I was 13 years old and living in Bootle, Liverpool. Along with a lot of other children I was evacuated to Southport, but my stay was short. In those days we left school at 14 years old and so I was soon home again.

During the period, March to May 1941, the Bootle docks were set alight by incendiary bombs. That had the effect of creating fires which guided the bombers back to the port time and time again.

We had a particularly bad period early in May 1941, when the bombers dropped their loads on Liverpool on nine consecutive nights. It wasn't long before that started to get people down so that everyone had the same idea and that was to get out of Liverpool for just one night to get some sleep!

My uncle drove a furniture van so, as we felt the same as everyone else, I remember he filled it with mattresses, pillows and blankets and the whole family piled in and uncle drove us off to St Helens.

There weren't many people left in Liverpool that night. The funny thing was that when we got home again next day,

we heard that there hadn't been a raid! At this time my father was fire-watching at the Bootle Bakery near the docks where he worked as an electrical engineer.

One night the bakery garage was set alight by incendiary bombs and Dad braved the flames to drive most of the vans out of the garage but he didn't mention it to us at the time but we read about it in the *Echo*.

I used to stay with my grandmother and aunts and uncles quite a lot. Their house was situated right beside a railway track. One day when I was there my aunt and I were on our own when we heard some loud explosions and we cowered behind the sofa waiting for them to stop. Afterwards we found the blast had blown open the back door, which was locked. An ammunition train in the sidings had been hit by incendiary bombs and the brave railway workers had managed to release the wagons which had not caught fire, which helped a lot.

Each morning as I set off to work in a confectionery shop, I just didn't know what would greet me. On more than one occasion the shop window was shattered and one time I found machine-gun bullet holes in the wall! I had already at that time passed Walton Church, which was on fire.

My father had a lucky escape when a window in the house blew in on him while he was sitting at the table, and he climbed out of the pieces of glass and broken frame with just a small cut on his head.

What I remember most though is the way that the war brought out the best in people. The streets were pitch black and no lighting was allowed, only torches, and they had to be partly covered. My friends and I were not afraid to go out at night in the quiet periods. Everyone was so kind and helpful.

But we were after all in the 14-to-19-year-old age group when we were supposed to be enjoying life, so we made the most of it despite the limitations. Towards the end of the war I volunteered for the ATS and became part of the Royal Army Pay Corp. I was stationed in Yorkshire and then in Wiltshire and enjoyed it immensely.

Joan Wallace

I certainly have memories of the Blitz! From September 1940 to May 1941 there were not many nights when we were not bombed. I often used to wonder how the people went to work after such awful nights. You couldn't make a cup of tea because there was no electricity or gas, and you had to wash in cold water, that's if there was any. But they did go to work and I never heard anyone say that we wouldn't win the war, and our spirits would be lifted by listening to Winston Churchill even if the news was bad. We all felt that at least he told us the truth, and I remember being in London and seeing him clambering over rubble, and felt somehow that even though he was the Prime Minister he was one of us! I certainly feel more afraid for the world now than I did in the war!

Lord Haw-Haw (William Joyce) used to give regular broadcasts over German Radio. A lot of people used to listen to it because sometimes he would give the names and numbers of prisoners-of-war at the end of his programme. I remember one particular night we had all been through about ten hours of bombing and we were all worn out and desperately tired. It was a Sunday morning and Dad switched on the radio.

I remember Lord Haw-Haw saying, 'Good morning, have you all come out of your holes? Now you haven't any meat ration today.'

My mother heard him and she was furious and dashed to the kitchen returning with a piece of meat in an instant. I can see her now dangling it over the radio and shouting out, 'You are a bloody liar. We are going to have a lovely dinner today and tomorrow I'll make a pie with the bits that's over!'

To cap it all she then turned on Dad saying, 'I'll deal with you later for letting that man tell such lies.' Dad to my knowledge didn't listen to him again!

It was after the Blitz and I suppose it's not directly related to it, but it does show the sort of life that we had to live during the war. I had a friend who lived further up the hill in a bungalow with her little daughter of two and a half. Her husband was in the navy. It was 1944 and the flying bombs were beginning to fall.

On this lovely summer day I remember she stopped by my gate and said, 'My Jim's coming home on leave on Saturday.' Her little daughter Susan was dragging her golliwog. She walked on up the hill to her bungalow, and five minutes later a flying bomb dropped on her bungalow killing them both.

There are, however, some funny stories. Back to the Blitz again. My grandmother lived near the Elephant and Castle in a block of tenements. My parents lived near Hornchurch Aerodrome and on one Saturday night after a dreadful night of bombing my father and I went to look for Gran. There was nothing but rubble where she had lived. Her home had gone. We found her with a friend, but she refused to come home with us.

She was rehoused and again after a bad night of bombing we went to see if she was all right. This time the house was still standing, but there wasn't a window left. The building next door had gone, and yet Gran was clearing up soot in the living room.

'Look what that bugger Hitler has done,' she said. 'I only had this chimney swept last weekend.'

I can remember clearly saying to her, 'Oh Gran, if Hitler could see you now he would give up.'

She still refused to come back with us, saying that she had lived in London all her life, and '"he" isn't going to make me leave'. She was so typical of all Londoners who were so determined and resolute through what were terrible times.

Finally, as we lived near Hornchurch Aerodrome we used to hear the alarm go there before the general siren. I was visiting my parents and I remember Mother saying, 'In the shelter all of you, the alarm's gone on the aerodrome.'

My sister was in the bath, and we all hurried to the shelter except my sister. Everyone had forgotten all about her! Suddenly the general alarm went and almost immediately the bombs began to fall, and a very frightened wet sister almost fell into the shelter as naked as the day she was born!

Doris Gosden

I have spent the whole of my life in Fulham. In 1940 my son John was born and I was rushed to St Mary Abbots Hospital in an ambulance with a very young air-raid warden. Halfway there I was doubled up in pain and I was so afraid that my baby would be born there and then in the back of an ambulance in the middle of an air raid.

I remember still the cheeky young face leaning over me and saying, 'Cheer up, luv, I can cope.' I was shocked in my day. These things were so private. We arrived amid loud bombs, and my son was born, and after a rest I was pushed into what I first thought was a big empty ward. But then I heard noises all around and saw that all the women were on mattresses under the beds! At first I couldn't understand it and then I found that every time the sirens went we had to get under the bed leaving our babies each in a cradle fixed to the bed. Eventually when the nurse wasn't there we got to the stage where we all used to creep out and take our babies with us under the beds and on the mattress. Of course, when the nurses came back they were very angry!

I went home eight days afterwards but as we lived on the top floor of a block of properties I went to stay for a couple of days with my sister in Fulham Court. My younger sister and mother were on a visit when the sirens went, and it was very bad at first, but then there was a lull and my young sister and mum decided to go to my other sister's flat, leaving her with the children. We went to make a flask of tea, but my mother was very tired and so she laid on the couch and went to sleep.

All of a sudden there was a terrific bang. The whole building shook. My sister jumped on Mum to wake her, but as she did so she slipped and her elbow jabbed in Mum's eye! We rushed to the door and there was dust and smoke everywhere. I had an awful feeling that there was no balcony, but of course there was and so we made our way to the shelter, afraid, however, that even that might have been hit.

Suddenly we saw my sister screaming, 'My mum and sister are in there!' thinking that the property we were in had been hit. Of course she was wrong and was she glad to see her 'dead' mum and sister alive and well. The only thing that did come out of that raid was that Mum had a terrible black eye for weeks!

My husband was unfit for the army because he had a weak heart. Our house backed on to the Heckfield Police Station and we could see the siren. On one particular night we were so tired that we decided to stay in our own beds! We left the window open so that if the sirens went we could at least hear them. We were all so tired that we all slept in a deep sleep for 12 solid hours. I can tell you that my husband was really pleased to have got some good rest and I was as well.

Next morning we went downstairs to the toilet and the woman on the floor underneath said to me, 'Didn't you come in?' I told her we had not gone out to the shelter and what a grand night it was with no sirens and bombs for a change.

She stared at me as if I was mad and said it was the worst night she had ever had! The sirens apparently had been going off all night and bombs had been exploding everywhere and we had slept like babies right through the whole lot!

These were the funny sides of war, but there were sad times as well. One night sitting under Fulham Court in the air-raid shelter we heard what we called a string of bombs. An hour later a man came in and said a milk bar in Putney High Street had got a direct hit. The milk bar had been packed with young people and underneath was a dance hall also full of young people dancing. I can clearly remember that he was crying and said that there were arms and legs everywhere.

These are only a few of the stories and recollections I have, but there are many more, some of them funny. Such as the three months we spent in Yorkshire where a man I remember ran around the house where we stayed in Ingrow with other mothers and children screaming we were all German spies! Apparently he was very drunk and received three months in prison for his trouble!

Rose Gallagher

I still have in my possession a letter written by me at the age of 15 years to an aunt Annie living in Applecross, Ross-shire, three days after the Clydebank Blitz in March 1941. I was living in the west end of Glasgow at the time where many of the bombs were dropped, and this is what my letter says.

148 Beechwood Drive
Jordan Hill, Glasgow

Monday 16 March 1941

Dear Auntie

We are still alive, and I suppose you heard that last Thursday and Friday we experienced the full force of the Nazi planes. From nine o'clock on Thursday evening until quarter past six in the morning we heard the German planes continually flying over and over our house. We sat in the kitchen the whole time. There was terrible damage done across Crow Road in Abbey

Drive where a landmine dropped in the garden of a house. In Dudley Drive another mine was dropped on three tenements killing over 20 people and injuring many others. Our Boys Brigade staff sergeant was one of those killed. Another member of our BB company was trapped under the rubble and survived on a bag of sugar which landed on his lap before he was rescued three days later. His mother and sister were killed, and as his father died before he is the only one of the family left.

Dr Alex Gillies, right.

When we went down to see it that next morning we did not know that there were still people alive and dead in the rubble. If the Blitz had occurred the previous evening (Wednesday) we would have been coming past that area on our way home from the BB in Hyndland School about the time the first bomb was dropped.

The Nazis concentrated their attack on Dalmuir and Clydebank. What destruction. There is hardly a house standing and those that are still standing are being blasted down. The Yarrow shipyard was badly hit. Oil wells at Old Kilpatrick were set on fire and are still burning. We can see the smoke. We could see the terrible blaze on Thursday night when we looked out of the back door to have a peep during a lull. When Dad went into the dining room to see if Pete our budgie was all right he was astonished to find him flying down from the ceiling skirting on to his shoulder. The amazing thing is that he had been in his cage with his spring door shut, and also a cover over the cage. How on earth he got out of his cage we don't know, but he must have been terrified at the noise.

Over a hundred planes took part. The anti-aircraft fire on Friday night was very fierce and I believe a plane was hit. We collected a lot of shrapnel in our garden. It is pitiful to see the homeless coming up from Scotstown and Clydesbank in lorries with nothing left of their belongings but themselves.

A time bomb and a landmine were dropped in Crow Road. The landmine exploded killing some people including two in a car but we are still waiting for the bomb to go off. No trams or buses are going down Crow Road for the bomb is in the park alongside the road. A bomb fell on Crow Road and landed just beside a telephone kiosk and the handle of the telephone landed in a rugby pitch about a mile away. There was an awful smell in Crow Road near Anniesland Cross so a bomb must have hit a gas main.

We had three windows blown out and part of the front door, also part of the ceiling came down from the washhouse next to the kitchen.

We went to school today. Nearly all are present but some evacuated. A boy in Hector's class was killed.

Jordanhill and Hyndland are a sorry sight. Hundreds of windows were blown out. Everyone is boarding them up. We have a few daylight 'alerts' but nothing happens. A plane was shot down on Saturday afternoon.

We were more frightened on Friday night, after seeing the damage. Dad read Psalm 91 to us and it helped. I hadn't heard it before.

I am sure you are all thankful you are not here.

Love Alex.

Dr Alex K. Gillies

I lived with my parents and my brother was expected in 1940 so that my mother was under strain apart from the war. It was a council rented house which had a party entry with each door and this served as our air-raid shelter. It was supposed to serve the four houses but everyone in the street crammed themselves into 'our' entry as we had such fun in there every night.

As soon as the sirens sounded we would all crowd into this entry and the man from the fourth house always brought a crate of beer or some other drink in with him, and other people would bring food, rugs, hot water bottles, etc. We all sang the songs of the day which I loved, 'The White Cliffs of Dover', 'We'll Meet Again' and 'Run Rabbit Run'. It became so enjoyable that I really began to think that we all looked forward to these nightly meetings! My father was an air-raid warden and I remember that on one occasion we were all in the 'entry' and heard a very loud bang quite close which made one lady from a house across the street remark, 'My God that was close.' What a laugh everyone had when we found that we were in the middle of an air raid, and it was the front door banging after my father's return from duty.

Another funny episode was when my father had to go and fit people out with gas masks and he used to do this on a certain number of evenings. I remember that he came home one night and said he would need to go to one house again the following night even though he had spent all night at this particular house already. Apparently there were 14 children in it and it was taking all of his time to fit them out!

I used to have to take my gas mask to school every morning and when the siren sounded we all took to the shelters which were always full of water and very uncomfortable. On one occasion I was talking through the railings to my mother when suddenly everyone vanished and I was left alone. My mother said, 'You had better run to the shelter,' so I promptly did so, only to find I was in one with children and teachers I had never seen before. Also it was pitch dark and I slipped

*Marion Higgs
is far left.*

and went up to my waist in water and had to be stripped off in the teachers' common room!

There were many incidents during the whole of the war years, but the thing about it all was the 'oneness' that existed and the friendly feelings between everyone. I feel that although it was horrific mostly for the people serving and the killings, etc., it certainly was a more caring world and it is sad that war has to happen to create this atmosphere.

Marion Higgs

My experience is of the 'Big Blitz' on Sheffield and Rotherham. As you probably know, Sheffield and Rotherham are united by their suburbs as one big metropolis but there were greater links. The craftsmen of these two places were universally accepted as the best steelmakers in the world, known affectionately and locally as the 'Little Mesters' and what household in this country still hasn't got some Sheffield cutlery!

At that time one could travel for ten miles along the Rother Valley and on each side of the road there were continuous rolling mills, blast furnaces and coalmines. They were a great prize for the German bombers, because of the big blow that their destruction would cause to our war effort.

I was a young lad of 17 at the time, and an apprentice iron moulder at a large steelworks. My work was defined by the government as 'essential' and, consequently, I was deferred from any call-up for the Armed Forces.

On the night of the 'Big Blitz', my mate and I had arranged to go into town to a dance at the swimming baths. 'Modern' dancing was all the rage, and the smallest village hall to the largest town hall or swimming baths held dances six times a week. All the music was 'live' with from five to twenty-five musicians beating out the rhythm of the 'Big Band' era: Miller, Goodman, Dorsey, Basie, Ellington, etc. There was 'Jitterbug' and 'Jive' from 1/6d. to 2 shillings (7½p to 10p) and one could have a couple of pints of ale, a packet of fags, a big bag of fish and chips, bus fares to town and back, for no more than 50p!

During the dance the air-raid sirens were heard. Quickly that was followed by air-raid wardens entering the hall and asking us all to go to the nearest shelter. But knowing that all public transport would already be cancelled and used for emergency services, we decided instead to walk the three and a half miles home. That had steelworks and factories all the way.

As we stepped out in the street we were met by a strange quietness that was most eerie. Although we were in the centre of town it was pitch-blackness from the smallest house to the biggest building. There wasn't a chink of light any-where and all the steelworks had already put their 'safety nets' up, which involved drawing large sheets of steel along the roofs of the mills, so hiding the glow of the furnaces from the sky. Yes it was, I am proud to say, a complete and total blackout. So we cautiously made our way, picking a route through total darkness for the first half mile or so. But things were getting really bad. First of all we heard the dull thud of bombs dropping, and the black sky was continuously lit at intervals by the ack-ack fire and then the shrapnel and bomb splinters began raining down all round us, sounding almost like heavy hailstones on the tin and slate roofs. At that stage we decided enough was enough and dived in the first communal shelter!

These shelters were brick-built with an 8 foot concrete roof and were situated between 300 and 500 yards apart in all built-up areas and they could accommodate from 30 to 100 persons. As we entered the shelter we were met with an amazing sight. There were about 50 to 60 people inside, ranging from young babies to elderly persons, and each family had brought along blankets, rugs, mats, paraffin stoves and lamps, together with stools and chairs and food and drink. We found our own little area on the floor and were very soon comfortable and cosy.

A big old-fashioned tea urn was standing in one corner, and would you believe it, someone had brought in an old piano, which was obviously permanently stood there, and soon it was thumping out national and war songs, and everyone was having a real old sing-song. We were met at the entrance to the shelter by a lady holding pint mugs of hot cocoa and a pastie, and every person entering the shelter got the same treatment. I can still taste that lovely cocoa today!

We stayed about half an hour, joining in the singing, and chatting, and although gun and bomb fragments were constantly peppering the roof, the talk wasn't of the air raid or the war, but more serious things like Johnny grazing his knee at school, or Mary's doll had a broken head, because tomorrow would be another day but with the same problems.

The rest of the three-mile journey home was simply a question of running, weaving and diving into at least five more shelters. There we received the same warm welcome and food and drink, and eventually arrived home at 2.30 a.m., long after the 'all clear' had sounded and five and a half hours after leaving the dance!

I remember vividly laying in bed, trembling from head to foot. It wasn't from fear but from the sheer excitement. We were only young teenagers and all I could think of was the wonderful and exciting experience we had had.

I was brought sharply down to earth the following morning on reading the local newspaper. The steelworks had suffered very little damage but death and destruction in Sheffield itself was terrible to see, with thousands homeless and the remembrance of it affects me even now. My father always said that I grew into a man overnight.

We were excited, we were thrilled, and we were also a little foolish! But more than that when I remember the sight of Sheffield that morning and the thousands of homes that had been destroyed and the terrible problems that hundreds and hundreds of families were going to have to overcome, we were very very lucky.

Charles Green

Although I have lived in Yorkshire for 18 years, I was born in Portsmouth and lived there throughout the war years. I was married to a naval man who, like me and many others, endured years of air raids which took place along the southern coast of England. Some people escaped but others died. Time often softens our memories but we do not forget the horrors of it all. To my thinking, the sacrifices and suffering and courage of those who were killed or injured should never be forgotten.

The night of the Blitz I was alone with my small daughter as my husband was stationed further along the coast. During that day I had a chat with an elderly lady who lived across a narrow road from me. I remember that she asked me how I was coping and I said I was lonely as my daughter and I were alone throughout the many raids, and we felt particularly vulnerable, especially at night. I remember offering to take two of her grandchildren over to our shelter because she said that sometimes her son came up from the town with his children and her shelter became overcrowded. That chat was at seven in the evening and by ten o'clock that night they were all dead. I remember a baby of a year old being discovered with her dummy still in her mouth.

That particular raid was severe and, in fact, we didn't

know that it was much worse than that. I laid on the shelter floor and cuddled my daughter close to me and tried to shelter her with my body. I remember thinking that I was prepared to be blown to pieces to protect her. One bomb actually fell in the grounds of a hospital at the bottom of my garden, and when the 'all clear' sounded, a warden came to my garden and shouted out asking if anyone was there. I can remember that all I could answer over and over again was, 'I am scared, scared stiff.' I must have sounded like an idiot but my nerves were shattered and I can still suffer from panic attacks at the thought of all that.

My house was badly damaged. I sent a telegram to my husband and the navy granted him two weeks' leave. I suppose we were lucky that night in a way because the people in town suffered so much more. But we all got on with our lives. We must never as a nation forget what war means or all those brave people who died that we might be here. We rebuilt our lives. Now I am a widow still plodding on. I will never forget the Blitz on Portsmouth. It was all hell let loose.

Amy Hall

When the Blitz started in 1940 we were living in Hendon, Middlesex. I had just left school and was working in Tesco's, not the big store as it is today, but a small open front shop. At first the manager sent all the girls to the shelter when the siren sounded, but after a while it was decided we should stay in the shop as we were spending too much time in the shelter! We didn't have the same intensive bombing as

London or other big cities. But we did spend many hours in our Anderson shelter listening to the planes overhead and the mobile guns on the railway. But from November 1940 we could no longer use the shelter as I was very ill with rheumatic fever.

My father joined the ARP first as a part-time, then as a full-time warden. One night during the air raid he was on patrol around the streets when he heard a thud and was

Florence Wymer's father.

showered with earth. On looking over the hedge he found an unexploded bomb had dropped in the front garden, right next to him. He helped evacuate the occupants of the house and neighbouring houses. Later that night the bomb exploded.

The next morning when they went to check all was well before allowing the people home, to their surprise they found about six chickens still running around without a feather between them! The blast had blown every one off!

I can remember Dad coming home with a straight face asking Mum if she had some spare time to do some knitting. At first Mum said 'yes', thinking some poor family had been bombed out and lost their clothes. But when Dad told her it was woolly coats for the chickens she was not at all amused! However, later she did see the funny side of it.

I heard Dad tell this story many many times, in fact we call it 'Dad's chicken story'.

Another night my father was on duty alone at the warden's post when he thought he heard a knock at the door. As he opened the door a bomb exploded a few yards in front of him. There had been no warning at all. Apparently an enemy plane had slipped through our defences.

Dad was severely injured and very ill for several weeks. At this point my mother decided a visit from me would improve his condition. I could only walk a few steps, so Mum borrowed a wheelchair and pushed me to the hospital. Dad was so pleased to see me and from that day on he began to get better. The doctor said my visit did him more good than all their medicine and within a few weeks he was home, but it was a long long time before he was fit to go to work again.

On looking back I wonder how my mother coped, visiting Dad every day in hospital, two children at school and fostering a 'baby'. Rheumatic fever had left me too weak to be of much help to her. There were thousands of mothers like mine. I believe it was their courage and determination to carry on as usual 'come what may' that brought us through the dark days of the war.

Florence Wymer

I have so many memories of the Blitz. They say children soon forget but when you have lived through it I can tell you that you don't! One incident I remember clearly. The siren went and we all bundled into dressing gowns and went to the back door. We just started to run to the shelter in the back garden, when I remember my mother shouting out 'Stop!' As children, at that time, if your mother said stop, you stopped! You didn't ask why!

A few seconds later she said, 'Right, off you go,' and we scampered to the shelter like little rabbits into a burrow. I can remember that above my bunk bed in the shelter I had a Shirley Temple picture! After the raid we usually trooped back indoors to our own little beds but occasionally we had to stay in the shelter until morning. The ARP wardens used to come round checking each morning that the families were safe after a raid and on this particular occasion my mother took them out into the back garden where a hole had suddenly appeared! They dug carefully around it and suddenly unearthed a large piece of shrapnel just where I had been running to the shelter. Call it a mother's instinct but if I had not obeyed instantly when she

Mrs Harris's four-year-old brother, with the kitbag and wooden gun made by their father.

shouted 'Stop', I honestly believe that I would not be here now. She always maintained that she had heard nothing, she just reacted to a feeling. I can only say that I am glad she did!

A little while later the bombing became even more intense and my father, who was on leave from the army, insisted that my mother agreed to being evacuated with us children to Lincoln, where he was stationed. So for seven weeks we became evacuees, sharing a house with a London family of six, and later, would you believe it, another family was crammed in as well! But I can always remember as we left our home to start our journey to Lincoln, my brother turning round and waving his hands and saying, 'Goodbye little house.' My mother said that that almost changed her mind but Dad insisted we had to go to Lincoln to be safe and that our house would be safe and sound still when we returned.

The communal shelters, which housed probably 20 to 30 families or more, were made like long underground tunnels. They were quite simple in design with double bunks down one side and long bench seats down the other, with the centre aisle free. The shelters were sectioned off every so often so that families had a little privacy, but for the most part they were open plan, to allow movement of air. I remember that in our shelter there were several air ducts, and there were wide steps down to the doors from the ground level, and then a 90-degree turn to enter the underground chamber. Those not near enough to get a communal underground shelter all had their own Anderson shelter in the back garden.

These Anderson shelters had a small ladder to get down into the entrance and then straight into the shelter itself. They had sufficient room for bunk beds and a third bed on either side. We had a little oil lamp in ours that our mother lit every night, regardless of whether we went down or not. Consequently the shelter was always warm and lit if we had to go down there. There were biscuits, tea, milk and sugar put there as a routine every evening, together with a tiny calor gas stove with a camping bottle, small saucepan, and some tins of soup. We children found it fun as we were so young and didn't realise the seriousness of it all. To us it was camping out with our teddies and dolls and our mother's undivided attention, especially if it was a long raid, as my mother could weave stories about anything!

The shelter protruded about three foot above the ground and it was turfed over, and it made a wonderful hill on which to catch grasshoppers and ants.

When the war ended these same Anderson shelters were removed if you didn't want to keep them. Some people kept them, above ground, as bicycle or tool sheds, but most people thankfully saw them unbolted in sections and removed by workmen onto trucks.

There was another kind of shelter for nursing mothers. That consisted of a full sheet of steel plating for a top and a bottom, with three sides of fine steel mesh. It was as large as a double bed and about three foot high, and when my little sister was born, we were issued with one for two weeks. Every night we were crammed into it. How horrible for my mother! Thankfully that was

removed after the two weeks and we all returned to our 'dugout'.

When my father was issued with replacement trousers, his old ones soon became a perfect replica in miniature for my four-year-old brother, including a small kitbag with a number painted on it, and Dad made him a small, wooden gun and taught him to march, salute and present arms. For a little chap he was good!

He became an officer in the RAF and taught flying of RAF jets, so he certainly kept up the 'Forces' tradition.

Patricia Harris

My memory of the Blitz is of sitting under the balcony of my favourite cinema, the famous Commodore in Hammersmith. The film showing was called *The Last Train to Munich* and indeed it was a night never to be forgotten.

The air-raid alert was flashed on the screen, telling everyone to take shelter in the street air-raid shelter or at the rear of the huge cinema but I decided to stay put. But I know now that had I gone out and made my way home I would certainly have been killed.

Suddenly the lights went out as the cinema shook and the balcony seemed to be falling down. People screamed, others, including myself, rushed out into the vestibule, only to be stopped by the uniformed attendants. I could feel my heart throbbing with fear and excitement but despite that I sat down with the others in the seats. I distinctly remember a lone lady walking out on to the stage as we sat there and in the silence I could feel the tears coming to my eyes as, to calm us down, she began to sing 'Land of Hope and Glory'.

Of course, the film was cancelled and so I eventually made my way home. In doing that I fell into a large hole in the street and got out wringing wet. I could see bodies laying still on the pavements, with policemen bending over them. I remember arriving home, trembling all over.

A stick of bombs dropped that night and a block of flats near to us was sliced in two. I don't know how many were killed that night or injured but it must have been hundreds.

Tommy Morgan

I was in London from September 1939 to July 1941, which was the period of the Blitz on London. The first bomb I heard was on a Saturday afternoon and on that occasion we just got under the stairs, as my father thought it was the best place. But when the raids got very bad, my mother and I went to a private shelter. It was long and narrow and just wide enough to walk through and have a bunk on either side.

You had to walk down some steps so it must have been nine feet or more under the flowerbeds. One night I remember they seemed to be dropping bombs in lines. The first line seemed to be in the High Street then the second line in the back gardens and then one bomb dropped so near to the shelter door that five people were killed. There was a husband and wife and two girls, and another man just a few feet from my bunk. The only way we got out was through the emergency door. My poor father, who was only by the bottom of the stairs, was embracing an elderly lady, thinking it was my mother! Mother and I had dark hair but when we looked at each other we were white from the dust of the bricks. If you could not go back to your home you were then taken to a school or a hall for the rest of the night.

Next morning we both went to the local swimming baths. I think we were the only customers! Sixpence first class. Lovely hot water! I did ask Mother what she would do if the sirens went.

'Stay in the bath!' she said.

When we got home most of the windows were out. The clothes that were hanging near the door were full of holes. So we took up the lino from the floor to cover the windows and so complied with the blackout requirements. We went to the Salvation Army Hall. There they were very kind to people who had lost all their clothes and home. I can remember it took an awful long time to boil water for a cup of tea because the gas pressure was low from all the burst mains.

My father worked at Hay's Wharf at London Bridge, so the usual procedure was that after I got in from work and had some tea, Mother and I would catch a bus to London Bridge, which was about half an hour's ride. It was always nice to get over the Thames before the siren went.

One night when bombs were dropping, I remember that one landed on top of the railway arch by the station. It was full of people and they were all killed. The arches were not really shelters. They were only brick arches and really couldn't provide protection.

I remember that we were sitting on our beds one night when we heard bricks breaking and rubble falling and thought 'this is it', but we were lucky. The bomb landed so close that my ears were damaged by the blast, so that for many years they were always wet and running and I had to permanently have a bag of cotton wool with me.

Mother and I would get the first No. 35 bus from London Bridge in the morning, back home, to get some breakfast. I remember one time we stopped at Liverpool Street Station and saw people who had been sleeping in the Underground all night coming up. They had been sleeping in the only clothes that they had, or struggling out with bags and blankets and baskets. Obviously they had been bombed out of their homes.

One night it looked as if all London was alight. There were no buses and you just walked home and the roads were full of hosepipes and buildings still smoking, and some were just rubble.

Eventually I moved to Herne Bay but we had to write to the police to explain why we were coming to live here and to get an authority to move. So I was here when they bombed Canterbury on a Saturday afternoon. My husband and I were out for a walk when the siren went, and looking across the fields to Canterbury we could see the planes almost 'hopping' over the city. Large shops were busy and full of people doing their Saturday afternoon shopping, and many died during that daylight raid in the afternoon.

Throughout the war I did war work – working on the pier making camouflage nets. It was very hard on the hands. It was very cold in the winter being close to the sea, but it was lovely in the summer! All of the time there were troops here, until one weekend in June 1944, when the town suddenly emptied. D-Day had arrived. What a blessing.

But I must conclude by thanking the WVS ladies who did a super lunch (costing 9d, 4p in new money) all the time we were working. That included a cup of tea, and we did work I can tell you. No days off!

Irene Hawkins

I was in the army in 1940 and evacuated from Dunkirk. On my return to England I was posted to Hull Prison, which the war department had taken over. It was in Hedon Road, right alongside the docks. My wife and children joined me there and took up residence about 200 yards away.

At least every week, and very often every night of the week, there were air raids, and my wife and children always went to bed in the air-raid shelter. There was a great deal of damage during the raids, as you can imagine, and I actually saw a house in the next street after a bomb had exploded at the side and literally cut the house in half. In the half that was left standing, I saw the body of a girl who had been

killed simply by the blast of the explosion.

By May 1941, the German air raids on the docks were intensifying and, as usual, when that happened, very often bombs were falling short and were landing on houses. Eventually the army evacuated many of the civil population who lived close to the docks area and, in fact, I was evacuated with my army unit to a park outside the town and my wife and children evacuated to a farm in Fridaythorpe on the North Yorkshire Wolds. It took me a week to find out where they had gone. Later my family visited Liverpool to see our parents but they were caught in the air raids on Liverpool Docks, and spent more time in the Anderson Shelter than visiting my parents! My father-in-law was killed in a direct bomb hit, where in the region of 100 people were killed in the shelter.

My most vivid memory is of 9 May 1941, when our house and the immediate area was surrounded by fire as incendiary bombs fell. They set fire to a timberyard next door and a nearby garage was also set on fire. I remember a bulk petrol tanker exploding and a car that had been parked near the garage was actually blown onto our roof with the force of that explosion. I remember that we were surrounded by fire and I can remember the heat and the fear as if it was yesterday. Fortunately we were able to find a way through on to the main road but I will never, as long as I live, forget that inferno.

Bert Gregory

When the Second World War broke out I was 21 years old and working as a junior contracts clerk in the Ministry of Supply in Westminster. Nothing very much happened that first year, the year when someone coined the phrase 'The Bore War'. Then came Dunkirk and then soon after that the real bombing began. I look back now and wonder how any of us survived, either physically, mentally, or spiritually.

To begin with it was very frightening. In fact it was always very frightening but as time went by it became a way of life. There was nowhere to run and no alternative, so gradually we began to adapt. I was living in Streatham and as the bombing raids increased it began to take longer and longer to get to work.

Transport became very difficult. Buses were constantly being diverted to avoid badly damaged areas and bomb craters. Getting home was equally difficult. There would be long queues of passengers waiting to get home before the air raids began. But people were wonderful at offering lifts. One would be offered lifts in all kinds of vehicles! I went home in a hearse once and certainly very often in lorries and, in fact, anything from a Rolls-Royce to a dustcart! Anything on wheels was welcome. The great thing and in fact the most important thing was to simply get home.

Then it would be a quick meal, change into a siren suit, and off to the shelter because as sure as God made little apples, the sirens would begin to wail as the evening closed in.

I sheltered with about 40 other people in a cellar underneath a row of shops in Streatham High Street. It was reinforced with steel girders and I suppose was as safe as could be expected. Obviously we all got to know each other quite well in time and soon we organised a fire-watching system. We took it in turns to stand by the stirrup pump at the top of the shelter to deal with any incendiary bombs that landed nearby, each of us spending an hour in turn. I learned to knit in that air-raid shelter. I read *Gone With The Wind* for the first time and, would you believe it, even got a proposal of marriage! When the 'all clear' sounded, usually at about 6 a.m., we would be off to our homes to get ready for another day's work.

One morning on my way to work the bus that I was travelling on was held up in Kennington. There had been a very heavy raid the night before and a high-explosive bomb had scored a direct hit on an air-raid shelter that held 250 people. I was sitting on top of the bus and though the canvas screens were up I got a view of the horror that had occurred. Ambulances and covered lorries were lined up and the dead and dying were still being removed.

The huge block of flats opposite, where most of the people in the shelter had come from, had also been hit. A huge slice had been removed from the entire block and it was extraordinary to see what looked like the inside of a gigantic full-scale doll's house.

That same morning, as I reached Westminster and was about to pass the houses of Parliament on my way to Tothill Street, I suddenly heard a bomb screaming down. I stood there petrified. I was literally rooted to the spot. It must have been only for a few seconds but it seemed like an eternity. Then someone hurled me to the ground and flung himself over me. There was a tremendous crash and then I sat up very shakily and watched the Paymaster's Office opposite going up in a cloud of lath and plaster.

I remember that amazingly there was a feeling of euphoria as I got up and dashed across the road and, in fact, almost under the wheels of a lorry! The lorry was a mere detail compared to the closeness of that bomb!

'Missed me!' I yelled to some unknown German pilot. In fact, he hadn't quite missed me. My left eardrum was damaged by the blast but an ear here and there is a minor detail when there is a war on!

In the meantime my mother, Sarah, was going crazy with worry and kept urging me to come home to Bristol where I belonged. I resisted her pleas for a long time as I didn't want to go back to boring old Bristol! Although London was a

dangerous place to be in, it was also very very exciting. If you were young and reasonably good-looking then the sky was the limit!

But the pressure was on. Sarah was determined that I should leave, so finally I applied for a transfer to the Timber Control in Bristol. The day that I left there was a hell of a raid at Paddington and as I waited in the Bakerloo Line for the 'all clear', I thought 'Well it won't be this bad in Bristol.'

And for a whole week it was absolutely peaceful. So much so that my sister and I went to a Sunday night concert at the Colston Hall. That also turned out to be the night that Bristol got the really heavy raid that destroyed the whole of the centre of Bristol for ever.

But that's another story!

Paula Knight

I have been living in Ramsbottom, Lancashire, for 20 years now but I am Welsh, being born in Neath, and living in Cardiff for most of my life.

During the war I was living at home in Birchgrove, Cardiff. They had built a Royal Ordnance factory about ten minutes' walk from where we lived and I was lucky enough to get a job there instead of going into the Forces. The factory was not far from Caerphilly Mountain where there was an anti-aircraft gun site and searchlights. We used to work there for two weeks on days and then two weeks on nights.

I can't remember the exact date but we were on night work when the sirens sounded and we didn't go to the air-raid shelter unless there was imminent danger. On this particular night the German planes were just passing over but the searchlights were on and the guns were firing.

I had just turned from my machine and I remembered no more until I started to regain consciousness. I was lying face down on the floor in dirt and rubble and all I can remember plainly saying is, 'I mustn't die, I mustn't die.'

Nancy, who had been stood with me by my machine, was lying dead beside me. Luckily the lights were out as there were about 12 other people killed and many horribly wounded. They told me later that the whole section of the factory was a dreadful sight.

I was very lucky. I did have several bits of shrapnel down my right side and still have stitch marks on my right arm and leg.

The really awful sad thing about this is that apparently it was a shell from one of our own guns that had failed to explode in the air and had come down and hit a girder in the factory roof, right over the section where I was working. I can remember it all quite clearly but I am not sure of the dates.

But how quickly it all happened and how terrible the results, even though with all the wounds that I suffered I can regard myself as being one of the lucky ones. At least I survived it, not like those poor souls who I was working with but who died in an instant.

Joyce Robson

During the Blitz, my family, which was my parents and four children, lived over a shop opposite the docks in Hedon Road, Hull. During the months we used various types of shelter during the raids, going when the siren sounded with our blanket bundles and gas masks and sandwiches, etc. The first shelter was some distance away and it was a brick-built structure, one of many. However, when one of those received a direct hit and all its occupants were killed, we stopped going there. It was all very illogical. I suppose the same thing would have happened whatever form of shelter received a direct hit, but somehow we didn't think they were that safe now!

So we decided to start taking refuge in the cellar. That was below the three-storey building in which we were the sole occupants at night. The thought of being under all the rubble that the building might be reduced to was no deterrent to our staying there!

As time went on we didn't always get up during an air raid. My mother sometimes took precautions. The four of us laughed one evening when she pushed a chest of drawers to the side of the double bed where my two brothers were.

'What good can that do? It's on the wrong side away from the window.' She may have mentioned something about 'the blast', I am not certain now. I only know that when we heard a landmine explode a block away, and much structural damage was done to our home, my brothers bumped their heads as they tried to get up! A huge window frame had been blown out and was across their bed resting on the chest of drawers. Isn't it funny – my mother had put it in the wrong place but as it happened they would almost certainly have been killed by that heavy window frame if it hadn't been where she put it.

So we were 'bombed out', as it was called. We spent a few days in a local church hall which was ready prepared with beds for the homeless. Then we were fortunate enough in being provided with a 'furnished house' by the council until my parents were able to find rented accommodation. That accommodation had an Anderson shelter at the bottom of the garden.

One morning my mother went to the local shop, leaving my young brother in bed. When she returned she was stopped by a policeman who said, 'You can't go along there, madam, the whole area is cordoned off.' Apparently there was an unexploded bomb in the immediate area! I remember that she told me she shouted 'But my little boy is in bed!' and physically forced her way through the crowd to get to him, which thankfully she did.

As a child of 11 in 1941, I cannot remember being afraid, even when a piece of shrapnel dropped and sparked in front of me! I accepted the sirens and the searchlights and the droning planes and the anti-aircraft gunfire just as almost a normal part of life. What I do remember particularly, however, is the tiredness of having to get up and the knowledge when going to bed that the rest would probably be very brief! I marvel now, however, at the courage of my parents, who faced the real possibility of death and destruction at any moment, not only for themselves but for their four children and everything that they loved.

I should add that I was quite happy when the sirens sounded when I was at school! Lessons were usually suspended and we were hustled into the brick air-raid shelters. Here we would have informal entertainment and as I saw myself as a 'budding authoress', I took great pleasure in reading my stories to what after all is the author's dream – a captive audience!

Rose Robinson

I was about 10 or 11 at the time of the Blitz. I remember that it was close to Christmas and for a few nights the German bombers had been very active bombing Sheffield, a city 20 miles to the west of the village where I lived. That village was Woodlands near Doncaster.

The particular night that I remember was starlit with no moon. Earlier that evening my friends and I had been listening to the engines of the German bombers as they passed over the village on their way to Sheffield.

When we went to bed on this December night, the raid seemed to be over. But around 1 a.m. the air-raid siren sounded with that wail that we had all come to know and hate. When it sounded, my mother came into the bedroom where my older brother and I slept. He was home on leave from the army, and wild horses would not have dragged him out of bed! My mother had already left my father in bed because he also would not get out! He had not long since finished his shift at the local colliery.

I was taken out of bed and shepherded to the air-raid shelter, which was in the school playground just across the street. It is still there – underground. My mother was terrified and thought that every bomb was aimed at her personally, hence our rapid exit from the house and an even faster entry to the shelter. In retrospect it was a very sensible thing to do!

We found ourselves in the shelter with other people of the same mind, sat on uncomfortable wooden benches in a cold damp tunnel, the only light coming from hurricane lamps suspended from the roof of the tunnel.

Up until this point with me it was always a game. The conversation between the adults around me was over my head really and I was left with my own thoughts. Sitting next to me was a young lady of about 18 years who hadn't said much to anyone the whole time, but who seemed a bit edgy.

Nobody had been paying much attention to the outside world. I suppose people were doing their best to try and forget what was happening. It was then that I heard a faint whistling sound. It gradually increased in volume and then became a shrieking that got louder and louder. As the noise increased I didn't need to be told what was causing it. It was the sound of a falling bomb.

At this time I was also aware of another sound, this time coming from the throat of the young lady sitting next to me. She had her hands clamped tight over her ears and was screaming her head off, terrified out of her wits. Her fear was rapidly transmitted to me and suddenly in that brief moment came the realisation that this war business was not a game. I was badly frightened.

The bomb exploded close to some houses about half a mile away as we later found out. The girl was comforted by her parents and eventually was calmed down. After the raid was over we returned to our home in the early hours. Would you believe it, my father and brother were both still in bed fast asleep! I went back to bed but as you might imagine sleep was a little bit difficult to come by.

The next day my friends and I went to where the bomb had dropped, searching for shrapnel. The bomb had exploded at the side of a main road, leaving a huge crater, but no major damage to people or property.

It was thought that the bombers had been aiming at the colliery. If so, they hadn't been far out because the nearest bomb of the three that had been dropped landed in a lime pit about 150 yards from the colliery shaft, covering all the trees and hedges with wet, sticky lime. My bomb, the only one I had heard falling, came within half a mile of the shaft.

Later on in the war we had a few more air raids but none scared me so much as that first raid and it remains firmly in my memory. There were other incidents but they are not so clear in my memory. I remember a parachute mine fell on houses in Royston Avenue, which is at Bentley, about three miles north-east of Doncaster, and about three miles as the crow flies from where I lived as a boy. This bomb destroyed several houses in the street and I believe a number of people were killed. This happened on a Saturday night around 7 p.m.

I remember that only my brother and myself were in the house at the time. Even from that distance the blast from the bomb shook the house and rattled the windows, but it was the noise of the explosion that was the most terrifying. I remember it scared me witless. To me it was just as if the bomb had gone off next door.

I also remember my mother's cousin, whose name was Madge Cadman, being killed by the bomb as she waited at a bus stop. The bomb dropped on the opposite side of the road to the Sun Inn public house on the Old North Road, three miles north of Doncaster.

A bomb also fell on a garage opposite the Grand Theatre in Doncaster. The blast from this bomb blew a friend of mine, Alan Thompson, through a shop window. This same person had friends who spotted a parachute coming down. Thinking it was a German airman they ran towards the parachute. It turned out to be a parachute mine which exploded and killed three of Alan's friends. They were Alf Norberry and his brother, and a lad called Guy Elves. They would be about 17 or 18 years old at the time.

I remember that a stick of bombs were dropped near to my house. There were seven bombs in total and the last one of the stick fell about 60 or 70 yards from the nearest house and blew out the windows of a house not 30 yards from where I now live.

After writing this article I had a conversation with a Mrs Thompson, who was married five days after the dropping of the bomb that I have written about when I was in the shelter. She told me that it fell not on Royston Avenue but in an alleyway that runs along the bottom of Royston Avenue and other avenues parallel to it. Fourteen people were killed and there is a memorial erected to them in the local cemetery at Arksey.

Mrs Thompson was 24 years old at the time and remembers the event vividly. She remembers that the blast from the bomb blew the roof off 62 Royston Avenue and there was soot shaken from the chimney of her mother's house that covered her wedding cake which was in the house and still had to be iced! She says that she remembers her mother dusting the cake off, with the remark, 'What the eye doesn't see the heart won't grieve over.'

Mrs Thompson also remembers a family who had taken to the air-raid shelter. It was a couple and their daughter and they were buried under the debris of a collapsed house but were rescued unhurt.

Finally, to confirm that when troubles come they really do come, Mrs Thompson also remembers that people who had been bombed out were rehoused in a street called Yarborough Terrace. These people who had already lost their homes were promptly flooded out when the River Don burst its banks a few days later.

Yes, life was really hard at that time.

J. Morrell

I was a child at the time of the Blitz, and my daily life was full of fear. The dreaded air-raid siren then the drone of bombers overhead. We lived in the south-east of London in Erith, North Kent, right in the thick of it all. My maternal grandparents, Gran and Grandad Clark, lived nearby in Belvedere, and their house actually fronted on to the railway line which carried supplies in London to the port. The house is still there today.

My grandparents were indomitable. They refused to take shelter. Six times all their windows were blown out. Grandad used to be outside, sweeping up all the glass, but stubbornly refusing to admit that 'old Hitler', as he called him, had got one over on him! 'I'd sooner say I'd done it myself,' he would say.

Time and time again the Germans tried to score a direct hit on that vital railway line but they never did. Grandad used to laugh. 'Rotten shots those Jerries, you know, they can't hit anything for toffee!' he'd say.

But one bomb did eventually land virtually on their doorstep, right in the front garden, missing the railway line by only a few yards. Grandad went out and looked up at the sky.

'Bad shot, old chap,' was all he said.

The damage was so extensive you could see through the party wall into the house next door. Even the foundations moved. In fact, the whole side of the house had to be demolished. The rescue workers rigged up a huge tarpaulin from the roof. My grandmother surveyed the debris and then said she had best get on with her work!

When my aunts and uncles went to help them, they found her as always, sitting on her couch, busily rug-making, with a little electric fire balanced incongruously on the rubble! She was a gifted craftswoman, forever crocheting and lace-making, dressing dolls and knitting cobwebby fine shawls. I remember that she was even making baby bootees in the final weeks of her life when she was 85 years old! The year of the bomb she was making lovely rugs and her attitude was that neither Hitler nor the Luftwaffe were going to stop her! The air raids were ceaseless. Once they had some visitors who, when the raid started, dived under the table during one loud explosion, only to emerge at the 'all clear' to find Gran and Grandad still calmly sitting there. Grandad always used to say that he was proud of Gran!

Originally we had an air-raid shelter in the garden but I don't remember it. The one I knew and hated so much was a big ugly Morrison shelter erected in our front room. It was made of corrugated iron and I remember being ill and having to go down there from our warm bed, all cold and sleepy and frightened. Later on in the war when the doodle-bugs came over, we would hear them droning overhead, and then they would cut out and there was a terrible, terrifying silence before they exploded as they landed. I used to watch my mother's face – always calm and reassuring. She never panicked. Only years later did I discover that she had been badly burned and injured in an explosion in which many were killed when she was a munitions worker at Kings Norton during the First World War. Her nerves were totally destroyed and any sudden noise would shatter her. Yet such was her courage that she bore all the terrors of the Blitz with unflinching bravery in front of us children.

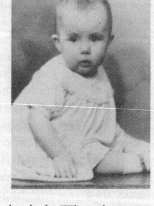

One night we were all in the shelter and my sister and I were crying because our cat was out in the dark! When there was a lull in the bombing, Mother went to the front door, calling into the pitch dark, 'Puss, puss, puss.' She hurried back with a frightened cat, very relieved to be safely inside. The problem was that when she got inside she found the cat wasn't ours! I think all the terrified cats in the area came to our front door that night – then the next wave of bombers came over and the cat had to fend for itself!

I don't know how old I was at the time they bombed the docks but I recall one night standing at our front door and all the sky glowing crimson to the west over the riverside. It was like daylight.

The sirens would wail out any time of day or night. Much as I loved *Dad's Army*, I still feel a lurch of fear as the air-raid siren wails. For many years after the war I instinctively shivered at even the sound of civil aircraft, thinking we were to be bombed again.

I was the youngest of a family of seven children, six of whom lived. Another sister, ten years older than me, rushed in one day, saying that if the Germans invaded us, her friend's mother was going to be in their street with a carving knife at the ready to greet them. What would we do?

My mother quietly replied that we would get on with our

lives as best we could and do what we have to do. What else can ordinary people do but survive with dignity as best they can?

Yet there was hope. Somehow our mother showed us there was another way. At Christmas, all through the war, there were always presents. I don't know how she did it – books, precious books. How we used to love it when she got down the little folding tree and pulled out the branches. There were some silver bells and green and red chenille swags to decorate the room. Her compassion knew no nationality. Once two fighters managed to separate a stray German plane from the rest and chased him over the houses. All the neighbours were in their gardens, cheering as they drove him towards the heathland to gun him down. I remember that she wept for those young German men and my father angrily told her to go indoors.

Every year I rage at the Remembrance Day Service when the words of Binyon's poem are read out: 'They shall grow not old as we that are left grow old.' They wanted to grow old, they didn't want to die, drowning in mud. Military history fascinates me. The more I read the less sense it makes. My paternal grandmother used to say that she would sooner see either of her sons dead than in uniform. I do not know any answers. It seems to me that nothing ever changes except the technology with which men kill each other. Maybe it all taught me an invaluable lesson early on in my life – that there is no such thing as security. My own philosophy can be summed up by the words of a poem I once read.

> *Out of the pit that covers me*
> *Black as the night from pole to pole*
> *I thank whatever gods may be*
> *For my unconquerable soul.*

(From 'Invictus', William Ernest Henley)

I always think that the reactions of the ordinary people summarised in the stories they have written, particularly about my grandparents' indomitable courage, conveys an enormous amount of information about the hidden qualities of the British character. As Hitler is supposed to have said: 'The problem with the English is that they are beaten but they won't acknowledge it.' I have worked with overseas countries for most of my career and I perceive that there is an elusive quality in the English character that still mystifies them.

Rosalie O'Hanlon

I have many vivid memories of wartime happenings and still vivid is the night our home in Sheffield was bombed on 12 December 1940, in a full night's Blitz when all the world seemed to be on fire and bombs came down for many hours. 'Like shelling peas,' as my father said.

Mother, sister, grandmother, live-in maid and I were rushed into the cellar by my father. Part of it had been reinforced and water and light had been laid on together with some seats. Then he dashed back up the steps to fetch some earplugs out of a sideboard drawer in our hall. At the same time we heard the whistle of a bomb and in that instant our home was no more.

Dad was blown back into the cellar and all of a sudden the water and lighting was gone but we were lucky and we survived because we happened to be in the safest place. Two yards away a big panshion, which is an Ali Baba-type stone jar, was shattered by the blast. It was full of eggs in isinglass and every egg was smashed.

We stayed in the cellar. There was no alternative, yet at about 11.30 p.m. another bomb seemed to fall in the same crater, so it was hardly surprising when they told us later it was the biggest one in Sheffield. It was 30 yards wide and 30 feet deep, taking over the whole of our front garden and part of the road.

We sat there all night in the dark with the front and side of our home gone and even the stone cellar steps all higgledy-piggledy. At around midnight we suddenly heard a voice through the grating above our heads, shouting, 'Is anyone alive down there?'

It was the air-raid warden on his round. Tragically, only a stone's throw away, his house received a direct hit and his wife and daughter were both killed.

My father was convinced that the remnants of our house would fall at any time. So at about four in the morning, during a lull in the bombing, we made our way down the back garden to the Anderson shelter but we left Grandmother behind because she thought she might as well die where she was as in the cold and damp of an Anderson shelter, and she steadfastly refused to move!

I shall never forget the sight that greeted us. The whole sky was red with fire so that it seemed that even the moon was on fire and the lawn was littered with debris from our ruined home. The 'all clear' went at about 5 a.m., and soon after one of our neighbours sent a message for us to go across for a cup of tea.

We spent the next few days salvaging what we could and, of course, had to split up until we were able to get another home together. Three days later I set off to work at Sheffield Electricity Department and the ruins all along the Moor, which was the main shopping area, were still smoking with hosepipes and water and debris all over the main roads. There were just no buses or trams at all.

There were some horrific stories told about that December

night. One about a big pub in Fitzalan Square that was set on fire. Everyone had gone into the cellar and the beer literally boiled and there was no way out.

Having hit the shops and suburbs that night, the raiders were back on the Sunday night to bomb the works in the East End. By that time my sister and I were staying with an aunt at Meadowhead, only about a mile from the ack-ack which had been brought in and my aunt had me going round the house, turning pictures to the wall and lifting mirrors down!

When I got back to work I was really touched. The girls gave me a pair of Lisle stockings, a scarf and a pair of navy knitted gloves to make me feel a bit better! There was so much bravery, hardship and suffering during those six years. Yes, we had our comical moments but they were comical moments in a really hard time.

We had just put up our Christmas tree on 12 December. Next day it and the house had gone. That was a strange Christmas but at least we were lucky to be alive!

Mary Dimond

Yes, I remember the Blitz, as having knowledge of babies my mother and I took hundreds of bombed-out babies from ten days old to four years old. We travelled the length and breadth of Britain and Wales, sometimes doing 90 hours a week. This was in the then WVS involving nurses and the Ministry of Health. Lots of experiences and scares.

We travelled in the blackout on trains with no lights in them. One scare was a journey down south. We were sitting in a train at Waterloo when a bomb dropped during a raid and it seemed for a second as if the train had been lifted off the line. Of course, eventually we got out, but I remember that when that happened my mother and I covered the babies with our bodies to protect them.

Our home had 74 panes of glass blasted out and doors blown open. But we got brushes and brooms out to sweep

away everything so that life could continue. Tar felting was used to replace the glass, but when we complained that as a result we couldn't see, the problem was solved for us. That night it was all blown out again! So then we had a kind of white material put up.

I did refreshments in a park shelter while the poor souls who had been bombed out sat on benches against the wall. I lived in Maida Vale, London, where I was born.

There is just one particularly sad story about a baby we took away. He was about 18 months old although we didn't know his precise age. He had been in hospital some months. He was scarred all over and was found under the rubble some days after his home had been destroyed. He was the only survivor of his family.

We took the babies from all over London. They were taken to three nurseries in London to be medically examined, and there they were given wherever possible new clothes from America or Australia.

I have to say that everything was well arranged. Although we were working 90 hours a week we loved our work. We used to take very little notice of the babies when we picked them up, but before long they dearly loved you! Although that was a very terrible time I can still remember all the love that we got from those babies.

Dorothy V. Curtis

My earliest recollection of the Blitz is as a toddler going shopping with my mother and youngest sister still in her pushchair and I can remember the excitement, mingled with fear, when the dreadful wailing mournful sound of the sirens filled the air. Lots of shouting and crying and urgency all around as we had to make for the nearest underground shelters which were dotted at regular intervals where there was sufficient grass, and always within minutes the streets were empty. Each shelter held about 40 people and we would all be led into singing to take our minds off things and so we didn't hear the planes overhead and the bombs that were falling.

While at school there were four shelters situated underground beside the huge oak trees on our playing field. If the sirens went our headmaster would ring two hand bells continuously up and down the corridors and the whole school would march *very* quickly and orderly, with books and gas masks, to the shelters, praying we would get there in time. We weren't allowed to run, scream or panic. It was all very matter of fact and necessary to avoid hysteria when dealing with young children.

One such occasion caused some consternation amongst us children when, on entering the first shelter, we found a 'real live tramp' who had spent the night there! Funnily enough that induced more fear and curiosity than any of the Jerry planes! It was a fairly affluent area and it was a rare thing indeed to see a vagrant. The teacher turned him out and he was very scruffy with a bushy beard and he very sheepishly sloped off, with a bent back, and looking at us as if we were aliens. No doubt we had disturbed his sleep!

Gas masks were always a daily occurrence. We thought it was quite fun actually and the younger children's Mickey Mouse masks would bring hoots of laughter, especially from amongst the boys.

Another time my twin brother and I were halfway to school. Luckily our house was five minutes' walk away when suddenly the sirens went. We ran like the devil, when suddenly my brother stopped and stared and choked and vomited. He had swallowed a boiled sweet that had been stuck in his throat! They were on ration then and Mother gave us one sweet each a day before we set off to school.

The dilemma I remember feeling was 'What should I do?' Run back home. Stop and try to thump the sweet up as he couldn't breathe. Would he die? Will we get killed if we stay in the open and deal with it? Actually, the reality was that while all this was going on in my mind we kept running and we kept saying, 'We must get on and get in the school shelter where the teacher is.' My poor brother barely made it and was sick several times in the shelter! The teacher gave him something to drink to help wash it down and he eventually recovered as it slowly melted. Even today I feel claustrophobic in a dark enclosed space, unless I can see or know of an exit beforehand. I used to try to be last in the shelters because then I'd be near the entrance door where a bulb was! We had to go to the far end first and on entering you couldn't even see the children who had already gone in because it was so black and only as wide as a bus, with long slatted bench seats each side and a central aisle. I was scared that a bomb, or blast, or debris would block the exit and I would be trapped down the far end in the dark with no escape.

At home life went on much the same. We got used to having our meals in the lounge on the big, metal cage which was the Morrison shelter, which had a thick steel top. At night we all slept under it. Mother put quilts on the floor and we laid on those covered with blankets. The Anderson shelter had to be outdoors. We slept in our own beds unless an attack was imminent. We would be carried in blankets by Mum and Dad in the middle of the night to the outside shelter if a raid took place. There were two bunks each side, one on top of the other, and I think my sister, the youngest, was slung in a hammock, but five of us somehow fitted in it. We were too young to know what the war was really all about. We grew up with it and therefore accepted it. That is, that it was part of life and the 'norm', although we did appreciate with very real understanding that bombs fall and kill and houses get blown up.

Bedtimes were a ritual of putting up the black sheeting at the windows or black roller blinds behind the curtains. Many a night I lay listening to the noises of the battles in the air and what I do remember is always being scared. As the Blitz progressed I continually marvelled, even as a child, that we were still alive, and whenever I heard a plane dive I thought, 'Poor devil, he's going to die but I hope it's not one of ours.'

I think when you live with possible death every day, you grow up valuing life very highly. We were certainly not deprived in any way. Our education continued regardless. Food was rationed fairly and with true British grit we all endeavoured to live our lives as normally as possible. Everyone but everyone cooperated regarding blackout laws and curfews and whatever. If we hadn't imposed that discipline on ourselves then, one thing I am certain of is that we would all have suffered a lot more.

Heather O'Neill

I was 23 when the war started and we had moved in May 1939 to a new flat. This was in the East End of London and part of Dockland. Of course, we had a lot of bombing being near the docks, but the worst time for us I shall never forget was 17 October 1940.

Our neighbours and friends and ourselves were all in the shelters, as we were every night because of all the bombing, but I remember that particular night at five minutes to eight we heard and felt a loud *whoosh*. Water started to come in and everyone tried to get out but my sister and I had our elderly mum to look after, but we got out and we were told, 'Don't look back.'

However, nosey me did look back and saw that all the flats opposite ours were gone. Getting Mum through the streets was a nightmare because she was crippled with arthritis. We eventually got to a Billiard Hall and they told us to 'get under the tables'. It was pitch black and, of course, there were no lights and so I felt with my foot until I found an empty space. We got in it and felt safe. In the morning we found we had spent the night under a trestle table!

Well, my sister was bombed out the following month and in the December we managed to find a big house to take all of us. Five people had been killed in that raid which had destroyed those flats, including my brother-in-law.

Later in the war my husband was sent abroad. I was expecting our first child and she was born in April 1943. We then had to suffer doodlebugs all day and all night and I seemed to spend all my life bent double from holding my baby close to me and trying to shield her from harm.

Margaret Murray

Lodged in my now middle-aged memory I have pictures and sounds of the wartime bombing by the German Luftwaffe. A child then, aged seven or eight years, I became accustomed to the mournful wail of the air-raid sirens churning out their 'warning' day and night. Heavy with lament and foreboding, their chilling tones were a constant interruption to our lives.

Apart from a short period when we were reluctantly evacuated to the Midlands, my mother and my younger sister and I lived in the outskirts of London for a large part of the war. There we occupied a small terraced house in dilapidated condition, along one of the many streets built for factory workers at the turn of the century.

When the bombing began I must admit that I found it quite exciting. I used to watch fascinated as the brilliant searchlights swept the dark skies, scanning for enemy bombers. Only once did I see the broad beams of light illuminate a German aircraft. First one searchlight held the silvery shape, then other beams caught it in a criss-cross of brilliance. Anti-aircraft guns began a barrage and shellbursts spattered the sky all around the plane. Like the gunners I was hoping for a hit, but the aircraft droned steadily on, intent on its deadly business.

My mother regarded the raids as 'wicked and terrible'. If she was frightened she hid the fact well. As children, my sister, Janet, and I accepted the wailing of the sirens as part of life. We were not scared by the air raids, simply because we did not understand the dangers that threatened. For adults, of course, those times were fraught with the imminence of death and destruction.

During air raids Mum would hurry us down our uneven path and settle us as quickly as possible in the relative safety of our Anderson shelter. This was a corrugated metal structure sunk deep in the earth, its rounded shape covered with soil. Once inside we would scramble on to the bunk beds and pull the makeshift wooden door across the entrance. By the light of a battery torch or a night-light (a short candle set upon a saucer) we would make ourselves as comfortable as possible. Like primitive cave dwellers we would huddle in the cramped space and pass the time talking and playing and indeed sometimes quarrelling until the sweeter and happier tones of the 'all clear' siren signalled our release into the wider world of house and garden.

Sometimes our freedom would be curtailed rapidly by yet another 'warning' and then we would be bundled, protesting, back into the dank atmosphere of the shelter. In the dim light we would either look at picture books or comics or talk or squabble. Sometimes, tired of inactivity, we simply played boisterously, disturbing flakes of rust above our heads so that they showered down on us and made our scalps itch.

In quieter moments I used to arrange a few of my lead soldiers on a metal ledge where they would fight imaginary battles. Occasionally a live spider would join the proceedings to be instantly 'fought' and killed mercilessly. My little sister, Janet, lived in perennial fear of creepy-crawlies!

Often we would hear the 'crump' of anti-aircraft fire as the gunners tried desperately, but usually unsuccessfully, to bring down the enemy bombers. Whenever the guns began firing, our cat, Blackie, would race in from the garden and somehow squeeze himself into the shelter with us. Once inside he would disappear into the deepest part of the shelter and we would have difficulty in finding him again!

The duration of the raids varied. Sometimes the 'all clear' would sound after about five minutes. At other times we could be down the shelter for hours. Mum tried to keep certain necessities stocked in the shelter such as biscuits and milk. I suppose like all children we tested our mother's patience at times, especially by protesting our need to either a hot drink or a visit to the lavatory! We had to learn to be patient, but I recall that Mum would occasionally make a brave if somewhat foolhardy dash into the house to fetch a coat or blanket or something that we felt we needed to remain comfortable or fed.

As the air raids became more frequent, with more and more interruptions to our lives, we spent more and more time in the Anderson shelter. At first we used to sleep in the house, only to be awakened in the middle of the night to put on our coats over our nightclothes and stumble sleepily down the garden path in the dark and cold. I must have been still asleep as I was dragged downstairs. I awoke halfway down the garden, the gravel hurting the soles of my bare feet. My slippers had remained in the bedroom during that air raid and I eventually fell asleep in the mustiness of the shelter, quite oblivious to everything!

Tired of the continual to-ing and fro-ing, we eventually decided to settle ourselves in the Anderson shelter every night whether there was an air raid or not. Usually there was one! We would carry our heavy stone hot water bottles, freshly filled, together with other necessities for a night's stay in the shelter. A round enamel chamber pot was, I remember, the most essential item!

On Sundays Mum would cook lunch, or dinner as we called it in those days, in the house. Then she would shepherd us with our dinners down into the shelter. There at least we could eat our Sunday dinner without being interrupted

Note the bombed-out house in the background.

by the wail of the siren. If an air raid started then we were at least able to eat on without undue interruption. We were still using that same shelter when the flying bombs arrived. These flying bombs with their throaty engines and their black shape ugly against the sky were a sinister threat to the people of South-East England. When a flying bomb reached the end of its range, the engine would suddenly cut out and with the sound of rushing air or a whistling noise the unmanned aircraft would plummet to earth, exploding tremendously somewhere beneath.

One summer evening I was in the shelter with my mother and my young sister. We heard the rumbling engine noise and I knew it was the sound of an approaching doodlebug. The noise grew louder and louder and my mother became agitated. When the noise of the growling engine sounded as though it was over our heads, there was suddenly a deathly silence as the motor cut out. Mother cried 'Oh my God!' and pushed my sister and me down on to our bunk. She then swiftly pressed pillows over our heads and covered us with her body, using herself as a shield.

Despite having the pillow over my head I heard clearly the terrifying 'whoosh' of air as the bomb descended. My heart was in my mouth. I felt sure, even at that young age, that the end had come. There was then an almighty explosion which shook the rust down from the shelter roof. There followed a short silence, during which I realised we were still alive. Then came furious 'plopping' sounds, which must have been falling debris. Once over the initial shock, Mum raised herself from our bodies and cautiously pushed open the wooden door of the shelter. She climbed up and stood just outside the door, telling us firmly to stay where we were. Filled with curiosity I pushed towards the doorway, looking out past my mother's legs. Astoundingly the clear evening air was now a foggy night. A huge cloud of dust and smoke hung like a blanket in the sky. I could no longer see our house, only a barrier of grey dust. Within a couple of minutes the dust began to clear and then I saw that our house was still intact but an upstairs window I noticed had a curtain flapping through a hole where the glass had been. There was a distinct smell of something burned or scorched.

As Mum stood outside the shelter there was suddenly a single 'plop' sound. She stopped and picked up something from the ground and then dropped it immediately with a shout.

A few minutes later, having turned the object over with her foot, she again attempted to pick it up. This thing that had fallen from the sky, narrowly missing her left shoulder, was a piece of jagged twisted metal. I remember the expression on her face as she held it out for me to touch. She looked amazed. 'That just missed my head – feel it, it's still hot.'

Gingerly I felt the chunk of metal and it was indeed still quite warm. Had she been standing a foot or so to the left ... In that instant I realised the implications of her shocked expression.

By now there were noises in the evening air. The rapid clamour of a bell, probably an ambulance, overlaid the general hubbub. Out in the street at the front of the house people were running round and shouting. Someone was blowing a whistle with long shrill blasts. Realising that our house had not been hit, we hurried through to the front door and anxiously peered out into the street. A man on a bicycle pedalled past, shouting and waving one arm above his head. He was an air-raid warden in uniform and steel helmet. People from all along the street were emerging from their front doors and craning their necks to see to the end of the road. Down at the bottom end of the road there hung a thick pall of smoke. Voices chattered noisily and a few men ran towards the smoke, eventually disappearing from our view. Now that I was no longer in a state of fear I stared in fascination at the turmoil, taking in the scene with its confusion of sights and sounds and smells. I was shocked but curiously excited. Just then a figure emerged from the smoke and strode purposely towards us down the centre of the road. His thick mop of grey hair framed a rugged face of a man of about 50 years. I remember distinctly the streaks of blood which were still running down the side of his face. He was shouting for people to go back, telling them not to go down to the scene of the bomb. The police had arrived by now and there was a call for calm.

We were then told to return to our shelters as it was quite likely that there would be more doodlebugs on the way. The 'all clear' had not yet sounded. At that stage I suddenly became frightened again at the prospect of yet another flying bomb. My mind just could not accept the possibility. But somehow my sister and I slept that night. Before we succumbed to tiredness we lay and listened to the sounds of the street. The cars rumbling by and voices calling out hoarsely. We fell asleep, not knowing the whole story.

Whether it was the following day or a day later I am not sure but my next vivid memory is of setting eyes on the large crater made by the flying bomb. By a stroke of good fortune it had apparently nose-dived into some allotments at the end of our street. But nevertheless the blast from the explosion wrecked the houses on both sides of the street, with the sad result that one little girl, aged about ten, was killed by falling masonry. Although I only remember her vaguely, she had attended the same school as me. Her face had been familiar to me in the playground although I never knew her well. Briefly, a short time after the bomb, I remember seeing her mother gazing forlornly at the remains of her house. I looked at the woman's back as she stood motionless for several minutes. Strangely, the thing that sticks in my mind is her short hair and her bowed shoulders. I think her daughter's name was Christine.

Peering through the allotment railings near the crater I could see no signs of wreckage. All of the flying bomb must have exploded into fragments which had been hurled skywards. I stood and thought of the flying pieces and especially the jagged chunk which had almost killed my mum. To my young eyes the saddest sight at that moment was the scattering of dead sparrows which lay on the pavements beneath the splintered branches of the nearby trees. Their tiny bodies lay pitifully around. The air was still and no birds sang.

I moved away from the scene, past the remains of buildings which had once been people's homes. I returned to our house, feeling somehow sadder and older. Although I was not aware of it at the time, there would be more air raids to come and more bombs. More children and more little birds would die somewhere before the war ended. When that day came, with the end of the war with Germany, it left us with our bomb damage and our grief. Today's casual observer will find new houses standing on the old bombsites of the 1940s. There the scars of aerial warfare are barely visible but in the memories of many the devastation will always remain.

Keith V. Perryman

My memory of the Blitz is of a warm sunny morning. I was just nine years old with a younger brother and sister. Normally we would have been playing nearby that day but as my mother often remarked later, 'It was a miracle that we were all in the garden together and that it was the school's summer holidays.' Earlier I had been to a lady's house in the next road to see if I could take her baby out but she told me that they were going out. My brother and sister had changed their minds about going to the park on their skates.

Mother had just cleaned all the windows and was cooking some mincemeat for our dinner. My father was at the local hospital, having a check on his finger. He had had an accident at work when he had lost part of it. It was twelve o'clock lunchtime when the siren sounded. As it sounded we three children ran down the garden and jumped into the shelter and by the time we did it, I remember that bombs were falling already. I remember that Mum turned off the gas and the water and ran down the path and as she did so a blast from a bomb actually blew her into the shelter. The noise was terrific and in the middle of it the shelter door came open. My brother had been playing with the lock the previous day.

Dirt and dust came blowing in on top of us. I remember my mother was holding the door with one hand and trying to comfort us with her other arm around us. There was a sort of 'singing' noise in the shelter and I remember that part of the shelter had been lifted out of the ground. It all happened very quickly but my strongest memory is of being very frightened. The 'all clear' sounded and we came out. What a terrible sight we saw. There was shrapnel lying all around which was still hot when we tried to pick it up. There were firebomb craters at the bottom of the garden and in the school field at the back of the garden there were 27 craters. The school had been set alight by incendiary bombs.

At the bottom of the road was an army camp and I remember how quickly the soldiers came to see if we were safe. Our house didn't have any windows left and all the ceilings were down. There wasn't a place in the house where we would have been safe had we stayed indoors. The lock on the back door had been blown by the bomb blast through the kitchen, into the hall and in some upward swirling movement upstairs and was lying on my bed! Even my doll had shrapnel lying on her where she lay in the cupboard.

I remember saying, 'You wouldn't think they would want to hurt a poor little doll.' I can remember the lady next door saying, 'Oh my poor house.'

My mother replied, 'I don't care about my house, just as long as my family are all right.'

When we looked at our

dresser in the kitchen, the cups were all broken with just the handles on the hooks. I remember everything so vividly. The front door was propped up in the hall, where it had been blown completely off. The 'bus stop' sign was lying on the front lawn.

The first dead person I had ever seen was an old man across the road. He had been coming home from his allotment and had a barrowful of flowers. My brother ran down the alley and nearly trod on a dead woman. There was shrapnel and bullets all the length of the alley and our two cousins, who we had been playing with the previous day, were both killed. One was 12 and the other, who was just 18 months old, was killed in my aunty's arms. My aunty had her arm blown off. A few doors away another little friend had her arm blown off.

Another little friend was killed, with his mother, sheltering under a table. In the next road a family of six were all killed. There was a direct hit on their shelter. There had been 29 people killed and 27 injured and the casualties would have been far more if it hadn't been the school summer holidays.

I must admit, as children, things were very exciting. We ran to the shop across the road and because the front had been blown in, we were all helping ourselves to the jars of sweets. One boy had a card of combs and was distributing them to us! The authorities came soon afterwards to board the shop up. At the time we didn't seem to realise that it was wrong.

The road was in a terrible state. You had to climb over debris to get anywhere.

My mother told us to stand at the top of the steps and wait for Dad so he could see us from the top of the road when he returned from the hospital. I remember he told us that as he neared home he heard a woman say to another, 'Here comes Mr Harrison now.' The sight that confronted him was like nothing he had ever seen. I remember him telling me that the first thought he had had was that we were all dead.

He and all the neighbours boarded up the houses as best they could with sacking and bits of carpet and wood. For several days there was an endless stream of people passing through our street. They came to gaze at the terrible damage. No one had ever seen anything like it before. I am glad I was only a child. We were just excited about it all, but it must have been terrible for the adults.

After the trauma of the day my father went to see his boss at the paper factory where he worked. He told me that we were unable to sleep in our house due to the extensive damage. I remember that my dad found room for us in a tunnel under a chalkpit but my only memory of having to move there was that it was so clean and nice! The inside was whitewashed. Everyone had bunks with their own bedding and also there was at least some privacy for each family. There was a canteen at one end and families had 'get-togethers' at the end of the evenings. I remember my father remarking how lucky we were to get in there as there was only a limited amount of room!

Dad later went into the army and I remember that terrible time when we received a letter from the War Office saying that our darling dad was missing. Mum went to pieces. She never washed herself or combed her hair. I remember thinking that she looked like a witch. It lasted a fortnight and then she had a letter from Dad, before she heard from the War Ministry. He had been taken prisoner and she was transformed immediately. I remember as a child thinking how wonderful it was!

We used to sit in the shelter with cushions on our heads and we would hold our ears when the raids were bad. Strange to think that if your head is covered and your eyes are closed you will somehow be safe. Such innocence.

I remember a German plane being shot down near us. My brother got on his bike and got to the scene before the authorities. He came back and said he had seen the pilot buried head down to his shoulders in the ground. His hand was completely off. He came home very excited, telling us how he had nearly brought the hand home because it had a nice ring on it. It sounds terrible now, but we were children at the time. Being children and not understanding these bizarre events in a way was a godsend. These distressing happenings, in some ways, were like a game of 'pretend'.

Another funny story. Some friends who lived in London had a father who often refused to go to the shelter but one night there was an extra-bad raid and he decided to go to the shelter. As he sat on the edge of the bed, a very private part of him got caught in the spring so that as he went to get up the spring closed together! Needless to say he didn't go to the shelter! He was a cockney and they said that his language on its own was enough to send all the German bombers home!

My father was a prisoner-of-war for four and a half years until he escaped a few months before the war finished. Sadly, my darling father died in July 1989, aged eighty-five and a half years. He died so peacefully while eating his breakfast. He deserved to die that way after all that he had been through.

Beryl Petersen

I was living in the Hockley district of Birmingham on the night of the big Blitz. I was sitting waiting for the 'all clear' when the front door bell rang and on the steps stood a policeman.

'All out, madam,' he barked. 'As quickly as possible!'

Before I could question further he had gone. I retreated in panic. I had one sick husband on my hands and a child of three years old and I was doing the best I could when the bell rang again.

'Madam, why are you still here?'

I explained the circumstances and also that the car was at the back of the house.

'Give me the keys and be ready in five minutes,' he ordered.

So in our dressing gowns, with the sleeping child warmly wrapped up, we were waiting when the car arrived. I had presumed that I would be driving and the police helped my husband into the back, with our daughter also there, still asleep. Certainly I was allowed to enter the driving seat, but as I approached it the officer called me back and in sotto voce said, 'There is a landmine in the house next to yours. I want you to get into the car but do not turn on the engine!'

He pointed. 'There are crowds of people in that shelter and their lives are in your hands. Any vibration and that mine could go off.' I asked him what he wanted me to do. 'My officers will give you a push and tell you when it is safe to start her up.'

So with one man on each running board I taxied slowly and silently down the hill. At the given word I started the engine and we were away, to my mother's house in Handsworth. Twice on the way we were stopped by the police and diverted because of landmines.

Later, the mine in Lodge Road, Hockley, was detonated and the landlord of the Conservative Club, for that is where it had fallen, gave me a piece of the parachute and a yard of the cord. But the heroes of that shocking night were the police.

There are some other stories that I remember from the Blitz.

My brother, with his wife and child, were sitting in the Anderson shelter, waiting for the 'all clear' and when it went my brother decided to take a look round as, during the raid, he had heard a definite thud on the top of the shelter. When he went looking he found an arm lying on the top of the shelter.

He rang the police and they told him to wrap it in paper and take it to the station because they told him that as far as they were concerned, 'it was nothing new'. I know that he was always haunted by that picture in his mind of the arm as he wrapped it in the newspaper.

My husband, being a doctor, had an evening surgery that he held in Key Hill, Hockley. He had given up driving the car, so when surgery was over, he would ring and I would call to collect him. That night the call came early and knowing that on such a bright night the enemy would certainly be soon over England, I was particularly glad.

It was while my husband was having a bath that the sirens sounded. Soon it was followed by the heavy guns doing their best and explosions everywhere. The Germans target was, of course, the centre of Birmingham, but on the way over they did quite a bit of damage elsewhere in the process. One of the casualties was my husband's surgery which had a direct hit and I remember thanking God that he was in the bath and not in the debris.

Writing about my husband, I remember that one of his patients died and the funeral was all arranged. That very night a house in the Hockley area received a direct hit and not only the corpse but all the guests were blown sky high.

Another story about the blackout. I remember I was sitting alone, immersed in a thrilling detective story. From the sound of the guns there was quite some activity going on and I had just arrived at the point in the book where the stalwart bobby stands on the doorstep, when the bell rang and there he was, tall, young, handsome and officious.

'Good heavens,' I cried, 'are you real or in my book?'

I wasn't sure whether I had got mixed up between fact and fiction!

'I'm real all right,' he said, with not a glimmer of a smile. 'If you don't do something about your light you'll be booked.'

'What light?' I asked, puzzled.

'Come over the road with me and you will soon see.'

I was in my dressing gown but nevertheless I followed him and then I saw that a bedroom light had been left on and through the smallest chink imaginable, a tiny streak of light could be seen!

I promised to pull the curtain that extra half-inch but I couldn't help wondering what fabulous eyesight the pilots were supposed to have to be able to see that! Still, rules were rules, and we abided by them for the safety of us all.

Florence B. Gaston

Stourbridge where I live is a small town 12 miles from the 'Second City' of Birmingham. When war broke out and now knowing what was in store for us, my father cleaned out our cellar, whitewashed it and shored it up. My mother and I, being nervous types, slept down there.

It was horrible. It smelled damp and musky and as we lived next door to a corn shop we regularly saw mice running across the beams!

Every morning I caught the 8 a.m. train to Birmingham where I worked. Leaving Stourbridge behind, everything standing as it was the day before, to arrive in Birmingham was a shattering experience. There was often a sign saying 'diversion – unexploded bomb'. And we would start the detour. There would be baths hanging out of windows perilously balanced, ready to drop into the street. The sound of piles of glass being swept up from broken windows. The acrid smell of burning wood.

I always reached my office and found it safe. At one o'clock lunchtime I would go to the library to change a book, just as if times were normal, and find a poster pinned to the door giving the names of those who had been killed in the air raid. Yet finding the inside of the library carrying on just as if nothing had taken place.

At six o'clock, going home time, I always had to run like mad to catch my train. I carried a big sheet of white paper across my chest so that any on-coming people in the black-out would see me. On boarding the train it was so very dimly lit that many times I accidentally sat on someone's lap! Oh the relief to get back to Stourbridge before the sirens wailed, especially if it was a 'bombers moon'.

Olga Male

We had an Anderson shelter installed in our back garden and my father, being an electrician, had made it reasonably comfortable with heat and light and fitted bunks, leaving a space for a carry cot beneath the bunk on one side.

We prepared food and hot drinks and large containers of food to take with us and after my son was born we used to put him to bed in his carry cot so he was ready to be transported quickly to the shelter without disturbing him too much. I remember a night when we all huddled over the cot with the kitchen ceiling falling down on our shoulders as we hadn't got out of the house quickly enough. Then we made a dash, one by one, to reach the shelter.

Bristol's first air-raid warning siren was sounded at just past midnight on 25 June 1940. Between then and 25 September 1940, there were 150 warning sirens, but the 151st siren heralded the daylight attacks on Bristol Aeroplane Works at Filton. I was in the Bristol Maternity Hospital at Southwell Street, Bristol, following the birth of my son on 15 September. Most nights were disturbed and the patients were taken in the lifts on camp stretchers to the basement, until the 'all clear' signals.

The Bristol Maternity Hospital was on high ground, overlooking the city. At 11.30 a.m. on 25 September, there was a commotion and the nurses were rushing around checking and climbing up into the window recesses with binoculars, giving us a running commentary on the planes crossing from Knowle across the centre of the city to Filton on the outskirts. During the early evening of that same day, 25 September, a patient was brought into our ward in a very distressed state. Her husband had worked at the aeroplane works and was one of the missing workers. I understand that 168 bombs were dropped on the British Aeroplane Works in 45 terrifying seconds, causing a very high death toll and much havoc. The staff were all wonderful to this lady and enquiries were going on all through the night. There were about six of us in the ward and I am afraid that nobody had any sleep that night. We were alternately sympathising and crying with her.

Then in the early hours the matron herself, Miss Nora Deane, came into the ward with the news that the patient's husband had been traced to another hospital and he was not too seriously hurt. She had a taxi waiting, with a nurse escort, to take the lady to see her husband and to put her mind at rest. That was a wonderful moment for us all to share, even though it was a rather damp one. She returned in about an hour and her own baby was born later that day. I cannot remember her name or whether she had a boy or a girl but the circumstances are as vivid to me today as if it was yesterday. We were all as thrilled as she was and I often think of her although she is unknown to me personally.

In November 1940, one Sunday night, we had a very heavy air raid on the main shopping area of Bristol, covering mainly Wine Street, Castle Street, Old Market and its surrounds. The large departmental stores of Jones & Baker, Bakers in Wine Street, were flattened. The Regent Cinema and the News Theatre in Castle Street were all destroyed. Had this been a Saturday the roads around here would have been crowded with people. On Good Friday, 1941, after a heavy raid, we walked to the end of the road and saw our local church, St Francis in Ashton Gate, ablaze

Mrs Poore and David.

from end to end and we could also see the timberyards of Taylor & Low and May & Hassell and several others on Cumberland Road, all alight.

My memories go on beyond the Blitz. My husband was called up and so my mother and father and son, David, had the opportunity to stay on a farm about ten miles out of Bristol. My husband was sent overseas to India and on to Burma and he was there until he returned in November 1945.

From the farm we could see the air raids over Bath. We were only one mile from Lulsgate and one Saturday afternoon I was walking with my son in his pram and we saw several aircraft approaching very very low and obviously in trouble. Then we saw several of the crews eject and parachutes floating down. Looking back on this it was a wonderful sight to see the airmen floating down in brilliant sunshine but as this was during the period that we had been warned to look out for parachutist landings, we didn't appreciate the effect! My first thought was whether I could reach the farm with the baby before the airmen, as one was only 50 yards away in the adjoining field. Unfortunately they had all bailed out much too low and most of them were killed on impact, but my father helped the nearest one into the farm. He had a broken leg. Several of the planes managed to get to Lulsgate on one engine. The planes were returning from a raid on Lorient. David was 14 months old then and was more than five years old and at school by the time my husband returned. This was a very traumatic period as my mother and myself had worked very hard to keep his dad's memory alive to him. He had his own photograph and a book of 'Daddy's Boy', which was read to him every night. We made such a good job of this that at one period when he was ill and delirious, all he called for was 'his daddy' and not us!

My husband was, at this time, still in Burma and I remember the day after Victory in Europe Day, I was in a local shop and everyone was in high spirits. Someone then reminded everybody that the war with Japan was still going on but they laughingly said that that didn't concern them as it was too far away. Naturally I was very upset and when the shop lady explained that my husband was out there still fighting, they were all very quiet.

Sue Poore

We lived just ten miles from Manchester on the flight path of the German bombers who regularly gave Manchester a battering. As soon as the sirens went Mum got myself and my brother up and took us down into the cellar. We were aged 10 and 13 at the time. I distinctly remember that this was the only time that Mum was religious! She would suddenly be transformed into a cross between a missionary and a mum, insisting that we all sang hymns while she repeated the 23rd Psalm!

It didn't take Dad long to get fed up with this and go up into the yard, watching the searchlights criss-crossing the sky and watching the glow of the fires in the distance in Manchester. He told us that one night while he was doing this, he saw the elderly lady next door tiptoeing across the yard and when he asked her what was the matter, she said

Mrs Rennison, centre, with her parents and baby sister.

that she didn't want the bombers to see or hear her! Of course there was no bathroom inside in those days – just an outside loo!

I don't know which was more alarming as a child. The thud of the distant bombs and the anti-aircraft guns thumping away quite close to us – or Mum's nightly salvation performance! However, after a few months we got to the stage where we just ignored the air-raid warnings and stayed in bed! Thankfully we all did survive.

Mavis Rennison

I lived with my parents on a smallholding called 'Bushey Fields' in Bushey Field Road, Herne, near Herne Bay, Kent. On this particular Saturday afternoon my mother and I had been shopping in Herne Bay and got off the No. 6 Canterbury bus at the top of Herne Common Hill and walked along Curtis Road. As we approached the T junction with Bushey Fields Road, intending to turn right, I saw two very low-flying aircraft a short distance ahead, flying from right to left of us. Suddenly the planes made a sharp left-hand turn and flew along Bushey Fields Road, almost at treetop level.

Realising the danger, my mother pushed me into a roadside ditch and followed me, complete with shopping bags! I remember hearing the swish of bullets through the cornfield on our right, and the roar of engines only a few feet overhead, and the aircraft shadows darkening our hiding place for a split second, and then the silence, except for my mother saying that she was worried about a bottle of vinegar which may have got broken when thrown into the ditch! I was later told that vinegar was very scarce during the war.

As my mother lifted me back on to the road I heard my father shouting from the direction of our bungalow. He knew that we were due off the Canterbury bus about that time and guessed what had hap-pened. I remember that my father ran to find us, keeping close to the hedge. I can remember seeing the effects of the burst of fire, which appeared to have been aimed deliberately at us. In fact, all I saw then was the bungalow with some of its windows and doors and roof, with all the tiles, destroyed.

Although I do not personally remember the consequences of this, I was later told by my parents that the two aircraft were FW190s and they were part of a raiding force that had carried out a bombing raid on Canterbury that afternoon. When the aircraft flew to the other end of the road, where it joins the Canterbury road near the Fox & Hounds, both of them then attacked the bus that we had just left, and also a passing bus, the No. 6 to Herne Bay. At least two people on the buses were killed and some injured when, as a result of the attack, one of the buses crashed into the woods, so as you can see my mother and I were lucky twice that day.

Robert Port

One night during an air raid I was with my family sitting in the air-raid shelter outside in the garden. I was aged ten years and at that time and at that age we didn't realise the seriousness of things. Even though the bombs were still falling I remember someone rushing into the shelter and shouting out, 'I think the school is on fire.'

Nobody could stop us. We were out and away non-stop a hundred yards to the top of the hill even though the raid was continuing. We could see the school and it was certainly on fire. In fact we watched it and saw the roof fall in. By God it was great! The Germans had done us a great favour. No school next day. Nor for the next six months. Believe me it was heaven!

But there was another side to things. I remember two school chums of mine found a live shell. So they decided to hit it with a stone and see if it would fire. It did! It slightly wounded one in the shoulder and grazed the other on the head. They were certainly very lucky!

Finally, I have always been a collector of film stars' photographs and autographs and I used to write off to the film stars for them.

One day the postman brought in a large box. It was from America and I was puzzled. To my astonishment when we opened it, it was a food parcel and it was from Groucho Marx. It was well received! There were tins of beef and everything we didn't have and needed! I was very grateful and I have never forgotten that incident. It was so very kind.

Eric Cameron

A t the beginning of the war I joined the Royal Marines and served until March 1946, but of all the action I saw the most traumatic was the Blitz. I was 20 years old in July 1940 when I was posted from Lympstone in Devon to the Admiralty in Whitehall.

My job was to guard the Admiralty and to take my turn on an ack-ack gun on the roof of the building. The episode that I cannot forget took place around seven o'clock one night. I had been across to the crypt of St Martin-in-the-Fields where servicemen could buy some sausages and fried bread.

The sirens went and the searchlights lit up and the guns started firing and so I rushed back to my post. It was only a matter of 200 yards but suddenly as I was running a bomb dropped very close to me. I was physically blown to the ground by the blast and I can distinctly remember still being dazed when I got up. I started to run back to my post but then I remember seeing a girl who was fairly near to me and she was still lying on the ground in a twisted position. Her eyes were open and I didn't know at that time that she was dead. I carried her to a first aid post, although bombs were still falling

everywhere and it was only when I got her there that I was told that she was already dead. I can distinctly remember that she would be about 18 years old. She was a bonnie lass, and although I had never met her in my life before I cried myself when they told me. I never forgot this girl. I had only ever seen one dead person before and that was when my dad died when I was ten. But somehow this all seemed far far worse. A few minutes earlier she had been alive and young and everything before her. Now she was dead.

We later heard that a film star called Movita had been killed that night in an air raid and I often wondered later if it was her but it didn't matter. The loss was just as great whoever it was.

Later the raids got heavier. People were having to sleep in the Underground railway platforms and the streets at night were deserted. The sirens seemed to go off promptly at six o'clock every night, and the 'all clear' seemed to be equally prompt at six o'clock the next morning. But the amazing thing was that I never saw any panic. People seemed to help each other and although, of course, hundreds of shops were bombed and their windows blown in, I never saw or heard of any looting. We were on duty all night and next morning we had to help to search ruins with the Civil Defence, for people who were often buried in their homes. After a while the effort of that all-night duty and then physical work the next day took its toll on many of us.

All the people in the Armed Forces and, in fact, all the civilians and the Londoners were magnificent. Night after night in their own job and in their own way they fought against tremendous odds. I have actually seen bombs falling, that's how close the enemy was. I lost one of my hometown mates in October 1940. He was a fighter pilot and the same age as me. But, in particular, I must remember to commend a group of men who were very often forgotten. That was the men and indeed the women of the fire brigades. They never stopped working under the most appalling conditions and in the most terrible danger, and if they hadn't done what they did do, things would have been far worse.

I find it very hard to write about it all but I never forgot those wonderful Londoners, even though later on in the war I was on the ship that helped to sink the Bismarck, when over 1,500 men were lost, and I was there on D-Day but the Blitz will always be in my mind and, in particular, that lovely young girl that I never knew who had not even started living.

Norman Robinson

I was seven years old when the war started and remember vividly that Sunday morning walking home with my father from church. The announcement that England was at war with Germany had just been on the wireless and my mother was sobbing as if her heart would break when we reached home. The appalling thing was that she was sobbing her heart out and that I had never even seen her crying before.

I also remember my sister and I were to be evacuated but my brother was just a baby and he had to stay behind with my parents.

We took part in a rehearsal which involved going down to the station in Bradford with all the school and the teachers, carrying our gas masks and some sandwiches. We were all marshalled on to the trains where we sat for some time but, of course, we didn't move and then we went back to school!

On the morning we actually did leave, my sister and I got chicken pox and so we didn't go with the rest of the school. We had to follow at a later date. However, my parents decided things were not bad enough by then so we didn't go at all! Our friends were evacuated to Ingleton and we managed to visit them and I remember one particular friend telling me that she had started to wet the bed and the people who had taken her in were not at all impressed!

We then moved to Leeds. Things got worse there with more raids and more bombs falling. We had an Anderson shelter in our back garden. Dad was an air-raid warden and when the raids started Mum and my sister and brothers would all be in the shelter where we would be tucked up in bunks to sleep but I would just sit holding my mum's hand, which would just tighten as we heard the bombs whistling down.

She never let me know how frightened she must have been but I can remember knowing how frightened she was and how frightened I was by the tightening of her hand as the raids went on.

For years afterwards, through habit, I used to put my clothes in order at night, ready to pull on quickly if the sirens went.

There are funny things that you remember. The first is that I can distinctly remember the water standing under the wood slats on the floor of the shelter. Why I remember that I don't know. There is something else that I remember and I can understand why I remember it. To keep our spirits up, to pass the time, we always used to sing songs and one I can particularly remember singing is the following:

> Underneath the spreading Chestnut tree
> Mr Churchill said to me
> If you want to get your gas mask free
> Join the blinkin' ARP!

There were many songs we used to sing but that was the one that sticks in my mind!

Patricia Roberts

During the Blitz on London, street 'fire parties' were formed to provide a back-up to the fire brigade and fight the fires in their own streets that had been started by German firebombs. These street 'fire parties' were government-sponsored and were staffed by volunteers suitably equipped with steel helmets and stirrup pumps. These stirrup pumps resembled extra-large bicycle pumps that had been fitted with a length of hosepipe. The way to use this pump was to immerse the pump in a bucket of water and pump furiously while a companion held the end of the hose and directed the resultant jet of water onto the fire.

My father and I were part of a street 'fire party' and we worked to a rota system whereby two firefighters would keep watch overnight and raise the other members of the team if firebombs fell in their particular street. Air raids were a nightly occurrence and this rota system was necessary in order to obtain at least some period of rest.

One particular night it was our turn to stand on watch

and we dutifully retired to our shelter at the end of a garden and paid periodic visits to the street to ensure that no fires had broken out.

In spite of the fact that an air raid is noisy with anti-aircraft guns and falling bombs and explosions and human cries and fire bells, familiarity can nevertheless breed contempt and so we used to play dominoes to while away the time!

On this occasion we must have been more lax than usual because when I paid a delayed visit to the street I found suddenly that all hell was let loose. The streets had received several direct hits from incendiary bombs and the resultant fires were burning in the roadway and in the upstairs rooms of three houses. There was no need to rouse the team because they were all present, but I hurried back to my father and we gathered the stirrup pump together and ran to a burning house to do our duty.

My father was a window cleaner by profession so he climbed the ladder with the hosepipe in his hand in preparation to direct the jet of water through the upper bedroom window and onto the fire. Due to the bombing there were very few windowpanes left and so it wasn't necessary to open the windows. Most windows had translucent waterproof paper over the openings to keep out the bad weather. On this night it was quite dark and drizzling with rain. There was no paper on the window so we supposed it had been conveniently removed.

I started to pump as fast as I could and the jet of water spurted from the hose that my father was holding as he directed this towards the glaring incendiary fire. Another of the team kept my bucket supplied with water and I pumped and pumped and pumped. I remember calling out to my father, 'How's it going?'

'All right,' he replied, 'but keep on pumping.'

I carried on pumping but suddenly became aware that I was becoming very wet. However, I supposed that it must

*George Kenway
on the left.*

have started to rain more heavily and in fact I remember hoping that this would help to put the fires out!

After I had emptied about five buckets I was becoming quite breathless, and so I looked up to see how my father was getting on. I looked at the window in front of my father and then the reason for my saturation became suddenly apparent.

I could see the reflection of fires on the windowpanes in front of my father and realised that they were still intact and not missing as we had thought! My father could hardly be blamed; his sight had been failing for years and he refused to wear spectacles in the street, so all the water that we had believed had been directed at the fire was in fact cascading down on me!

We soon put things right by disposing of the glass. Fortunately, we never had a similar experience that would have made it necessary for me to remove obstacles from my father's sphere of action before he did his bit! At the very least this experience did dampen my enthusiasm somewhat!

George Kenway

I remember the Blitz! I lived in Liverpool at the time and there were events there then that are etched on the memory of anyone living through those years.

It started with air-raid sirens sounding and nothing much happening and just waiting and wondering. Barrage balloons hanging in the air. They themselves looked menacing, as if waiting for the planes that didn't come. Then the sirens used to start as I was on my way home from work. My friend and I would arrange to meet late in the night at a hotel that had turned their cellar into a shelter, and we would all congregate there and think it was rather fun.

But it suddenly became more serious. When the planes went over we used to try and guess were they 'ours' or 'theirs'. Eventually when they came over in large numbers and we watched the incendiary bombs dropping to light up a target, there was no need to guess any longer!

My father used to put his ARP uniform on and go out and do his bit. My family and another one used to get inside the small Anderson shelter and listen all night to the planes coming over and wait fearfully for the whistle of an approaching bomb.

Sometimes we used to chance a visit to the cinema and on the way home we would fling ourselves on the floor when we heard the familiar whistle. One of the worse nights was after emerging from the shelter as daylight came to find our homes were without windows and water and beds were filled with glass and plaster.

That night the landmines had floated down and a sailor friend had watched as one was directly over my home, only for the wind to blow it on to the next street where all the houses were completely demolished. Whole families that were known to us in that street were killed. A theatre which had an underground shelter was eventually sealed up to entomb the dead. Not an isolated case.

My fiancé was on leave and on his way to visit me when

he met families emerging from shelters in the morning light and people waiting for buses to take them home.

Yes, I certainly remember the Blitz! How we used to sit in our large pantry under the stairs and sing so that my mother would not hear what was happening outside!

Let us pray those days never come back.

Lily Knowles

I was a nurse during the war in London during the Blitz. I trained at St Leonard's Hospital in Shoreditch and I can remember that we all slept downstairs in the sitting room in our uniforms. I still have mine! That way we were instantly ready to go into action as soon as the sirens went.

The casualties I remember were terrible. The City of London Maternity Hospital had a direct hit, as did the Bethnal Green Station. We had mothers in labour and both patients and nurses badly injured and terrible wounds, and all this time while we were trying to treat them and to cope with the situation there were bombs falling everywhere around us. We just carried on doing our duty as best we

could and trying to ease the pain and the suffering in the most appalling conditions and trying not to show the fear that we felt. Later on I went to the Lister Hospital in Hitchin as a staff nurse. At Christmas time I produced the shows for the patients and the soldiers that we had there. I remember particularly we had a ward of German soldiers and the funny thing is that I can remember at Christmas that they all sang 'Silent Night' to us in German. It was lovely to hear and my eyes still fill at the memory of that song.

I worked at Colindale Hospital for a year. It was next to Hendon Aerodrome, and when we were off duty we used to go to dances with the RAF chaps and have a good time! When I say that at one of those Saturday night dances I danced with Neville Heath, older people will remember who he was! He was hanged for murdering women! Obviously I didn't know it at the time when I had a dance with him and I can only remember how very handsome and kind he was. Obviously he wasn't as kind as I believed!

I have organised reunions every five years since, always in different places, one of them being at St Paul's Cathedral and one at the Café de Paris. I still have all the photographs and newspaper cuttings of those days, which strangely enough still bring back happy memories, even though they were very terrible times.

I could write pages and pages of the war years and my memories of them. When Hendon Aerodrome was closed down I was invited back as a special guest, and the lovely part was that the Queen Mother was there. I wore my nurse's uniform which I had last worn 40 years earlier but it still fitted and I felt very proud!

Rebecca Rosenfeld

My memories of the Blitz are numerous. Some are sad and some had their humorous side, but the one that will always remain uppermost is the night of 28 December 1940, the night that the German Air Force burnt the City of London.

It was my duty night with my St Johns Ambulance Division, which was held in the building where I worked. That was situated next door to the Guildhall in the City. We got the first siren at 7 p.m., which meant that the planes were at the coast and so it would not be very long before they would be reaching their targets. It wasn't long before we realised that their target that night was the City; incendiary bombs and ordinary bombs all rained down on the City and it was but a very short time before the whole square mile of the City was burning. The fire brigades were soon at their work but it was a mammoth task to cope with.

The bombing and incendiaries went on until well after midnight, and by that time everywhere was a raging inferno. Wherever you looked all you could see was fires, and the smoke nearly choked you. The Guildhall roof had burnt right through and the burning timbers had all fallen into the beautiful hall below and started more fires. Sad as it all was it was a wonderful sight to look to the east of the City to Ludgate and see St Paul's Cathedral silhouetted in the smoke and the burning buildings.

Officially we went off duty at 7 a.m. but we did not think it safe to go outside to get to the station to return home, so we stayed on. At 9 p.m. one of our party ventured out to spy out the land and see if it was safe for us to come out. A fireman told her that we could chance it if we didn't mind climbing over piles of hoses.

And piles there were! I have never seen so many in my life. We had to make several detours because so many of the streets were closed owing to fires still burning, and others because of unsafe buildings and falling masonry.

Eventually I got to Cannon Street Station hoping to catch a train back to Sidcup where I lived, only to be told that the signal box at Hither Green had been bombed and that no trains at all were running! So I decided the only way for it was to start walking.

I had to retrace some of my steps to get back to the street that was open so that I could get over London Bridge. In doing this I had to walk up a street called Walbrook, and it was there I saw the most sad sight of the day. There was melted silver running down the gutter! I had to stop and ask how had this happened and was told it was all the communion silver from the crosses and candlesticks of the high altar. They had melted in the heat of the fire at St Stephen's Church in Walbrook.

There were over a hundred churches in the City that were burnt to the ground that night, but only a small number of them were rebuilt. St Stephen's was one that wasn't.

Eventually I reached London Bridge and commenced my long walk home. I was quite lucky really because I got as far as Lewisham which had also had firebombs that night, but I managed to catch a bus from there to Eltham and then I only had a three-mile walk to Sidcup! I eventually got home at 1.30 p.m., much to the surprise of my parents because they had heard on the radio all the news of the raid on the City. I am sure they were glad to see I was safe.

Emily Green

We lived in Deal in 1940 and my husband worked at Tilmanstone Colliery, after working for many years at Betteshanger Colliery. When France surrendered and invasion was threatened, he had to stay in Deal working in the pits while I and my son moved to Sheffield where our family came from.

We were in the Sheffield Blitz. I remember I always had Thursdays half-day off from the Mecca Cafe where I worked, right in the middle of Sheffield and near to Fitzalan Square. I remember that I always objected to having to have Thursday as a half-day off because that was the day that all the shops were closed!

Funnily enough that particular day I can distinctly remember cleaning the house out for my mother, with whom we lived. She had taken my son out for the afternoon. He was five at the time. It's funny how little things that seem irrelevant stick in your mind. When darkness came I had nearly finished. Suddenly the siren went and it seemed that the bombing started almost straightaway. It was heavy and regular and after a short while we realised it was going to be a very heavy raid and so my mother and I and my son went to sit on the cellar steps. It was cold and it was dark, except that we had a number of small candles which were used very sparingly to give us a little light.

Although we were sat on the cellar steps we could clearly hear buildings falling and the thump and crump of bombs that somehow seemed to be almost next door to us. The terrible part was the feeling of isolation and not knowing what was happening. I think if we couldn't have heard anything it wouldn't have been too bad. The terrible part was hearing all the noises but not being able to go out and see exactly what was happening.

My mother had just turned 60 but already she was becoming rather deaf and I remember in the dim candlelight, sat on those cold steps, she was watching me all the time to try to judge from my reactions what was happening. She knew something serious was going on and she knew the terrible danger we were all in but she didn't know what it was all about or how to cope with it. I just kept telling her everything was all right.

The raid finished at about 6 a.m. the next morning and I can remember that a short while later, despite having sat on those cellar steps for 12 hours, my friends who I worked with set off with me for work just as usual! Throughout the night I wondered what was happening and I thought in some way that I had prepared myself for what I would see next morning. But it was far far worse than I had ever dreamed of. When we got to the city centre where we worked, the whole of the city was a shocking sight. There were fires still burning everywhere and flames still licking out of shop windows and into the streets. There were hosepipes twisted across the roads and a scene of total chaos but funnily

enough the thing that upset me most and, in fact made me weep, was the sight of all our lovely Sheffield tramcars lying shattered and overturned everywhere.

The whole of the city centre had been destroyed in one night, including our lovely Mecca Cafe. There was rubble and a stench of burning and although it was now morning, the whole sky was grey and it just seemed as if the end of the world had come. I had been born in Sheffield and in fact lived within 200 yards of that city centre, and I knew every building and every alleyway in it, and in 12 hours it had all gone. I suppose that I ought to be thankful for having to have that Thursday afternoon off, otherwise I would have been still working in the cafe when the sirens went or certainly by then on my way home.

The water mains, I remember, had burst. Everything in Fitzalan Square and the surrounding streets was wet and I can remember the feeling of contrast of all the water in the streets with all the smoke and the fires that were still coming out from all the shops or what remained of them. There was a Burton's outfitters' shop near to our cafe. All the windows had been blown in and the wax models had been sucked out by the blast and were lying all over the road. All the old familiar places had gone and my friend and I just stood there and wept and wept until there were no tears left to cry. Our Mecca Cafe had been totally destroyed. There wasn't one wall left standing. It was as if a giant's hand had come down and swept right through the centre of the city and left nothing but one smoking ruin.

This was all in early December just a few weeks before Christmas 1940. My husband came straight away and we all went back to Deal. It was only 20 miles from the German guns but somehow it seemed safer and although I loved Sheffield as I loved my own life, I just wanted to get away from it. We had the shelling for four years from the French coast and, of course, our own 'minor' Blitzes, but whatever I went through with my husband and my son, I shall never forget my hometown and how in one night all the places of my lovely childhood memories were wiped out. It was in ruins but, of course, it has now been rebuilt and a lovely city it is but to me it will never be the same as it once was. Happy days before the war.

Florence Shaw

It was winter and I was in London. I arrived home to find a glowing coal fire and the wireless on and tea ready, but my attention was focused on a small bundle of fur scampering on the floor. It was Timmie, the kitten I had been promised for my recent birthday. He was black and white and bright-eyed and friendly.

We all loved him. He was always on the lookout for me when I came home from school and in the early evening he would be waiting to greet my mother on her return from her wartime job as a fitter's mate for the London Passenger Transport Board.

A year later Timmie was sitting on my knee in the basement of our house during a very heavy air raid. One after the other the bombs came down, each getting closer. Three, four, five … and the sixth one landed very close. In an instant our house crumbled about us and windows shattered and we were plunged into darkness. Even now, so many years later, I can still feel that sensation of Timmie leaping in terror from my lap and disappearing.

We survived. We were taken to a rest centre, shaken and covered in dust but unharmed apart from minor scratches. The next day my mother returned to the house to salvage what was left of our home but there was no sign of Timmie. I never saw him again but at least the story has a happy ending. What we did not know was that while I was at school and my mother at work, Timmie spent the day with the manageress of a local laundry! She grew extremely fond of him and it was to her that he fled when his little world fell apart and left him homeless and afraid. She took him to her home in the country where I'll always believe that he lived happily for the rest of his life!

Winnie Sebley

I was 27 when the war broke out. We lived in Smethwick and we were there during the whole of the war. I can vividly remember the first air raid. It lasted hours but I remember it started as I was drying the washing up, and I ran down the garden to the shelter, clutching the drying up cloth and the carving knife in my hand! I can also remember my mother running down the path with me and she had some white washing on the washing line and I remember snatching it off because I was certain that the enemy would see it!

My father had made an underground shelter of railway sleepers. What he didn't know at the time was that a stream ran underneath the garden and it ran into the shelter! So every evening my sister and I had to take it in turns to scoop the water out with a hand bowl. But how it hurt my knees! I can still feel it even now!

After the 'phoney war' the cinemas and theatres didn't stay closed for long, so we were able to have a little entertainment. One night my friend and I went to the cinema when it was flashed on the screen that the sirens had sounded. We all left and kept dodging up 'entries' to avoid flying shrapnel and glass; suddenly we heard a voice roar out in the darkness. 'What are you playing at!' An ARP warden promptly grabbed hold of us and marched us to the nearest shelter! There we had to stay until the 'all clear'.

Later on the air raids came night after night without any break. We would all sit down to our dinner at 6 p.m., more or less knowing that the sirens would sound at around 7 p.m. It got so regular that we always aimed to get washed and dried up and cleared away before they went! What we did know was that there would be a warning. What we didn't know was how long we would be in the shelter. Very often during that period it was all night and when we came back in at six or seven o'clock in the morning we still had to do a day's work next day.

Unfortunately I developed rheumatism and the doctor wouldn't let me go down the shelter for a long time, so every night I had to sleep under our good old-fashioned dining table in the house. My distinct recollection of that was that every time I heard a bang during an air raid, I shot up and used to hit my head on the table! I seemed to have a permanent lump as big as an egg. I slept there for a long time but I never did get used to that table.

I remember the night of the awful raid on Coventry. It sounded as if the sky was full of planes, and next morning we had to pick our way through broken glass and rubble which littered the pavements, the roads and the gardens. Another night of the raids was when my place of work was burnt down.

When I arrived next morning for work it was still blazing fiercely and as it was a cake factory, the smell of burning sugar nearly choked us. We couldn't salvage anything so we had to go to the canteen, which was in a separate building, and try to get started again somehow. With a lot of perseverance somehow we did it, although I am not certain how! I had a friend who was in the Auxiliary Fire Service and was always away for hours during the Blitz on Birmingham. Two of his friends were killed at that time.

I was one of the wardens around our area and we had a rota which worked out that twice a week we had to patrol the streets throughout the night. Some nights it was impossible to see your hand in front of your face. It was quite frightening on one's own.

There was a lovely spirit of friendship and comradeship and cooperation in those days. As an example in our offices we all used to put sixpence a week in a tin and then when it had accumulated we would give a party with whatever we could get for our coupons for wounded soldiers. It turned out nice for me in the end. A few weeks after the end of the war we were giving our last party and it was there that I met the man I was to marry. I was 33 and I believe that we fell in love with each other immediately! He was such a handsome man. Six foot two inches but he looked so ill. He had been flown home from Malaya and had been a prisoner-of-war and working on the notorious 'Railway of Death', which was being built by the Japanese. He had suffered so much at the hands of the Japanese as indeed they all did but with care he gained quite a lot of his weight back over the years.

I haven't any outstanding story to tell. All I have tried to put down, in rather a disjointed way, is life as it seemed to me at the time.

Catherine Shrewsbury

I was an air-raid warden in Coventry in the 'Big One' on 14 November 1940, having, at the age of 21, already survived all the others! The raid was the longest of the war. Thirteen and a half hours, I believe.

We were hit at 5.30 in the morning while taking shelter in a cinema. It was in the Scala in Gosford Street.

The picture was *Dr Cyclops* and starred Albert Dekker. Eight people were killed when the cinema was hit and my sister was buried in the rubble but recovered, only to die a year later at 17. My then girlfriend was wounded in the leg and a girl who was a friend of both her and myself lost her right hand. They all worked at the cinema.

I sustained a shrapnel wound in the left lung. In fact, my topcoat saved my life. I was taken to Gulson Road Hospital and they evacuated us to a military hospital in Evesham where I had to stay for three months. While I was in hospital, would you believe it, my landlady's son stole my Post Office savings book and withdrew all my savings. The bloke had even visited me in hospital, expecting me to die, but then I suppose that's life!

I remember meeting and shaking hands with Wendell Wilkie, the Vice-President of the United States. But I remember even more the wonderful nurses at Evesham, particularly the sister and staff who looked after everyone so well. There were 45 patients in my ward and I can remember that Christmastime, the nurses with candles and lanterns singing carols to us.

There was a human warmth and gregarious camaraderie that people had for one another at that time but now it seems to have gone for ever and I think that generally only people of my generation realise what has been lost.

After I came out of hospital I served in the Fleet Air Arm and there I had wonderful experiences, including meeting Sir Laurence Olivier and Sir Ralph Richardson, and one thing I learned was the value of positive thinking!

James Smith

I was eight years old when war was declared on 3 September 1939, and I was the youngest member of our family, my two elder brothers being aged 16 and 21 years old, respectively. Therefore, I was the only one too young to join in any of the Civil Defence services. Both of my parents joined the ARP, my mum full-time and my dad, who had a job in industry, joined for part-time service. My eldest brother was in a reserved occupation so to 'do his bit' for the war effort he joined the Home Guard and my 16-year-old brother joined the ARP Messenger Service until he was called up later into HM Forces. It was because everyone but me would be on duty during any air raids that we as a family were not allocated an Anderson shelter. A hole was dug in the garden in readiness, but we just never got one! But it's an ill wind that does no one any good, as they say, and we found that during the fuel shortage we were able to make use of 'the dig' as we called it. Our garden was part of a coalmining area, and lots of small coal came to light when we dug the hole, thus helping to keep the home fires burning!

When the air raids began I was sent to share next door's shelter, but the company did not last as our neighbours were natives of Lancashire and returned north to their families for a time. That left me – and my dog – as sole occupants of the shelter. For three weeks I slept there to save being disturbed from my bed in the house when the frequent alert sounded with that wailing siren. Funny, but I cannot remember being scared at being there with just my dog for company. I am certain that I would be more afraid nowadays!

When the terrible air raid on Coventry occurred in November

1940 my mum volunteered to help with clearing up after-wards and so this time I was farmed out to my cousin's home for four weeks so that I was cared for properly during Mum's absence from home. The younger of my brothers, now 17, went with Mum to help the distressed people of Coventry.

A few of my mum's recollections come to mind. The situation in Coventry was so bad that the water mains burst and the mobile canteen that Mum served with were given gallons and gallons of milk from the Cooperative Society. This milk was used for soups and beverages and even the washing up had to be done in milk because of the infection risk from the only water that was available which was dirty.

One little boy aged about five was found wandering alone and dazed by my brother. Both of his parents had been killed. Another man they met was a master plumber. He had dug himself out of the debris with his bare hands, which were still raw and bleeding. The amazing thing is that the thing he was most worried about was the loss of his plumb-ing tools!

It came as a complete surprise when one day quite unan-nounced King George VI came to see for himself the disaster area. My mum said that he was clearly close to tears as he looked around. She saw one little old lady rush up to the King and push past all the VIPs and grab the King's hand and say to him, 'God bless you, sir – you've got more guts than that Hitler bloke.'

One good memory is of the comradeship of all the people. Everyone helped everyone else. I wonder why it takes a disas-ter or a war to bring out the best of 'the man in the street'.

Another memory is of the night when a German bomber was shot down and it crashed on two semi-detached houses near to us. All the family except the husband from one house were killed. That husband was at work on night duty. The shock caused him a complete mental breakdown.

Some of the German crew were killed. It was reported

that the pilot of the fighter who shot down the bomber attended the funeral of those killed. How futile is war!

Patricia A. M. Rodwell

On the night of the Coventry Blitz I lived in the village of Eastern Green just on the edge of Coventry and about four and a half miles from the city centre. I was a 14-year-old schoolboy who attended Leamington College for Boys, ten miles from Coventry.

When the siren went in the early evening I had only just got home from school after a ten-mile train and four-mile bus journey, and I was having my evening meal. We didn't know what to expect and as there was a very large aero engine factory only half a mile away we felt particularly vulnerable.

The local searchlight was on and the barrage balloons were up and soon we could hear the sound of bombs falling and ack-ack guns firing. Then the fires began and we could see the blazes four miles away silhouetting the famous three spires which was our normal view in the distance. On and on went the bombing through the night and we were still in trepidation worrying that the bombs would get closer and closer to us. However, although we stayed up through the night, we were fortunate in that the nearest bombs were over two miles away.

After the 'all clear' everyone's thoughts went back to a

normal day and my father set off to cycle to his work three miles away. I went off to catch my usual 7.35 a.m. bus to Coventry. At the Bus Terminus were some passengers for earlier buses and it soon became obvious that no buses were running so we all just set off to walk!

On my route I saw a few bombed houses but continued

walking on towards the station, meeting other rail travellers on the way. At the end of Station Road we were turned back by a policeman because there was an unexploded bomb in the station and so I began the long trek home.

The following morning, though a Saturday, was still a school day for me and so I borrowed my father's old 'sit up and beg' BSA bike and cycled the ten miles to Leamington to school. When it came to the maths lesson Bonzo (Mr Onslow, the maths teacher) asked me for Thursday night's homework and then sent me to the headmaster for not having done it!

Apparently they hadn't even heard the sirens in Leamington!

Godfrey Kent

I had always said from being a teenager that I should have a different kind of wedding myself, after being bridesmaid in five similar weddings in one year.

Little did I guess how different.

On 13 November 1940 I had a telephone call at the office to say that my fiancé was coming home on embarkation leave and telling me to arrange the wedding! The girls in the office said they would bring ingredients for the wedding cake. There was rationing but we couldn't have a wedding without a cake!

Meanwhile I rushed into town during the dinner hour to get a dress or suit. The girls were true to their word but the suit had to be left for a slight alteration. It was all 'go' and excitement I can tell you!

Just on seven o'clock that evening a bomb was dropped. 'Jerry' had come early tonight! Everything was dropped quickly on to the kitchen table while the whole house emptied as we all rushed off to the Anderson shelter. Then all hell was let loose. My most vivid memory was sitting under the neighbour's canary cage and having sand and dirt showering on me every a time a bomb came close! Yes, the canary was in the shelter with us as well!

At seven o'clock the next morning the 'all clear' sounded and we all staggered out of the Anderson to see utter devastation. Six houses had been demolished and five people were buried in them. Miraculously all of them lived. My brother, who was an air-raid warden, had been thrown amongst the debris and was one of the walking injured.

Despite all that he staggered about all day trying to salvage things and help anyone that he could. I can always remember particularly that he had a triangular bandage over his head with his tin hat on top of it! No one cared about appearances in those days and looking back there were some queer sights around I must say!

I hopefully set out to fetch my wedding dress but there was no buses and, in fact, no transport of any kind. So I set out to walk across the city. Funnily enough it wasn't till afterwards as I relived that walk that I realised that I had stumbled and staggered for over two miles through the devastation of Coventry city centre. There was nothing but ruined masonry and smouldering rubble. I did notice the three spires but no churches.

Another of Coventry's landmarks, the Market Hall clock, remained standing but I found no shop and certainly no wedding dress.

However, we were married in a little prayer chapel at the Central Hall the following Wednesday. The main hall had gone but somehow the small chapel was still standing. Unfortunately it was a different minister and he had got mixed up and took my sister-in-law as the bride, and I had to call out, 'No it's me!'

I had always wanted a wedding with a difference – and I certainly got one.

By the way, my husband was missing for a whole year but I never gave up. He was a prisoner-of-war for four and a half years. Somehow I just knew he was alive and we would make up for everything when he got back. We have. We have a daughter who is and always will be a great blessing to us both after a long wait.

Finally, I forgot to mention that our wedding breakfast was a cup of railway tea on Stourbridge Railway Station. There was one blessing though, I had many wedding cakes!

Everywhere I visited for months afterwards, the hostess would always say to me, thinking she was the only one, 'This is your wedding cake!'

We also had a delayed honeymoon in the Isle of Wight after he came home and that was certainly worth waiting for.

Frances Slack

I was nearly 17 when war broke out, and can recall many hair-raising nights of the Blitz on Liverpool as we lived very near to Gladstone Docks. Even now if anyone admires the moon I shudder with fear because a full moon meant an air raid. In my mind I can still hear the throb of the German bombers coming over.

I remember particularly when a landmine hit our street and many of our neighbours were killed. My dad was an Auxiliary Fireman and I could not sit long in the Anderson shelter and went out to help him dig for bodies. Being the youngest person about during air raids I was in fact sometimes called upon to identify any dead children or teenagers as I could recognise them quicker than the grown-ups.

The funniest thing I recall was the night we were bombed out. Bootle was ablaze and we were told to get away from the town and head inland. Although all the doors and the windows and most of our roof had gone, Dad insisted that he go back inside and pack a case with some clothes.

Now most households have a drawer full of odds and ends

which are hardly used. In our case it was a drawer full of things like my old Brownie uniform, swimsuit, etc., all of the clothing in fact completely useless. Dad managed to find a suitcase, but of course he also managed to find that particular drawer when he was packing the clothes. He was going by guesswork because he couldn't see in the dark, and of all the drawers he had to empty it had to be that one which was packed with clothing that was quite useless to us.

We ended up that night or rather 3 a.m. next morning in a henhouse on a farm outside Liverpool. There were bare boards I remember all dotted with chicken poo. We got a lift there in a baker's van.

I remember that we all stood in the field and looked towards our town with its red sky and blazing buildings, and feeling a huge sadness as we mourned the friends and neighbours we must have lost, but thanking God for being alive ourselves. Not a thought was given at any time I remember to any discomfort of sleeping on bare boards. We only had what we stood up in, but when we opened our suitcase next morning I can remember we laughed and laughed at its contents despite the fact that our home and everything else had gone.

Edna Thom

It happened during what came to be called the 'Sunday Night Raid'. Previously there had been a couple of light raids and a very heavy and terrifying Easter Tuesday one which devastated the Antrim Road area. Then one night the sirens wailed out that eerie sound which dragged us from sleep and made me shiver. At that time I was 12 years old. In the next room all was bustle as my mother lifted my sister out of her cot and wrapped her in a rug.

'Put your coat on over your nightie,' she shouted to me. 'And hurry up.'

We hurried. There was no question of not hurrying! Dad took care to leave the key in the front door lock as we joined the other families and moved towards the underground shelter. Keys were left in doors in case of incendiary bombs and the urgent need for air-raid wardens to get in

Rhoda Watson, on the right, with her uncle.

quickly with the stirrup pumps. They tell me now that there was a 'Bomber's Moon' that night but I don't seem to remember that aspect. After all it was a very long time ago.

The underground shelter had been dug out by one of the neighbours and really could not have been any more than six or seven feet down, as deep as a grave in other words. There were two wooden benches, a tiny oil lamp and a box of matches. The three families settled down to wait and the grown-ups were stern-faced, although I have to say that there was a lot of giggling among the children of the group. We didn't feel adult fears.

It seemed only a very short time before we heard the planes approaching. There was no mistaking the heavy sound of German bombers. Our own air force had quite a different sound altogether. The grown-ups exchanged looks and in the light of the little oil lamp I could see the pallor on their faces. Soon the first bombs dropped. They landed with a sort of pinging sound, which is hard to describe but which I will never forget. But then it seemed that all hell broke loose. In between explosions there was return gunfire from our side from what were known as ack-ack guns.

The ground rocked almost continuously from the blasts, which was a pretty alarming state of affairs. It was clear that night that the east side of Belfast was copping the worst that the enemy could do. I remember one woman started to cry gently and we children stared at her husband who patted her shoulder and stroked her hair lovingly. Was this the same man who worked at the docks and scared the wits out of us with his rough shouting sometimes? A lull came between the waves of bombers and my father and one of the others ventured upwards to have a sortie. They came back in double-quick time. In fact, they were blown in and blown off their feet by the blast.

Some said it was a bomb and some said it was a land-mine, but whatever it was it felt like the end of the world. There was a rushing sound, an incredible explosion, and we were all thrown together in a hotch-potch of tangled limbs, mixed up with upended benches, as well as a lot of muck. Of course the light disappeared. The women screamed and cried out but miraculously no one was hurt. Somehow we sorted ourselves out.

'That was close!' cried my mother.

I have never forgotten Dad's answer.

'It was not. There's nothing to worry about. It was a way down at Hollywood Arches at least!' And he started to whistle. I realised that this nonchalance was all an act when about five minutes later I overheard his whisper to a friend that he thought the houses had gone.

Eventually the 'all clear' sounded and we crawled out. The four houses belonging to the four families, who had crouched in our shelter, and the one beside it were no more. The bomb or whatever it was had ploughed a huge crater in the road and our houses had fallen into it. Like a scene from some inferno the sky blazed red from the flames of numerous fires, and barrage balloons flapped on broken cables. In the middle of all this devastation our front door could be seen standing upright in a pile of rubble, the key still intact in the lock!

Like many other houses which fell into holes due to the bombs, our house was rebuilt when the war ended. Not all the families who sheltered underground on the night of that raid returned. We were one family who did.

I lived there until my wedding day when I left to take up another stage in life. The underground shelter has long since disappeared. It's buried forever beneath the car park of the Park Avenue Hotel but the memories remain!

Rhoda Watson

My boyfriend was stationed locally with the Royal Engineers but his home and family were in the East End of London which, as most everyone knows, got a terrific battering by bombs. Nevertheless I went there whenever he was on leave without thought of danger. His mother used to come to tell us nearly every night: 'We'll have to get into the shelter – Jerries over again.' It's unbelievable now but I used to take all my Dinkie curlers out and brush my hair before I went down!

On another occasion we came out of the cinema and it was a very moonlit night. We could hear the planes droning overhead and we ran for our lives, hearing shrapnel dropping around us. We had to clamber over bricks and rubble to get into the shelter and all I was worrying about at the time, I remember, was my suede shoes getting spoiled! I can't remember it but they were probably the only pair I possessed!

I must emphasise that I was only there from time to time. The people who suffered day after day and night after night must have found that life was a nightmare. They lived from day to day really but although the pubs were knocked about and grubby, there were still pianos being played and

sing-songs going on. In fact I don't think I had seen much of life before – it was an education to be amongst them.

My strongest memory though is the shortage of everything during those years. Food, clothes, make-up. All of the things that we take for granted now were in short supply and limited but we didn't feel deprived because the 1930s had been bad enough anyway and we were all in the same boat.

We had all sorts of ingenious ways of trying to look nice. We made ourselves all sorts of things out of all sorts of material or cloth. I remember I once made myself a 'jigger coat', which was like a short boxy jacket, from cloth meant for car seat covering!

Insofar as my boyfriend was concerned we made up for the long dreary hours of continuous work and lonely hours away from home because our time was so short together that every minute was precious. A letter or telegram to say that leave was due was paradise and it kept us going.

We married after D-Day 1944. He was wounded, but not badly luckily, in the invasion of France. We spent 43 very happy years together with our family. I get his letters out sometimes. I kept some of them. I read them and for a little while I recapture my youth. All I can say is that, despite all the times we had, I have some truly wonderful memories.

Eunice Allen

During the war years we lived on a very lonely farm called Mobbs Wood Farm at Shilton, Coventry, which was about five miles from Coventry and every time Coventry was bombed the planes flew over our farm. My husband and our three children and myself used to watch them go over. We had no shelter. I can remember one night when there was some exceptionally heavy bombing, and the fir trees in the paddock on our farm were set alight. After the raid our workmen went to put out the fires and got a shock. They found 20 bullocks lying dead.

About an hour after that a man came to the door asking if we could provide he and his wife and baby with some accommodation. Apparently they had received a direct hit on their home and in a few minutes had lost everything. Of course I said yes, that they could come in as we had plenty of room because it was an old large farmhouse. So I told him to fetch his wife and children and I can especially remember that when I told him that he was in tears and said 'God bless you' and went running off down the drive to get them.

Two hours later we had just about given up any thought of seeing them again when my son came running in shouting that the army was coming! I went to see what he meant and, oh lord, what a sight! I was shocked. Women and children were just trekking along with just their night clothes on and some with no shoes, and all were in a state of shock.

I took one look and called them to come into the kitchen. It was a big room and warm. I never asked questions. I just told them to find a seat wherever they could while I got them something to drink. When I went to see how many needed a drink, and how many babies there were I got another shock. There were 25!

I nearly panicked, but I could see that they were at the end of their tether, so I just got on with getting the drinks as best we could. They could explain everything later. Luckily for them I had just had a baking day, so as it happened I had plenty to feed them for the time being. It was also past milking time, so we had a churn of milk ready for the children.

After they had been fed and rested one of the women became their 'spokeswoman'. She told me that they had heard the man tell his wife that he had found somewhere for them to stay, and so they had all decided to come along too!

Eventually I managed to find somewhere for all of them to sleep except for a family of five. I had to tell them that I only had room in the loft. They said that would do and so I found them a spare mattress and some army blankets and they went upstairs to the loft.

About half an hour later we heard a lot of screams and yelling and then all the family from the loft came running down the stairs.

It appeared that they had been cold and so they had lit a fire in an old fireplace but, of course, it was blocked up and as the smoke could not get out of the chimney it was filling the room. So they had opened the cock loft door to let the smoke out, and let a family of bats in which were flying around in the smoke. Of course, being town people, they had been scared stiff. What a day and what a night!

The next problem was how to clothe my visitors. I racked my brains and then I had a brainwave. I collected all my spare sheets and curtains and bedspreads and meal bags and I gave them to the women to do what they could with needle and thread, and the result was marvellous.

Next night was 14 November and the big raid on Coventry. It was hell. It seemed to go on for ever. I gathered everyone into the kitchen and had an old gramophone blaring away to help in some way drown the noise of the raid, but try as we might we could still hear the thump of the bombs as they landed.

Suddenly there was a long drawn-out screech and a big bang and then all was quiet for a few minutes. Then there was another tremendous bang and we all dived on to the floor. My husband had been outside fire-watching and I remember that he came in and said, 'Don't go out at all, not for anything.' He beckoned me outside and told me that a German plane had been shot down on our farm. I thought it would all never end.

Next day was fairly quiet until about two o'clock in the afternoon when six firefighters came to see if I could put them up for a few nights. But all the rooms were full. I could not help them, but one of them said anywhere would do, so I offered them the room where the water tanks were and they said that that was okay and it would do for them.

Then I remember one said, 'Do you know that Coventry is practically deserted? All the shop produce is being offered to anyone who can help themselves.'

So my husband took off straightaway in the horse and cart and it was true. My husband loaded his cart with tins and tins of stuff, mostly with the labels missing, and wrapped bread and for days my visitors were opening tins hoping for a 'lucky dip'! But despite the fact he had picked up so many tins and most had labels missing, it turned out that every tin was baked beans!

And all this was just four days only of my life during the war that went on for six years!

Elizabeth Hunt-Bond

I lived with parents and brother in a built-up industrial district of Birmingham. The raids had been very bad and we had not slept in our beds for weeks, making do with a straw bed under the stairs. I was 11 years old and my brother was five. The house was one of many in a large yard.

This particular night the raids started early and my father and grandfather, who was aged 74, were out fire-watching and we were in our usual place under the stairs. The bombs were very close and the dairy at the end of the road was hit. That was where the horses were stabled. They were duly led out to safety and tied to lamp posts, but you can imagine the cries and the scene, and my mother then decided to go to my grandfather's house just five minutes down the road which had a cellar. He had shored it up with supports as he thought that would be much safer so off we went.

At the yard where the bombing occurred.

Halfway down the road a man appeared from a doorway and asked where we were going. My mother explained her need to get to her father's house and the man insisted we all go down to this particular cellar as the raid was so bad. No sooner had we joined other people than we heard an almighty 'whoosh' and instinctively we all rushed up the steps.

We knew that it was a bomb and that it had landed very near, and when the 'all clear' sounded and we got outside, to our disbelief my grandfather's house was no more.

We found out that about 28 people were killed on that side of the road and most surely we would have been in that carnage had that man not stopped us.

God was surely with us that night. We just couldn't thank him enough. But my grandfather was never the same again. The shock was devastating for him.

Betty Hunt

I had been married for just ten months when the Second World War reached its climax. I was living in Rugby in the county of Warwickshire at the time. Having no children I was asked by the government to either take people into my home, have a baby or go out to work! Being newly married I gave it a lot of thought. I chose the latter course!

My husband was already working at the Armstrong Siddeley factory at Coventry. He was a toolmaker and cutter/grinder by trade. He could not go to war because his job was vital to the war effort. So he got me a job in the machine shop. If through bombing my husband was going to lose his life, I felt that I would prefer it to happen to me also, so that we would remain together even in death. Working in the same place made this a realistic possibility. It sounds morbid, but that's how we felt at the time.

We were both on nights so we had to leave our home at six o'clock. The train left the station for Coventry at 6.30. Sometimes it was late through no fault of the railway. I prayed very hard that we should arrive at Coventry all in one piece, because the German planes made a nuisance of themselves trying to bomb or machine gun the train. When this happened we were told to leave the train and hide down the railway embankment! It was exhausting because we still had to do a night's work from 8 p.m. to 7.30 a.m. if we were lucky.

Often when we did get to work the air-raid siren would go so we had to shut the machinery down. We were told to go to the air-raid shelter as soon as possible. To me this always seemed funny because it had been built inside the factory! If the factory was bombed the air-raid shelter would go too, and everybody would be killed, but I am glad to say that it never happened.

We expected the bombers to come every night, but soon got used to it. When the attack was not too bad we just donned our tin hats and hoped for the best. But time passed by and the raids became heavier. They even got to shooting down the barrage balloons so they could get through to bomb us.

I remember one time after the night shift we walked along Park Road to see what devastation the bombers had caused. The houses we had seen the night before were now all gone. Fires were still burning. People were still looking for their loved ones and salvaging what they could from the rubble. Tired firemen were packing up hoses and smelling of smoke and blood and sweat. I remember a lady seemed to come from nowhere to bring those gallant men a most welcome cup of tea. She was a real breath of life to them.

I saw a small boy about four years old with no cheeks to his bottom. He was covered in water and dirt. He was crying for his mummy and I carried him as gently as I could trying not to give him any more pain. I found a fireman and our eyes met, but not a word was spoken because I knew that he understood exactly how I felt. A Red Cross helper came and relieved the fireman of his precious charge.

My husband took me away with a loving arm around my shoulders. All that day I cried. Who was I crying for? Was it for that child or the dead and the suffering? Was it for all the suffering war brings to the world? I asked God, why? Alas, I never did find the answer.

Bombs fell every night. As the train passed a row of houses a board stood out from one of the upstairs fireplaces. At the end of the board was a child's potty. All the travellers on the train thought it gave us a little light relief by placing bets on how long the potty would stay there! Every one of the travellers put a sixpenny piece into a Red Cross box. How much money was collected I never found out.

Although we were very tired after a night's work and coping with the threat of bombs we still sang songs and told jokes just to keep awake. If we hadn't we could have travelled on to the end of the line and into London! We also shared our food because the ration was not enough for us. Many a time I went hungry to feed my husband without him knowing it. I can tell you this – we had no slimming worries in those days!

One night we lost the roof of our factory. Another bomb had been dropped on the graveyard next door to us. The next thing we knew were bodies, skeletons and coffins flying everywhere and through the roof like some sort of horror film.

Just across from our factory was my favourite public house. It was hit by a bomb blast. They found the pianist still sitting at the piano looking as if he was still playing there with not a mark on him. The blast had put an untimely and prompt end to his life. That same night three bombs dropped on an air-raid shelter. It was said to hold 400 people. I do not know whether there were 400 people in it, but if this was true what price they had to pay for the war. After those bombs had dropped there was nothing left of that shelter in the morning.

Soon afterwards I left Coventry. I had received some very good news for both of us. Yes, I was pregnant! Those years of living hell were enough for me.

When I did have my baby my husband had a night off from work to be with me. Then came devastating news. He had to go before a tribunal at work. He was found guilty and fined heavily because there had been no one to replace him. But he did not care as long as the baby and myself were all right. It was worth every penny! Now I have the time to sit and think, it still hurts to think of Coventry and the war.

Gladys Reeves

I didn't really experience the Blitz as such but I did four years in a Royal Ordnance factory. The shell cases were made in one Welsh factory and the cordite was made in another. I can tell you that our job was very dangerous.

We travelled by bus and train from our village to work, Glascoed to Usk, that was the train terminus. It was a station especially built for the factory. Wales being classed as a land of song, Sunday night was particularly happy. Everyone sang and Rhymny folk could certainly hit the top notes. I often look back now to those beautiful memories.

But there were tragedies too. One afternoon a German plane machine gunned the pathway to our workplace. No one was seriously hurt, but lots of girls were in a dreadful state of nerves. Believe me when the siren sounded there was a great panic, as one bomb dropped there would mean thousands of lives lost.

It doesn't take much to imagine what would happen with a bomb dropping in a factory full of cordite. We were told that Usk was chosen for the factory because it was regularly covered in mist, and so the factory was hidden. Whether that is true or not I do not know, but it kept us happy at the time!

I remember one particular accident at the factory that was terrible. We had a girl who was an inspector and she was testing a shell with a wooden gauge. No one really knows what happened, but it exploded. Sadly it killed her and badly disfigured another girl, and two lads who were working nearby each lost both of their legs. After months in hospital the two lads came back to work but they were now a liability. But their sense of humour was nevertheless wonderful and it is something I will never forget. They used to joke about all sorts of things. They made jokes about not missing their legs until the following morning when they went to put their boots on! I could go on and on, but the memory of those two lads will never leave me.

M. Hughes

I was a ten-year-old at the time of the Blitz and we were living in Middlesex at the time situated between Hendon, Heston and Northolt aerodromes. Uxbridge Royal Air Force Station was only a short distance away, and so when the German bombers came they could literally take their pick!

The war years were full of instances which stand out for me. The night an unexploded bomb fell in an open field, and my father with other ARP wardens crawled around looking for it with blacked-out torches. Only a little 'X' of light was allowed. While he was crawling around he lost his false teeth and he was so long searching for them that I remember that when he got home my mother gave him 'what for' because she thought he had been killed!

One night we were in the shelter and thought the Germans had invaded and were machine gunning the street. It turned out to be a new gun being tried out which sent up little round balls in quick succession and was called 'the flaming onion gun' and used for shooting out the flares dropped to light up a target. But it sounded like a machine gun to us!

During the severest meat-rationing period I remember that the meat ration was one chop per person per ration book. A friend of my father's who kept pigs (and everyone was encouraged to do this) arranged that when the time came to slaughter

he would keep one pig back for himself and one for my father, and send the rest to the Ministry of Food. To withhold more than one pig was illegal. Nevertheless it was all arranged that it was going to be done under the cover of darkness and obviously planned very carefully!

On the arranged night I was sent to bed earlier than usual, but like all children when something is going on I wanted to find out and so I sat quietly watching on the landing.

It appears that my father set out at dusk with the garden wheelbarrow and walked to his friend's house to collect the pig. After the transaction was completed a very happy dad put the pig in the wheelbarrow and covered it over with an old coat and came back home avoiding the main streets. Apparently throughout the journey he was thinking about the roast he was going to have on Sunday, but he hadn't gone very far when the air-raid siren went.

His step quickened and he started to sweat, and as he turned the corner of the street in the dim light he suddenly made out the shape of the local bobby coming down the road on his bike. What to do? As quick as a flash he heaved the carcass over the hedge and walked on. When the policeman was level with him he said, 'It's my advice you should take cover, sir. Don't worry sir I will get you back home safely.'

He walked the whole way back with my father, only

leaving him after he had gone inside the house where friends were waiting ready to divide up the pork!

After a great deal of mutterings and mumblings, and after the 'all clear' had sounded, it was decided that he would go back and pick up the pig before daylight. This he did, but search as he might there was no pig to be found!

But my father always said that whenever he saw that policeman afterwards he always saluted my father and it seemed that he was giving him a big knowing smile!

There are so many tales that could be told. Some are funny and some are sad. Most sadness was kept from me being a child, but sometimes I was touched by it such as when the ARP lady's son was shot down and killed. Again when a friend of mine whom I had been playing with in the morning was killed when a doodlebug fell in her street. I went to see her that afternoon to continue playing, and to my horror saw the houses destroyed and the Civil Defence workers and fire people trying to clear everything away, and my friend's leg poking out of the debris.

There was the time when my sister and I were booked on a Red Cross ship going to America. But because she was 18 she joined the WAAF and so we didn't go. That ship was torpedoed in the Atlantic and two of our friends went down on it. Just a few memories which will never be forgotten from the most traumatic time in our lives when children grew up quickly and young men didn't get any older.

Jeannette Chilton

I was only seven years old when the Blitz came all too suddenly to our family. To be precise on 26 August 1940. Until then there had only been a few windows broken and tiles dislodged in our vicinity. But then the Germans decided that South Birmingham was a good target!

Already in the Fire Service, Father had joined with neighbours in taking turns to stay up all night listening for the

Anne is on the left.

all-too-familiar sound of German bombers approaching. The unofficial wardens then knocked loudly on doors to warn families to run to their shelters or at least to take cover under the stairs.

On the night in question the siren, or 'alert' as it was known, sounded long after we were all in the shelter. By then the bombers were nearly overhead. I remember that their engines had a peculiar rhythmic hum, and there was no mistaking their mission. I remember hearing the stick of bombs dropping. They had a whistling sound, but surprisingly there was no bang on impact. This time six were dropped and I remember my father turning to my mother and I and saying, 'I am afraid we've been hit this time.' I can remember it was exactly 3 a.m.

There was a full moon that night and the Germans never missed the opportunity when there was good visibility. In that moon it was easy to see the devastating damage to our little house. The back half had completely disappeared into a large crater. Where my bedroom had been only part of the back wall still stood with a single wardrobe hanging grotesquely upside-down with my clothes occasionally floating down from it to the ground!

To a seven-year-old it was all very exciting and I had no conception of what a lucky escape we had had. My Pekinese dog had been left in the house because he was unwell and had been blown in his basket from the kitchen, now completely demolished, to the front door which was still intact. Amazingly and thankfully he survived unharmed!

My father was told that it was entirely his responsibility to make the house safe! But two days later when inspecting the damage he suddenly noticed a low-flying aeroplane approaching in broad daylight. No sooner had he spotted the swastika than he hurriedly ducked out of the way as he and two neighbours were machine gunned. The nearby shed was promptly riddled with bullet holes!

The house was subsequently rebuilt to exactly the same specifications, but by then we had moved to the Warwickshire countryside where we felt a good deal safer and where we only heard of the Blitz from our newspapers and our radio!

Anne Janes

My particular memory of the Blitz starts when I asked for a 24-hour pass and it was granted. I was stationed at Hothfield, near Ashford, and I dashed to a bus and arrived home at 3 p.m. at my parents' house in Ramsgate. We had a lovely tea together and I remember in the evening that Dad and I had a stroll along the cliff tops and seafront, something we hadn't done since the outbreak of war. Mother being an invalid stayed at home.

After dark, Dad and I joined a few other neighbours on the cliff top overlooking the harbour, which was only a few yards from our house. We stood there, watching and chatting, as the RAF bombed the invasion ports with Calais and Boulogne getting a real good pasting. Flares lit the sky above the sea and searchlights probed the sky above France. Sometimes they held a plane in their light like a huge moth. Sometimes that moth would fall in flames to the ground or into the sea. I remember about ten o'clock, Dad said, 'I'll go and see how Mum is then we'll be off to bed. Cheerio, son. See you anon!'

From me came a cheery 'Goodnight, Dad.'

Not long after there was suddenly a new note amongst the noise in the sky and I remember saying to myself, 'That's Jerry up there!' Nobody seemed to take any notice or get worried but I set out to walk to a safer spot! Suddenly I heard a bomber hurtling out of the moonlit sky and in fear and panic I started my run for the shelter. I remember as I reached the top of the steps which led to the long tunnels below the cliffs that there was an almighty bang and I ended up at the bottom of the hundred or so steps. To this day I don't know how I got there.

I got up and stood there shaking and then there was another explosion and a huge piece of chalk fell from the roof and missed me by only a foot or two. I remember a girl standing nearby, crying out that her family was up there and suddenly off she went up the steps. Then somebody shouted, 'They've hit Adelaide Gardens.' Our house was No. 35.

It transpired that the first bomber had flattened buildings only a few feet from where I had dived into the shelter, including a pub. Another bomber had hit the area where our house stood and yet another pub. The lump of chalk which almost hit me had been shaken down from the tunnel roof by the second bomb. In the moments that it took for the football-sized chunk to thud near my feet, my whole life changed direction and at the same time the life of my mother began to move towards its end.

I knew that I had to go up and see what had happened to my parents but at the same time I was petrified that I would get caught by a repeat attack. So I walked till I reached the spot where my brother sheltered each night with his wife and their son of three. A younger son, just a baby, had already died, mainly as a result of the conditions under which it had to exist. The four miles of chalk tunnel were cold and windy and damp and my brother, Joe, had severely injured his ankle on rubble as he searched for Dad in the ruins and wreckage which strewed the area and he was unable to carry on any

longer. I went back up into the beautiful moonlight, and back to the broken glass, and the murmur of the English Channel.

I yelled, 'Dad!' Silence. Again I yelled, 'Dad, Dad!' Silence. I gave what we called the 'family whistle' and knew that an echo would return if Dad heard it. That silence was bloody awful. Again I yelled 'Dad!' and suddenly a firm hand grasped my shoulder.

'What's up, son?' asked a kindly policeman.

I explained and he said, 'We have an elderly gent in the ambulance over there. Care to have a look?'

We entered the makeshift ambulance and I could see something very grim lying under a sack. At this point I hesitate to say what I saw, but if I do not tell you how can you know of my feelings? I had no desire to see what might be the dead face of the dad I loved so much and told the policeman so.

'He has a big toe which I would know for sure was his,' I explained. 'Let me see his feet.'

The sacking was pulled gently back to reveal two bloody stumps cut off at the ankles. I was shaken beyond description. 'It's got to be his face,' I declared.

Once again the police constable eased the sack away and again just a bloody mess was revealed to me. It was nothing more than a terrible pulp. The face had totally gone. Only the grey hair at the back of the head indicated that it was possibly Dad.

Back down in the tunnel I found Mother laying on a bunk. She was badly cut on the legs and asking where George was. Apparently on hearing the first bombs fall, he had seen Mum to 'safety' under the front doorsteps, hoping she would receive some protection from them. He had then gone out on duty as an ARP warden to see what he could do. As he got outside the garden gate, a 1,000-pound bomb fell and his remains were found on the very edge of the crater. Another bomb, a 500-pound one, had fallen at the side of the house, only feet from the doorsteps and Mother.

Before rescuers reached her, she had dragged herself clear and found her way along into the tunnel. It was there that she received medical aid.

The rest of the night was long and cold. I sat in a deck chair but sleep was quite out of the question. In the early hours, Police Sergeant Coosons, who was my dad's brother, paid us a visit and asked Mum if George had been circumcised. He also produced a piece of tie and asked if it was from the tie that George had been wearing. Till then she had clung to hope but now she knew the worst. At first light I ventured up to inspect the damage. Our house stood but was still unsafe to enter so it would have to be pulled down. Evidence of the horror of the night before still cluttered the road. What was left of my dad's nose and glasses and a grey hand-knitted sock cut neatly off at the ankle but containing his foot. I called a rescue worker who said it would soon be cleared away. I also found a slipper with a nasty piece of bomb casing stuck into it. Twelve pounds in notes which Dad had been saving for the rates just vanished into thin air. Ironically Dad had been left this house by a lady he worked for only six months earlier, hence he was saving to pay the rates bill.

That morning was a busy one. The gas main at the side of the house was fractured and the escaping gas caught fire. I assisted some ARP workers to put it out, using some small flimsy and hopeless-looking stirrup pumps. We were all pretty tense, expecting the whole street to blow up at any second, not knowing that as it was mixed with air and burning, it was quite safe. As fast as we doused the fire at one point it would pop up at another, but eventually we won. Soon after a rescue worker emerged from the basement carrying our canary and cage. The poor little bird was still singing away as though all was well with the world. That morning I sent a telegram to my unit, explaining the circumstances, and requesting extra leave. After all I had only been given a 24-hour pass.

Request refused! I had to go back! Nowadays they talk of treatment for trauma after violence. My 'treatment' was short, sharp and very sweet!

'Stand up straight, man.'

I was already standing like a guardsman.

'What happened?'

I explained.

'You say the bombs only split the house and didn't demolish it at once?'

'Correct, Sergeant Major,' I said. 'What's left will be pulled down.'

The sergeant major turned to the sergeant and snapped, 'There you are. I told you their bombs aren't as powerful as ours! Off you go, soldier.'

That was all the sympathy and 'treatment' I ever received from the British Army. Three months later I was discharged with recurrent TB and bad nerves and two years later Mum died at the age of 50, after one blow too many.

The price paid for freedom is absolutely appalling and few people appreciate the cost, especially to ordinary housewives and mothers who carry on through everything and without whom everything would collapse. No stars, no medals, no crosses, no glory – in my case just a loving memory that lives forever.

Harold Cossons

From September 1940 London was bombed every night for at least two months. The sirens seemed to try to deafen you at dusk and there would be no 'all clear' until daybreak. There was a nightly exodus to the Underground stations. Whole families could be seen carrying bedding or using prams or anything on wheels!

There were no air raids over the Christmas period of 1940, so London had a welcome respite for a short time. However, the German bombers were back in force on 29 December and the sirens sounded the alert as darkness fell. From the start this was to be an unusual raid as no high explosives were to be heard although some were to be dropped later. As my family were preparing to leave the flat for the shelter I happened to open the bathroom window

and was astonished to see the sky lit by patches of light blue. This was caused by thousands of small incendiary bombs being dropped. As I called my father to come and have a look, a shower of incendiaries came our way. One struck the building about ten feet below our window so my father never did look!

It was as light as day, but incredibly the 'all clear' sounded before midnight and so we made our way out of the shelters to the roof of our flats where we had a grand view of London burning. What a sight! No longer the roar of bombers or the crunch of bombs, just the crackle of flames. Instead of throwing off our clothes and jumping into bed, which we usually did with the 'all clear', many of us were up and down on the roof until dawn. It was too exciting for bed! A warehouse adjacent to the Etheld Estate where we lived was engulfed in flames. One floor after another collapsed until the building was a burned-out shell. All the time what I believe was tins of paint were going 'bang' and jumping up in the air. Quite amusing! And all that turned up to tackle the flames was a tanker lorry full of water, which cleared off when the couple of men using a hosepipe from the street had used all the tanker's water on the flames with no particular effect.

During the night I did a 'Norman Tebbit' and jumped on my bike for a tour of the sights but although I was 17 I only got to Southwark Street. That was enough! There were fire hoses all over the road and although the firemen were having a real 'go' I watched one building after another crash to the ground. That raid of fire created the biggest area of devastation in Britain, about one square mile north of St Paul's Cathedral, including the Barbican district. Etheld Estate where we lived had only been recently built and so at first shelter life was great for the young ones as we were all more or less new neighbours. We helped the older folk, tried to cheer them up, and generally got to know how nice our neighbours were. Someone would bring a portable gramophone down and we would listen to each other's records, although sometimes you could only appreciate them properly during a lull in the raids! Sometimes we would play cards or chat, and other times of course the family photos came out.

During quiet periods the younger ones would go to the flats and take tea and food back to the shelters. On one such occasion I was alone making tea when six bombs whistled down, the last landing on our estate. Luckily the bombs were only small but they still wrecked a number of upper-storey flats. You knew when landmines were dropped because these were said to be 50-gallon oil drums packed with explosives and dropped by parachute. You heard these as two very disturbing thuds! If close enough two terrifying booms in quick succession with the whole building shaking!

People slept in their clothes (there being no heating) but changed into working or other togs in the morning. The shelters certainly never smelled like the Underground where masses of people slept on the platforms! If Jerry got noisy, as the saying went, people woke up and got very frightened and apprehensive. The bombs seemed to drop on every street. Everyone had their own bomb story! To us old Londoners these stories are folklore now.

The closest ever bomb to the Etheld Estate fell early on in

the Blitz and demolished part of a facing tenement. The blast even blew off the shelter door but fortunately caused no injury. But for a while morale collapsed and people were very distressed. Another bomb fell on a bakery in the street market now known as The Cut. Some people died in the shelter under the bakery. The Young Vic theatre now stands on the site.

As the nightly ordeal continued our shelter became less popular. People went off to the Tube stations, if only to have a good night's sleep. Others went to what they thought were safer shelters, until only about 15 or 20 of us remained. But the most demoralising sight was of the bombed buildings, and of streets impassable with rubble. Many streets were roped off because of unexploded bombs but people often ignored this restriction on their way to work, even pausing to have a look down the hole to see if they could see it! I always travelled by pushbike and would look at buildings on my travels wondering what your chances were if you were caught in one when a bomb struck it. I would wander all round Central London during weekends viewing the devastation. For a lad of 17 it was a terrifying but exciting and fascinating time too.

I remember that in November when one night the sirens were silent everyone was amazed! We expected trouble later because we'd had two months of bombing every night! But no, nothing happened, although next night the sirens sounded again. This was the first of many raid-less nights and nights when the raids didn't last from dusk till dawn. Of course other towns were 'having it' instead, as the saying went. I think we had three clear nights when Coventry was bombed.

This was to be the pattern of the Blitz in future, with a heavy raid now and again, each seeming to be heavier than the last one! The worst seemed to be that of 10 May 1941. The last few weeks of the Blitz saw me taking my parents down to Waterloo Station, not the Underground, but to an underground shelter *under* the main line station, the Underground shelter being full. Such were the effects the last heavy raids had on 'Blitz weary' Londoners.

The sound of planes flying overhead was enough to hold millions of Londoners in fear and dread. The sound of warning sirens would turn your stomach. My courage ebbed and flowed. Some nights I really would be shaking. But always after a close bomb I had the courage of a lion! No doubt the excitement and the anti-climax. With the 'all clear' everyone would cheer up and you would see some of them trundling off to bed. A terrible time, but let me finish with two happier stories!

One of our mobile crane drivers returned one day to say he had just left Buckingham Palace after he had shifted a huge unexploded bomb there. He told us he had had tea with the King and the Queen. This man was 'Dido', an awful braggart who looked like a Sumo wrestler! Of course we called him a liar but after the war there was a picture of Dido and his crane at the Palace! I think he was decorated for shifting the bomb but I've still got doubts about the tea!

Then there was my friend Charlie who worked at a rag-and-bone shop near the Elephant and Castle. These shops seem to have disappeared but were incredible places, wide open to the road (no shop front) with mountains of rags to the ceiling. What a pong! The proprietor would sit out in front with a huge set of scales waiting for people to sell him rags. During the war all premises had to have fire-watchers and the employees of small firms had to take it in turns. Charlie was on duty on the night of the Great Fire Raid. On asking Charlie how he got on that night he told me the rag-and-bone shop was gutted!

'Did you try to put the fire out?' I asked.

'Not bloody likely,' he said. 'I rubbed my hands; serve the old skinflint right!'

Apparently Charlie was never paid much! As a final note Charlie finished up a prisoner-of-war in Italy for three years. When on the run and nearly starving he told me that in those circumstances your first thoughts are of food, then sleep, and sex came a very poor third!

Frederick Thomson

' John. Wake up. The war's started!'

These words, etched in my memory along with the recollection of precisely where I was, who spoke them, and the accompanying sights and sounds which were to become only too familiar thereafter, remain undimmed.

For someone whose powers of memory seem exclusively and inexplicably reserved for faces and telephone numbers, the unusual clarity of my childhood recollections surely underlines the unique nature of the experience?

I was sound asleep in the large double bed belonging to my parents in the upstairs front bedroom of the house in Dagenham where I had been born three years before. Yes, I had actually been born in *that* bed. Weren't *all* children delivered in their mothers' beds in those days? Delivered by the proverbial stork, no doubt! Certainly a step forward in the march of civilisation which had previously left babies under gooseberry bushes!

The sights and sounds which accompanied my mother's calm but unmistakably insistent command were tinged with considerable excitement. The stuff of boys' dreams.

Was I really awake?

I could hear guns going off. Through the window the usually stygian black night, from which only sleep itself could provide protection from the demons of childish imagination, was uncharacteristically alive and bright!

In one instant I was wrapped in a blanket and hauled up into my mother's arms and wafted down the stairs and into the street. Deserted as one would expect. The war seemed only to be happening to us. No one else was interested apparently!

We were on a short trip, a matter of yards to a neighbour's garden 'dugout'. The euphemism for the Anderson shelter whose construction I had been totally unaware of until that moment! Such shelters, commonly in use in those days, consisted of two pieces of something called corrugated iron bolted together and placed snugly inside a rectangular hole which had been 'dug out' of the garden, providing a temporary refuge away from the house which, if hit by a bomb, would have the effect of burying its occupants under much rubble. Some of these DIY constructions still survive intact usually as potting sheds! The fact of their survival bears witness as to their durability – at least against the unpredictable nature of the English climate. But it is difficult to imagine they could have afforded much real protection from a ten-ton German bomb still gathering speed on the end of a five-mile perpendicular path!

John Trustrum with his elder brother.

The street I found myself in was, as stated, in the sole possession of my mother and myself, and it was from the vantage point of being clutched high up near her shoulders that I looked skyward.

There were great raking beams of light flashing across the night sky, which was alive with a low and insistent droning sound. The bombers. German planes. Within a very short space of time the sound of German planes was easily recognisable from that of British planes. German planes had a rasping, whining, unfriendly noise. English planes were much more subdued, solid, dependable. Yes, English planes were much more *reassuring*! It's *true*!

Suddenly there was a flash of silver high overhead as one and then more of the slow-moving objects was trapped at the end of a searchlight's weakening beams.

'There they are!' I yelled. I could see them.

My mother made no reply but quickened her pace. There were other sights and sounds. Strange red glows dotted the horizon in all directions as I gyrated my head while my body was gripped even more tightly.

A cacophony of thuds suddenly let loose as the anti-aircraft guns broke into a barrage of angry retaliation at the intruders, dimly glimpsed and slipping in and out of the nocturnal mist.

Suddenly new sounds entered the scene. Strange strained high-pitched whistling noises. Not tuneful or melodic. Monotones. Getting louder and louder and culminating in a short silence almost instantly followed by the earth trembling and ear-splitting explosions. For the first time my excitement was halted. Perhaps this wasn't such fun as I had imagined? Men's games were more dangerous than boys' games, I thought. Can we play something else?

We were to spend many more nights in our neighbours' 'dugout' after that. My father had left to join the army and Mum was left 'holding the baby' – me! My brother had been evacuated to Llanelli in Wales, where (he wrote home) he had been billeted with a boy who suffered with acute acne! His description of 'covered in spots' was his non-medical diagnosis. Evacuations were frequent thereafter for both of us.

My father had gone to Dunkirk early in the war and he too was 'evacuated' or posted to various places in England and abroad throughout the duration of the war. My father was a picture of a man in soldier's uniform standing 'at ease' on top of the piano! Only years later were all these events set in order in my mind. I only ever remember being frightened once.

One night huddled inside the 'dugout' the now familiar high-pitched noise of a German bomb hurtling down through the night sky went on just too long! The whistle turned into a scream and it was obvious to me that this one was earnestly seeking our personal hideaway!

For a few seconds I recall the mind-numbing sensation generated by *fear*. This bomb was determined to obliterate me.

'But I am not old enough,' I protested inwardly. 'Can't I live a little longer? Please?'

There was a sudden deafening explosion close by. The inhabitants of the shelter, gripped in the tension of the moment, were silent. Then out of the silence a voice said quietly. 'Missed!'

Nervous laughter broke the silence, which rapidly developed and turned into guffaws of laughter. We'd been spared! Thank God! Spared to face more nightly threats? Praying for the 'all clear'.

This would remain the closest we should all come to extermination and live to tell the tale. How close we would come again in the months and years ahead none of us would know. The method of attack would change as the war progressed when buzz bombs and rockets were introduced, many of which probably landed even closer. Indeed buzz bombs were frequently sighted, wobbling out of control on the final silent approach, but that night in the bunker was my first and worst taste of *fear*.

At the point when fear reaches its culmination and that which we fear most becomes at least in our imagination a *certainty* – all thought ceases.

It is as though we have entered a black void from which all sensation is banished. Even the rhythmic pulsation of one's own body mechanism becomes suspended. Nothing exists in this void. Everything becomes – nothing.

Fate alone takes control decreeing whether or not a door will open to let in the light which restores life. That night fate opened the door to us.

Had this not happened we would have gone into that eternal darkness never knowing what lay beyond the door. Knowing nothing. Feeling nothing. Oblivious and obliterated. That night in the 'dugout' was, without doubt, my closest shave.

John Trustrum

At the time of the Blitz my children were aged four and eight and had to be evacuated. I lived in London and I was a widow and my baby was born seven weeks after her father's death. So my life was one long struggle, working to keep us all. But I had a good mother and relatives who tried to help us. I remember one day at 5 p.m., when the darkness fell and the siren went, and in came the enemy bombers. They just dropped their bombs. It was terrifying. I had got my children back because they had been evacuated to Bristol, which was also having heavy raids, and so I had to go home in the middle of a raid.

I worked at St Giles' Hospital and every night it was the same. Bombs going off and I having to get home in the middle of it all. I remember hopping from door to door because of the shrapnel. One night I had just got home when I heard a plane that seemed to be directly overhead, and I rushed through the house, collecting my children as I went and down the garden into the shelter. Then I heard a huge crash. I went out to see if our house was still there. It was but it was badly damaged and over the road all the other houses were severely damaged. Some of them had been demolished. I just missed it all.

And so it went on. Fires every night, to be put out, and then the bombing would start again. Everybody worked so hard. Young boys went out putting fires out. Such brave children. But it was a combined effort and everyone helped each other and shared everything and did the best they could to make life as easy as possible. They shared food and beds and what have you. The firemen, for a long time, faced the most dangerous jobs, very often tired out and lacking equipment. We had some firemen living in the school near us. Such nice men but alas they were all killed from a direct hit on the pub and the shop next door to us. They were all destroyed and our houses were all severely damaged.

I remember sweeping up the bricks and the dust from the third floor of our block of flats, down all the stairs to the front door, only to find that the front door was gone! All the neighbours were out doing the same. We were all wondering if next day the houses themselves would disappear.

Going to work in the morning they were still coming in bombing us. At first it was sustained. From five in the evening until seven in the morning. I used to walk over hosepipes and coke and coal and all manner of rubble and glass in the streets. Then there would be the sad part when we got to work. We'd be told of those of our friends who had been killed. We all looked out for each other directly we got to work to see if we were safe from harm.

One night the hospital was bombed. Three porters were killed and two of the Sisters and Matron and a Medical Officer were injured. The patients were all evacuated except for emergencies.

But when I look back and remember how the Londoners, with their cockney wit reacted, I feel so proud. They were so cheerful and never was there at any time a defeatist outlook. 'Hitler was not going to tell the English what to do' was the general feeling. No, we would wipe him off the map. Amidst all the suffering and terrible tragedies they faced, I consider the Londoners were a courageous lot, and I wasn't one, I came from Kent! But the cockneys were the salt of the earth. They must have been to be able to smile at such adversity. We had many laughs and fun though to see us through. Humour at that sort of time is a saving grace.

I remember a man, whose garden backed on to ours, who came round one evening. He was in a rage and said we had a light on up top and the planes were over. He was a warden.

My landlady said that we didn't have a light on. But it transpired that a young lodger had come in and, not thinking, had put the light on. Now we had an old soldier living in the boarding house and he was a marvellous man, always trying to help everyone, went to work in the docks by day, up all night giving any help that could be given. Anyway he 'flew' at the warden. He would not countenance cheek from a warden who, after all, was only doing his duty.

I couldn't believe my ears. They both got to the shouting and swearing stage and then the old soldier 'offered him out' for his cheek. They were going to have a fight! Would you believe it! The bombs were falling, the shrapnel was flying everywhere, and there were fires starting, and where they could find space for a fight goodness only knows! The landlady and I couldn't stop laughing. Anyway we told them – they may not have to worry soon – we might all be gone with the wind!

Would you believe it that two evenings afterwards, Camberwell was heavily bombed and the whole area seemed to be alight? The people at the back of us were trying to save what they could before the fires enveloped all the houses. The warden called out for assistance and the old soldier came to help him move his piano and furniture into the street. The warden's house was burning. Two days earlier they were going to take each other apart!

The old soldier jumped over the wall and started to help, calling me to catch the light stuff thrown over the wall. I remember shouting, 'You're all crazy. It's no good trying to save things. You'll all get killed.'

I went into the shelter and after a time all was quiet. The furniture had been removed and all the people were in their shelters but the fires were still raging.

Then bang, wallop, we shook. We thought that this must be at least a 1,000-pound bomb. I think it must have been. We went out and, of course, all the houses at the back and all the furniture were no more. The piano went on to play in some never-never land! Our house got a bit more hammering which left us without lights and water.

After a few more weeks we had all had enough and I went back to my mother's home in Kent. My landlady went to Wales. We had to do it after all the horror of seeing such tragedy, noise, poor dead babies and children, etc. When I read of the cruelty and mindless killing …

Joan Wilson

I would like to share my experience of the second night of the three-day Blitz of Swansea with you. My father, William Maddock, my aunty Louisa Matthews, my sister Ethel and myself had been visiting our relations in the Hafod. We were walking home along Ysgubor Fach Street when the bombing started. It was so heavy that the whole of Townhill was lit up, a sight I will never forget. We sheltered in a house in Ysgubor Fach Street, laying under a large kitchen table. Within minutes a high-explosive bomb made a direct hit, bringing the house down completely. My uncle Louie Balser shouted to us that help was on the way to get us out. Then we heard another bomb, the blast of which killed my uncle instantly.

By the time they finally got us out the tenants of the house were dead, and my sister's legs were badly burned. Also my father's legs had been injured. My sister was taken to hospital, which one we were not sure of at the time, and the rest of us were taken to a church crypt overnight. The following morning we had to walk home, amidst the smell of burning flesh, only to arrive home to find that our own house had been bombed. We couldn't find my mother, Gladys Maddock. She had been working night shift in Bridgend. She had actually seen people trying to dig us out while she was on her way to work but she had no idea it was us. We found her many hours later in a friend's house, where she had gone to look for us.

We then went to Mount Pleasant Hospital where my sister was. They had amputated one of her legs. Days later they had to amputate the other. Several weeks later she was transferred to Whitchurch Hospital, Cardiff. She made a good recovery, reaching the stage where she was preparing to have artificial legs fitted, when complications occurred and sadly after a very courageous fight she died.

During the time my sister was in Whitchurch, my mother stayed there with her. My father, who was almost totally blind, had to go to Llanelli to stay. I had to stay with several of my relations, and all this at the tender age of 13. An experience I will never ever forget.

Gwyneth Austin

I lived in a terraced Victorian house with my mother and two elder sisters in Woolwich, South-East London, during the war. Although I have recollections of the Blitz my particular recollections are of the period when the V1s or doodlebugs were dropping all over London and at that time I was just ten years old.

Being the youngest, my two sisters being 15 and 17 years old respectively, I always went to bed first and on this particular night I went to bed quite happily. I had that day just got myself a *Just William* book by Richmal Crompton from the public library, and so armed with that and a piece of candle I went into the Anderson shelter which was situated about 15 feet from our back door. This must have been about 9 p.m. and I read for about half an hour by the light from the entrance and then when it got too dark I dropped the blanket which hung over the entrance and read by candlelight for another half hour. I then put out the candle and went to sleep.

The next thing I knew was that there was a violent explosion. Although I was asleep I was literally flung in the air and crashed down on the double mattress with the bunk and rubble on top of me. One thing I'll never forget was the choking dust. I could hardly breathe. After a short while, however, it became a little more bearable, and so I crawled towards the entrance in the pitch darkness. But the entrance wasn't there. Just broken bricks and masonry.

I was buried, but strangely I didn't feel afraid. Maybe I had the faith of a child that told me that somehow I would be rescued. With that in mind I tried to collect my clothes and get dressed in readiness.

As most working-class lads did, I slept in my shirt and so I only had to find my shoes, socks and trousers as I had no underclothes! I scrambled around in the darkness and rubble and found both socks and shoes, but no trousers! I obviously couldn't find a small piece of candle or matches, but my main priority at that time, I remember, was my trousers. To a ten-year-old boy, being seen without his trousers in public was a fate far worse than being buried alive!

Pondering on this I had no idea of the passage of time. It may have been one hour or it may have been two hours before I heard a voice in the distance calling my name. It was my eldest sister, Joyce, and there were men's voices as well, calling out for me. There was a sound of digging, and that went on for a time. I can remember at the time I was shouting, 'I'm here, I'm here,' and then the back of the shelter was pulled away and there was the friendly face of a fireman looking at me. The hole was made bigger, and hands reached in to lift me out. However, my thoughts were still on my missing trousers and even as they pulled me out I grabbed a blanket to cover my modesty before facing the outside world!

We were given a bed when we got to the rest centre and a couple of blankets and a ubiquitous cup of tea. There were other people there as well who were in the same state as we were. I woke the next morning, but there was no sign of my sister. I found out later she had gone to the hospital to see my mother once she had got me settled. They were serving breakfasts from the school kitchen, but I felt too ashamed to get up without my trousers and so I just sat on the side of the bed with my blanket still clutched tight around me and probably looking thoroughly miserable!

Everyone seemed to be rushing about with problems of their own so no one spoke to me. Then an old lady who had been sleeping in the bed next to mine came up and asked if I was all right. I told her the story of what had happened to me and how I couldn't move without my trousers.

'You poor dear,' she said. 'I have got just the thing for you,' and with that she reached under her bed and pulled out a carrier bag.

She reached in the bag and produced, to my horror, a voluminous pair of bottle green flannelette knickers!

Forty odd years on I can shut my eyes and see them as though it was yesterday! They were faded through washing and certainly well worn and had elastic at the waist and knees.

'Put them on,' she ordered.

In vain, I protested I would be all right but she was most insistent and being only a small boy I did what all small boys and girls did in those days and did as I was told!

'Turn around! Yes, that looks fine,' she added. 'Now go and get some breakfast!'

As I walked the short distance to where some ladies were serving out food, I felt everyone's eyes were on me! It was a terrible ordeal although it could have only lasted for an hour or so until the clothing store opened. I remember I went into a room where there were hundreds of cardboard boxes marked 'American Red Cross'. A lady asked me what sort of trousers I wanted. Long ones or short ones? I couldn't believe my ears! In those days one had to be at least 12 years old to be allowed to wear long trousers! So, of course, I chose the long ones.

My father arrived later that afternoon. He had been given special leave from his unit somewhere on the East Coast. We went back to our house in the evening. The flying bomb had landed directly on the house next door but one, which had been completely flattened. A lady and her two children had been killed. I remember the daughter was about my age.

The front of our house as still standing but the entire back had come away and crashed onto the gardens which together with the house next door had buried our shelter up to about six feet in rubble. We had a three-storey house, and the roof and the interior floors were in various states of collapse. I looked up and saw my bed hanging out halfway into space with the roof collapsed on it. I found out later from my mother and sisters what exactly had happened that night.

Apparently it was about 11 p.m. and my mother and sisters were just talking when they heard the flying bomb droning overhead and then the engine suddenly stopped. Normally you would just listen, and then a minute or two later you would hear an explosion, the loudness of which would show how near to you it had landed. On this occasion my mother said there was the usual silence and then getting louder and louder, a rushing noise accompanied by a lot of metallic clattering which was probably loose panels on the bomb itself.

My mother at this point grabbed my two sisters and thrust them under the stairs. She dived under the table but didn't quite make it before the house collapsed. Her arm was broken in two places and she had extensive cuts and bruises.

The emergency services arrived very quickly and got everyone out. My two sisters were unhurt, and when they were asked if there was anyone else my sister Joyce told them about me.

To cut a long story short we were split up and I landed up with relations in Devon until my mother recovered and we managed to get somewhere else to live in Woolwich. The ironic thing was that we were evacuated the day before war broke out, but because we were so unhappy we were allowed back home when things got quiet in 1942/43. When we were evacuated at the height of the Blitz our house stood there throughout and was totally undamaged. Yet when we got back, within a year we had been totally bombed out and in the process I had lost my trousers!

Derek Drew

My father, John Smith, was an air-raid warden. He worked long hours at the UGB Glassworks but each evening he was out as soon as the sirens went, sometimes only getting back to bed at two or three in the morning and up again for work at five.

One particular evening was funny but yet it was frightening. The siren had gone one evening and my father made my younger and older sisters and my mother and myself go into the Anderson shelter in the back garden while he went out on patrol.

The sky was lit up with incendiary bombs going off in the streets around us, but not in ours. After half an hour everything went quiet and there wasn't a sound or a flare or anything for some time. At that time my older sister wanted to go to the toilet, which was about eight feet away from the shelter, but my mother said she couldn't go until my dad came back and said it was all right. When he returned she asked him if it was all quiet around us and he said yes, so she asked if she could go out of the shelter to go to the toilet.

He said yes, but don't make any noise! She had just taken two steps outside the shelter when an incendiary bomb was dropped outside our front door and it lit up everything all around our area.

Then at the same time we heard a bomb whistling down towards us and my father went outside and grabbed my sister to push her back into the shelter, but he wasn't quick enough. The bomb went off in the street near to us, and the blast threw my dad on to the ground and my sister back into the shelter.

What was funny to us at the time being only schoolgirls was my sister coming back into the shelter head first and I can distinctly remember saying to her, 'I see you got back quicker than you went out.'

What's more I can clearly remember her reply.

'Yes, and I've got a pair of wet knickers.'

Ellen Jowett

I was nine years old when the war began. We were living in Mitcham in Surrey, we being me, my sister aged three, my mother, father, grandmother and grandfather. We didn't have an Anderson shelter. Mother put a single mattress under the stairs where my sister and I slept, and Mother sat on an easy chair at the end. I can remember it used to be a ritual saying, 'Listen,' and no one spoke as you heard the drone of a bomber. I remember never taking my eyes off my mother until it had gone over!

After a while we all moved to Richmond. That was like jumping from the frying pan into the fire. We lived near Richmond Park, home for a lot of guns!

I remember one night we had the usual drone of a bomber, then what sounded like a mighty gush of air and then silence for a split second. Then all hell let loose. The doors and windows caved in and you couldn't see anything for dust. My father ran upstairs, his feet crushing glass as he went. My grandparents were still in bed, covered in glass but amazingly not badly hurt.

A bomb had demolished the house next door but one, but to this day I can still remember the awful smell of gas and dust and the cold night air that drifted in through the open doors and windows that didn't exist any more. There was a lot of shouting going on outside; air-raid wardens seemed to be everywhere, asking if anyone was injured. I remember Mum and Gran were crying.

Next morning I couldn't believe my eyes. I couldn't recognise anything. It was one heap of rubble and I couldn't imagine what was going to happen to us all. Then Mum's sister came over from Mitcham and took us back to live with her until we found another home – back in the same street we had left 18 months earlier! But now it had a large brick-built shelter in the road to house about 40 people.

Later we had some Italian prisoners-of-war at the back of our houses clearing the ditches. Mum made it quite clear we were not to look at them let alone speak!

I remember once as we passed by one of them smiled and waved but we ignored them. We had our orders! Then one day we were skipping and there was an argument if someone was 'out' or not when all of a sudden a young Italian walked over and got hold of the end of the rope and began to turn it, gesturing us to skip!

I looked to see if Mum was watching – she wasn't! So in I jumped! I couldn't look at him for long, he was so hand-some. And in his language he took over and was telling us who was 'in' and who was 'out'. Then all of a sudden he let go of the rope and burst into tears! He went to the fence and buried his head in his hands and cried and cried and we all felt so sorry for them all.

Next day I bought a Mars bar with my precious sweet coupons and put it in a bag and gave it to him. I remember when he opened the bag he smiled and got hold of my hand! I was fraternising with the enemy! But I felt so proud, and then it seemed everyone was talking with them, even the mums and dads!

Joyce McRickus

Acknowledgements

Without the stories this book could not have been produced, and so our thanks must go to all those people who wrote to us of their experiences, whether their stories have been published or not. There were so many moving stories that our greatest regret is not having space to include them all.

And again, our thanks to Shirley Cartwright, Judy Crawshaw, Jane Stew and Margaret Young for all the typing work and general assistance. They were all wonderfully helpful but we've listed them alphabetically so no one can claim they got a higher rating!

Our thanks to you all.

Frank and Joan Shaw

Index

Entries in *italics* indicate photographs.

Burma 69, 282, 283
Burnley, Lancashire 167–9

Cadman, Madge 253
Calais, France 327
Camberwell, London 342
Candy, Peter 156
Cannon Street Station,
London 296
Canterbury, Kent 243, 285
Cardiff, Wales viii–ix, xii,
128, 193, 247–8, 343
Carey, Bill 216–17
Carlton Cinema, Sparkhill 135
casualty numbers, Blitz vii,
viii
Catford, London 38
cellars as shelters 15, 26, 31,
75, 97, 98, 101–2, 114,
118, 148, 150, 169, 193,
200, 201, 245, 249, 258,
259, 260, 279, 283, 293,
298, 318, 319
Chesham, Buckinghamshire
88–9
Chiswick, London 160
Churchill, Winston 18, 84,
223, 290
cinema 4–5, 22, 25, 43, 78,
99, 101, 106, 135, 163,
198, 219, 240, 281–2,
293, 301, 304, 314
City of London Maternity
Hospital 294
Civil Defence 148, 288, 305,
325
Clacton, Essex xv
Clarke, Betty 37
clothing coupons 23, 76, 97,
98, 122

Clydebank/Clydeside,
Scotland ix, xii, 62–3,
227–9
Colindale Hospital, London
295
Commodore Cinema, London
240
communal/community shelter
81, 96, 187, 232–3, 238–9
Cooperative Society 306
Covent Garden, London
121–2
Coventry, West Midlands viii,
ix, xii, xiv, 53–5, 56,
77–9, 93, 95, 96, 110–11,
154–5, 209, 302, 303–4,
305–9, 315–22, 334
Crosskey, Harold 51

Dagenham, London 89,
123–5, 170–8, 336
damage assessor 132
dancing 45, 175–6, 181, 201,
218, 227, 232, 233, 295
D-Day 80, 243, 288, 315
Deakin, Bill 199
Deakin, Charlie 199
Deal, Kent xv, 297
Deane, Nora 281
Deptford, London 37–8, 48
Devon 12, 55, 85, 155, 286,
347
Donaldson, Tommy 33, 35–6
Doncaster, Yorkshire 106,
250, 252, 253
doodlebugs 13–14, 105, 153,
176, 177, 255, 265, 269,
270–1, 325, 339, 344
Dover, Kent xv
Drew, Joyce 345

Index of Contributors

Entries in *italics* indicate photographs.

Frank and Joan Shaw live in Hinckley in Leicestershire. They have four children and nine grandchildren. They were born and raised in Deal, Kent where they also spent the war. The idea for the We Remember series came when their granddaughter asked them about the Second World War for a school project. Frank and Joan decided more memories needed to be committed to paper, and they wrote to 700 local newspapers throughout the country asking just that. They were flooded with letters, which they then self-published as five hardback books, raising over £100,000 for the Royal British Legion.

Ebury Press are delighted to be republishing the books, starting with *We Remember the Blitz* and *We Remember the Home Guard*:

To find out more about our latest publications, sign up to our newsletter at: www.eburypublishing.co.uk